YOU AND ME,
NO MATTER WHAT

MINH VO

Copyright © 2023 Minh Vo
All rights reserved. ISBN: 9781916808157
Editor: Eman Najam
Printed in the United States of America.

No part of this publication shall be reproduced, transmitted, or sold in whole or in part in any form without prior written consent of the author, except as provided by the United States of America copyright law. Any unauthorized usage of the text without express written permission of the publisher is a violation of the author's copyright and is illegal and punishable by law. All trademarks and registered trademarks appearing in this guide are the property of their respective owners.

For permission requests, write to the publisher, addressed "Attention: Permissions Coordinator," at the address below.

Amazon Book Publishing Center 420 Terry Ave N, Seattle, Washington, 98109, U.S.A

The opinions expressed by the Author are not necessarily those held by Amazon Book Publishing Center.

Ordering Information: Quantity sales and special discounts are available on quantity purchases by corporations, associations, and others. For details, contact the publisher at info@amazonbookpublishingcenter.com

The information contained within this book is strictly for informational purposes. The material may include information, products, or services by third parties. As such, the Author and Publisher do not assume responsibility or liability for any third-party material or opinions. The publisher is not responsible for websites (or their content) that are not owned by the publisher. Readers are advised to do their own due diligence when it comes to making decisions.

In this book, it is important to note that the characters portrayed are based on real-life individuals; however, their names and certain identifying details have been altered for the sake of confidentiality and privacy. The intention behind this change is to protect the privacy of the people involved and to maintain the integrity of their personal experiences.

Amazon Book Publishing Center works with authors, and aspiring authors, who have a story to tell and a brand to build. Do you have a book idea you would like us to consider publishing? Please visit AmazonBookPublishingCenter.com for more information.

DEDICATION

In the loving memory of my beloved wife, Ally. You have made all the difference in my life and the many lives that you have touched. May your story continue to live on and help the many others who have and are still suffering.

This book is dedicated to my beloved wife, Ally, for your courage, strength, and love. Thank you for loving me.

THE

BEGINNING

CHAPTER
1
BORN TO SURVIVE

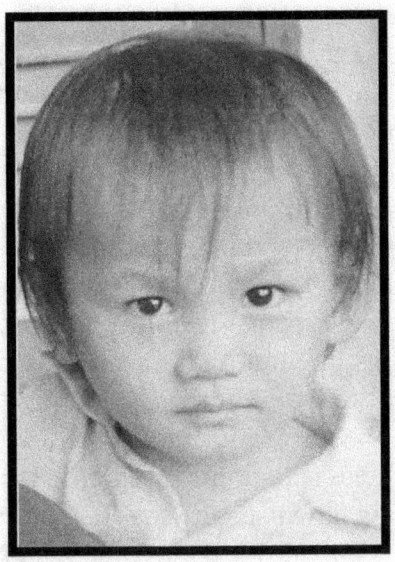

    The air buzzed with chaos and desperation as the hallways overflowed with a sea of voices, echoing and intertwining in a symphony of urgency. Shouts, screams, and tears filled the air, leaving me unsure of the cause, but the intensity on the surrounding faces was unmistakable. It felt like we were in an airport or an Army base, surrounded by soldiers in their green uniforms, carrying rifles. They guided and directed people through the crowd, bringing a sense of order to the commotion. Amidst the clamor, the distant windows framed a mesmerizing sight—the colossal planes preparing for takeoff. Their powerful engines hummed with anticipation, vibrating through the air and adding to the charged atmosphere. The scene was a sensory feast, with the noise and presence of the people and soldiers and the captivating view of aircrafts poised for flight.

Not long ago, my má, my sister, and I found ourselves amidst a crowd of desperate people, standing in line, eagerly awaiting the attention of an important man seated behind a desk. As my má's turn arrived, the conversation started calmly but rapidly escalated into a tempest. Tears cascaded down her face as she gasped and began screaming at the Vietnamese officer, pointing frantically at the papers she had brought before him. "I am his real wife. These are his kids," she wailed, her voice trembling with desperation. "Please, officer, please… believe me, please… please… help us. He can't leave us. He can't leave his family behind," she pleaded, her sobs filling the air as she clasped her hands together, beseeching the officer for compassion and understanding.

Standing beside her, my sister and I held onto her bell-bottom pant legs, gripping them tightly as if our lives depended on it. Though we couldn't see clearly or comprehend the unfolding events, we could feel the weight of my má's anguish. In response, we joined in her pain, shedding tears in an attempt to offer solace and stand united with her in that moment. It was an instinctual reaction, as most adolescents do when they sense their parents in emotional turmoil. At such a young age, my ability to articulate words was limited. Emotions became my primary means of expression, the only language I truly understood.

The officer remained silent, his eyes filled with questions as he scanned through the documents, studying their authenticity. After a brief moment, he turned his gaze towards my má, his expression inscrutable, before abruptly leaving his post with the papers in hand. My má's cries grew louder, her defeat clear as she rested her folded arms on the desk, burying her face within them, struggling for breath amidst her tears. What thoughts raced through her mind at that moment? Did the officer doubt her truth? Were we denied? How would she provide for her two young children? And where was my bố? Why wasn't he here to rescue us?

Amidst rapid, shallow breaths and her inconsolable weeping, my má began to whisper softly to herself as if gasping for air between each word. Perhaps she sought solace in prayer to the Buddha or desperately sought an alternative solution. Maybe she was grappling with how we found ourselves in such dire circumstances. Whatever her internal struggle, my sister and I could only contribute to the symphony of cries and tears, offering our own small voices of sorrow alongside the chorus of others nearby.

The passage of time blurred, as its measure held little significance in the face of my má's immense distress. To her, even a mere five minutes felt like an eternity in this gripping situation. Eventually, the officer returned to the desk, clutching the papers in his grasp. His voice broke the silence, carrying a message of liberation. "Mam, come this way. You and your kids are cleared to join your husband," he declared. The officer had likely sought confirmation from a colleague or superior to ensure the validity of our documents.

At the sound of the officer's words, my má raised her head from the desk, swiftly composing herself as she wiped away the tears that had drenched her face and hair. In an instant, tears of sorrow transformed into tears of joy. Overflowing with gratitude, she clasped her hands together in a prayer-like motion, nodding and fervently waving her hands to express her appreciation towards the officer. Then, with heartfelt sincerity, she knelt down and enveloped my sister and me in a tight embrace, her arms encircling us protectively. She pressed her lips against our tear-streaked cheeks, the gentle contact more of a sniff, a primitive and intimate recognition that only a mother knows by scent. Looking into our eyes, she assured us, "Everything is going to be okay now. No need for more tears. We are going to see your bố." Standing up, she gathered our suitcases nearby, asserting, "Be good and stay close to me. It's time for us to go."

The officer gestured with a wave of his hand, directing us to follow another soldier who stood nearby, holding a rifle or machine gun. This soldier would serve as our escort, guiding us toward the long-awaited reunion with our bố. Through a series of doors, we were swiftly led down a corridor until we reached a point where my bố stood, his arms crossed and his gaze piercing, patiently awaiting our arrival.

One might expect a joyful reunion marked by smiles and open arms. Instead, a new wave of yelling and screaming erupted as my má and bố came within reach, locking eyes for the first time. The shrillness in my Má's voice soared to ear-piercing heights as she unleashed her fury upon my bố. His retorts were laced with colorful language, defending himself amidst their tumultuous exchange, the phrase "Đụ má…"

frequently punctuating his sentences. During their verbal barrage, my sister and I were instructed to stand by the window and wait, removed from the conflict.

Eventually, the yelling subsided, leaving a silence that was somewhat unsettling. Standing alone in front of the expansive window, I pressed my forehead and arms against the cool glass. My má approached and stood next to me, her smile radiating warmth. I extended my right hand towards hers, seeking a connection and comfort, while my other arm supported my head against the window. Side by side, we stood in silent contemplation, gazing out at the airplanes on the tarmac through the towering windows. Gradually, my attention drifted to a solitary palm tree in the distance, illuminated by the bright sun as it gently swayed in the subtle breeze. Amidst the chaos of war, it appeared remarkably serene. I fixated on the tree, sensing a peculiar bond. Perhaps it symbolized a glimmer of hope in the world we left behind. Or perhaps it mirrored the profound sense of loneliness that often permeated my being.

My bố had endured significant challenges during the Vietnam War. He served as a special intelligence Green Beret in the South Vietnamese troops, known for their brave ventures into the perilous Cu Chi Tunnels. Their mission was to detect hidden mines and traps, protecting the American soldiers who ventured into those treacherous terrains. They were at the forefront of scouting new territories and defending against skirmishes.

Growing up, I would often hear my bố recount his war stories. One particularly vivid tale unfolded during a moonless night as he parachuted from an airplane, only to be met with a sudden barrage of enemy fire. The swarm of bullets illuminated the sky like fireflies on a sultry summer evening but with lethal intent. Each bullet had a straightforward aim: destruction and death. Amidst the chaos, a stray bullet found its mark, piercing my bố's side as he descended to the earth below. Despite the searing pain, he mustered the strength to clutch his wounded side, attempting to stem the bleeding. Gasping for air, he called out for help to the shadowy figures lying nearby. Regrettably, his plea fell on deaf ears.

Cautiously crawling towards the motionless bodies, he soon realized they had not been as fortunate as he.

The distant voices of Northern Viet Cong soldiers echoed through the fields near the jungle's edge, their presence intensifying as they combed the area for survivors to capture and interrogate. Panic and fear gripped my bố's mind as their sounds drew closer. In a desperate attempt to elude capture, he positioned one of his fallen comrades atop himself, striving to remain motionless amidst the advancing enemy. His plan succeeded as the enemy overlooked him, presuming he, too, was among the deceased. With the dawn came silence and tranquility, granting my bố a moment of respite to cautiously make his escape, embarking on a grueling journey out of the jungle. Amongst his platoon, he stood alone as the sole survivor of that fateful day.

There came a fateful moment when my bố's fortune abandoned him, and he fell into the merciless grip of the Viet Cong. His existence became a harrowing tale of suffering, confined to the desolate confines of a prison camp. Within those grim walls, he endured the cruel torments of starvation, brutal beatings that left his body battered and broken, and the unspeakable horror of a jagged blade carving its way across his back. The wound, reaching deep into his very bone, festered and oozed with infection, a haunting reminder of his enduring agony. Without proper medical care, his body weakened, consumed by a fever that threatened to claim his life. While the bullet wound in his side had spared him from immediate death, the festering wound in his back unleashed a relentless assault, pushing him to the precipice of the abyss.

Before the ravages of war shattered their world, my má reveled in a life of opulence and privilege. Her family's standing in Vietnamese society soared to great heights, their wealth intertwined with a myriad of successful businesses. They commanded influence and respect, forging deep connections among the elite and the corridors of power. Yet, it was my má's ethereal beauty that cast a spell over all who beheld her, earning her the coveted title of the Most Beautiful Woman in Vietnam. Admirers flocked to her side, offering their hearts and their fortunes, vying for her hand in marriage. But destiny had other plans as the ominous storm of civil war loomed on the horizon. The dreams of a bright future were put on hold as my má, a young and hopeful university student in Nha Trang, found herself caught in the grip of uncertainty and a nation torn asunder.

As the ravages of war engulfed the land, the Viet Cong Communist Party sought to extinguish the flames of freedom. Wealth was plundered, a cruel punishment inflicted upon those who remained steadfast on their homeland's soil. Amidst the chaos, university students were summoned to bear witness to the atrocities and pen letters of unwavering support to Vietnamese soldiers locked in a battle against the Viet Cong. In a twist of fate, my má, driven by an unseen force, drew my bố's name from the lottery, her heart pouring forth emotions onto the pages, offering solace and encouragement to an unknown soldier. Little did she know that her words, infused with love and compassion, would become a lifeline, weaving a bond that transcended the confines of war and suffering.

My bố was already acquainted with my má, familiar with her family, and captivated by her beauty upon receiving her first letter. As they exchanged their heartfelt words, a courtship blossomed between them, fueled by the youthful charm and irresistible allure of my bố, the dashing soldier with a muscular build. In a remarkably brief span of time, he easily won over my má's heart. Raised in humble circumstances, he embodied everything that my Má's family was not. Whether driven by novelty, rebellion or perhaps the guiding hand of destiny, my má and bố defied her parents' wishes and secretly united in marriage. However, this clandestine union inflicted great shame, pain, and sorrow upon her family. The weight of this shame and grief proved so overwhelming for my grandfather that he is said to have succumbed to a broken heart just six months later. Bereft of my grandfather's presence, my grandmother's passing followed soon thereafter. Abandoned by her remaining family, my má bore the burden of guilt and blame, a heavy load she carried throughout her days.

With the tragic loss of her parents, life became an agonizing journey for my má, compounded by the challenges that arose after her marriage. Deprived of her family's support, she was compelled to abandon her studies at the university, immediately thrust into the responsibilities of my bố's family's way of life. She was taught the skills of cooking and cleaning, transforming into a dutiful housewife, serving her new family, and embracing her new home. This unfamiliar way of life presented my mother with immense struggles, immersing her in the hardships endured by the less privileged segments of society. In the absence of external support, the family became their sole pillar of strength. Having children held great significance, as it meant extra hands to share the burdens of daily life. Like many new families, the desire for children took precedence. Soon after, my sister came into the world, swiftly followed by my birth. We were considered "Irish twins," born less than a year apart.

My early days in this world were marked by immense struggle, whether it was the consequence of war, poverty, famine, or the relentless grip of diseases sweeping across the land. From the moment of my birth, I became a fragile and sickly child, and my má carried me to the hospital week after week, desperate for answers. Countless days and nights slipped away as doctors tirelessly worked to unravel the mysteries of my ailment. But when I was a mere three months old, a grave turn of events unfolded. A raging fever engulfed my tiny body, and each labored breath became a gasp for life, leaving me lying in my crib, fighting for each precious intake of air. In a frenzy, my má whisked me away to the hospital, hoping against hope for a miracle.

Within the hospital walls, a doctor carefully examined me, measuring my temperature and listening intently to the rhythm of my lungs. With a somber expression, he diagnosed me with pneumonia, and my fragile lungs were weighed down by fluid. Urgency gripped the room as he instructed a nurse to administer a shot of penicillin to combat the fever and infection. But as the seconds ticked by, a dreadful realization washed over my má—something was still terribly wrong. In a matter of moments, my body erupted with patches of purple, my cries grew louder, and my breaths came in rapid gasps. An allergic reaction had seized me, ensnaring my life in a precarious dance. Witnessing the life drain from my fragile form, my má was overcome with terror. She saw the silent plea in my eyes, a plea for her help, a plea for salvation. Filled with panic, she rushed out of the room, screaming for the nurse's assistance, desperate for the doctor's immediate return.

Startled by my má's piercing cries, the nurse hurried to her side, asking in a concerned voice, "What's happening? What's wrong?"

With anguish etched upon her face, my má cried out, "My so…. Something is terribly wrong! He can't breathe, and he's turning purple! Where is the doctor? We need him here!"

Understanding the gravity of the situation, the nurse shook her head sadly and replied, "Oh no… The doctor just left. Maybe you can catch up to him if you hurry." She gestured towards the exit, her heart heavy with empathy.

My má darted towards the exit, her footsteps echoing in a race against time. Frantically scanning the area, she caught sight of a figure clad in a white medical uniform walking away. She sprinted after him, pleading desperately, "Doctor…. Please, stop!"

Startled by the urgency in a woman's voice, the doctor turned around, his eyes meeting my má's tearful gaze. She fell to her knees, her voice quivering with anguish. "Doctor…. My son, something is terribly wrong! He's turning purple, struggling to breathe! Please, come back and save him. I would give up everything, even my own life, to save him. Please, doctor, save my son."

Without hesitation, the doctor lifted her from the ground, his voice filled with determination, "Hurry, let's go back and see what's happening." Together, they rushed back to my room, their footsteps a symphony of hope amidst the desperate silence. Upon arrival, the doctor swiftly recognized the signs of an anaphylactic reaction to the penicillin. He rummaged through the medicine cabinets, searching for the antidote to counteract the life-threatening response. I lay there, almost motionless, my skin turning an ominous shade of blue, my very existence hanging by a thread. My má stood by helplessly, her eyes filled with tears, praying silently for a miracle to unfold before her.

With careful precision, the doctor administered the lifesaving medication. A glimmer of hope flickered in the room as my body responded, transitioning from cold and blue to feverish and flushed. Though my breathing remained feeble, the doctor instructed the nurse to place ice all over my body and position a large fan to cool the fever raging within me. Turning to my má, the doctor spoke words of reassurance, "I believe we made it back just in time. Your son appears to have an allergy to penicillin, but the medication I've given should help. With time, he should recover."

Overwhelmed with gratitude, my má embraced the doctor, her heart brimming with appreciation for his heroic efforts. "Thank you, doctor. Thank you so much," she whispered, the weight of her words resonating in the air.

"I will return in a few hours to check on him again. Until then, we must remain patient and pray," the doctor responded, his voice filled with a blend of professional assurance and genuine care.

As hours stretched into the night, I slowly regained stability, slipping into a deep, peaceful slumber. My má remained steadfast by my side, counting each breath I took, refusing to close her eyes. She whispered prayers of gratitude to the Buddha, forever indebted to the doctor who had saved my life. Such events recurred throughout the first fifteen months of my existence—incessant sickness, a weakened body, and countless hospital visits.

Following Vietnamese customs and traditions, a ceremony was performed to symbolically exchange my illness for a healthy child. With the guidance of my bà nội (grandmother), my má entrusted me to the care of a close friend. Prayers were offered, beseeching the divine forces to ease my ailments. As my má's friend returned me to her arms and was given the nickname Cu Được, which means "good boy." A name that carried hope and the promise of renewed strength. In the ceremony's aftermath, a remarkable transformation unfolded. I thrived, my perpetual illness gradually relinquishing its hold on me while my fragile body grew stronger.

And so, the indomitable spirit of my má, guided by love and unwavering devotion, shielded me from the brink of despair and granted me the gift of life. From the depths of those early struggles emerged resilience, shaping the trajectory of my journey and igniting the fire within me to embrace each day as a testament to the triumph of the human spirit.

In the aftermath of the Vietnam War, our homeland lay in ruins. The price of victory was steep, leaving behind a landscape marred by poverty, scarcity, and immense loss. The toll on American soldiers alone reached 58,000 lives, but for Vietnam, the cost was far greater. The nation mourned the loss of 3.1 million citizens, including soldiers and civilians alike.

In April 1975, the Northern Viet Cong seized control of Saigon, renaming it Ho Chi Minh City. The twenty-year civil war had come to an end, and it was time for United States soldiers and their allies to leave and return home.

My bố, being one of those allies, was granted priority for evacuation after the American soldiers departed. However, securing our departure as a family proved to be another uphill battle. We faced the daunting task of providing evidence of my parents' marriage and our birth certificates to prove our legitimacy. The clock was ticking, and time was running out to escape the grasp of the Viet Cong. It was a race against the odds, a race against the uncertain future that awaited us.

As I reflect on what I believe to be my earliest memory, I recall gazing out of a window, the view unknown. In my young mind, I imagined we were in Hawaii, perhaps on a layover en route to America. Our family had seldom traveled to glamorous or exotic destinations; our world was confined to our small hometown. But in my innocent imagination, that solitary palm tree outside the window symbolized a dream of Hawaii, inspired by an old Elvis movie I used to watch with my má. She adored Elvis, just like countless other women in the 70s. Together, we would lose ourselves in his movies and melodies, cherishing those moments we shared.

In the cozy corners of our home, my sister and I would belt out the lyrics, "You ain't nothin' but a hound dog, cryin' all the time…" as my má danced along, immersed in the joy of our makeshift performances. Clad in our vibrant red and yellow two-toned onesie pajamas, we would wave our hands and sway our hips, channeling our inner Elvis Presley.

My má adored Elvis to the core. She would often tell me, "It would be a dream come true to see Elvis in real life." Her longing echoed the sentiments of millions of women across the globe who shared a love for the King of Rock and Roll.

But as time went on, I discovered that my childhood belief of being in Hawaii was shattered. The reality was that we were at an airport in Vietnam en route to a refugee camp in White Rock, Arkansas, as the Vietnam War neared its end. This revelation made me question what other memories had faded since that moment I gazed at the palm tree through the window. The idyllic images of swaying palm trees, Elvis, and the movie "Blue Hawaii" were shattered. All I could recall was being a frightened two-year-old, relying on my parents as they guided us onto the plane that fateful day. Our destination: America.

CHAPTER 2

NOT YOUR TYPICAL SOUTHERN BELLE

On that eagerly anticipated first day of school, Ally chose a seat near the front, balancing being noticed by the teacher and avoiding the "nerd" label from the cool kids. With her long, dark pigtails neatly parted in the middle, she exuded confidence in her third-grade glory. Clad in brand-new jeans and a crisp, buttoned-up white shirt, she marveled at her reflection, thinking, "I look pretty cool but also smart."

As the bell resounded, signaling the start of class, the students hurriedly found their places. And then, in walked Rose—a blonde freckled-faced girl with a mischievous grin and an asymmetrical pixie haircut. Clad in punkish rock attire, she sported black tights, a white tank top, and a neon pink sweatshirt loosely hanging off her shoulder. The teacher introduced her to the class, announcing that Rose had just transferred from a local private Catholic school. Pointing to an empty seat, the teacher suggested, "Rose, why don't you sit next to Ally? She's one of my best students. I'm sure you two will get along just fine."

Taking a deep breath, Rose made her way toward Ally's desk, dropping her backpack to the side and slumping into her seat. Instantly, Ally straightened up and turned to Rose, a beaming smile on her face. "Hi, Rose! Would you like to be friends?" she enthusiastically asked.

Rose glanced at Ally, a hint of skepticism in her eyes, as she assessed her new classmate. As the new kid, she knew the importance of maintaining a certain reputation on the very first day of school—avoiding association with the "losers" was crucial. Perhaps she could establish herself as the Catholic schoolgirl turned rebellious. Pausing for a moment, Rose finally responded, "Do you know any bad words?"

Ally looked at her without hesitation and said, "Fuck."

With a smile of genuine warmth, Rose replied, "You bet! I'm Rose."

Ally, ever the compassionate soul, didn't let Rose's initial guardedness deter her. She still saw the potential for a genuine friendship. Ally possessed an unwavering determination to ensure that no one around her felt excluded or left behind. At home, she was a lively and exuberant child, but when it came to school, she chose to present herself as a quiet and obedient student. Ally made it her mission to always put her best foot forward in the classroom, striving to be an exemplary student. Her efforts consistently earned her the title of the teacher's pet, even though deep-down Ally had held a rebellious spirit within her.

Ally, born in the spring of 1978, was the second daughter of Marie and JB. From a young age, she exuded an energetic and joyful spirit. At just eight months old, while playing on the floor with her mother, a remarkable moment occurred. Ally pulled herself up, teetering slightly, and took her first wobbly steps. Marie, ready to catch her if she fell, encouraged her, saying, "Come on, you can do it!" With a radiant smile, Ally surprised everyone by taking not just one step but several before tumbling into her mother's waiting arms. Undeterred by the fall, Ally immediately got back up and eagerly attempted to take more steps. At that moment, Marie recognized the unwavering determination and spirited nature within her daughter. She knew Ally would be a force to be reckoned with as she grew older, never backing down from a challenge.

As a child, Ally had a penchant for carrying a doll or teddy bear in one arm, always accompanied by a small purse swinging from her other arm. Even at a young age, she yearned to embody the image of a grown-up imitating her mother's every move. One evening, while browsing the aisles of their local JC Penney, Ally's curiosity led her to a colorful display of pencils. Mesmerized by their vibrant hues, she halted in her tracks and turned to her mother, expressing her desire to purchase one.

Caught off guard, Marie paused for a moment, aware that Ally already had an abundance of pencils at home. However, captivated by her determined gaze, Marie asked, "Do you really want them?"

"Yes!" Ally exclaimed, her voice filled with excitement. "And I brought my own money." Ally beamed with pride, eager to show her independence. She delved into her purse, revealing a handful of coins to her mother. "Do I have enough money, Mom?"

Marie carefully counted the coins in her daughter's outstretched hand and replied, "Yes, you have enough, plus tax."

Perplexed, Ally furrowed her brow and asked, "What is tax?"

Taking a moment to explain, Marie replied, "Tax is a small amount of money that we pay when we buy something. It helps the government."

Ally looked at her mother incredulously. Ally's face contorted with dissatisfaction. "I'm not paying tax!" she declared, asserting her objection.

Marie gently responded, "If you want to buy this pencil, you have to pay the tax."

Ally stood there for a moment, contemplating what she had just heard. Then, with a determined expression, she placed the pencil back and started walking away. Marie, puzzled, called after her, "Wait, where are you going? Don't you want the pencil?"

With conviction, Ally replied, "No, let's go home, Mom. I'm not paying tax." At that moment, Marie realized she had a little rebel on her hands.

Every night, after her bath, Ally would race to her parents' bedroom, showering them with a big warm Ally hug and a kiss goodnight before preparing for bed. When it was time for Ally to attend nursery school, Marie would enter her room every morning, crawl into bed beside her, and playfully wiggle her nose, announcing, "It's time to wake up Sleeping Beauty." This routine never failed to bring a smile to Ally's face as she greeted her mother. The two would lie there for a few precious moments, engaging in gentle conversation, before Marie would slide out of bed to prepare breakfast.

Ally held a deep love for her mother during her childhood. Often, she would enter her mother's room with her hair ribbons in hand and ask Marie to brush her hair. Marie would playfully inquire, "How beautiful do you want to be today?"

Ally would always reply with confidence, "As beautiful as ever!" Pigtails were her most frequent request. Marie sought to teach her daughter that true beauty came from within, enabling her to radiate beauty on the outside as well.

From a tender age, Ally possessed an insatiable desire to be at the center of attention. Her laughter, resounding with exuberance, demanded the participation of everyone around her. Despite her intelligence and wit, it was her compassionate nature and nobleness that defined her character. Ally had an inherent inclination to bestow generosity upon those in her company, always offering anything and everything she had to make others feel cherished and significant. Her cleverness and playful sarcasm became her love language, a means to create lighthearted connections. Yet, alongside her vivacity, Ally embraced humility, often choosing self-deprecation rather than belittling others. However, despite her endearing qualities, she never truly believed she possessed the same beauty as her mother or her sister with blonde hair. To compensate for this perceived deficit, Ally embodied the role of the perky, fun-loving little girl. Consideration and thoughtfulness came naturally to her, complemented by a subtle southern drawl that lingered in her speech, eventually fading over time. She became known as "Miss Ally" among those who encountered her spirited personality and infectious charm. And if her charismatic presence wasn't enough, she possessed a secret weapon—a pair of captivating, blue eyes capable of melting hearts with their sheer beauty.

The strains of daily life often weigh heavy on individuals, and when combined with the responsibilities of marriage and raising young children, the pressure can become overwhelming. In those times, societal norms dictated that women tended to the home, cared for the children, and prepared meals until they were old enough for their mothers to return to work. Ally's father, JB, worked in real estate, a field that demanded significant groundwork, marketing, and networking to close deals in order to earn a living. JB's commitment to providing for the family often meant long hours away from home, frequently returning late past suppertime. The girls, including Ally, would grow hungry and often complain about the delay.

Marie felt neglected and disrespected because of JB's uncertain schedule. Minor disappointments, broken promises, and occasional white lies began to wear on Marie, causing her considerable misery. These patterns of behavior echoed the early days of their relationship, and as time went on, they intensified, leading Marie to reach her breaking point. Finally, upon returning from a week-long cruise around the 4th of July, Marie declared to JB, "I want a divorce." JB, taken aback and somewhat angered, responded callously, "Don't let the door hit you in the ass on the way out," effectively dismissing the matter.

A month later, when the couple found themselves alone, Marie broached the subject once more, her tone serious. "JB, I want a divorce," she stated firmly. "I'm tired of this. You're hardly ever home, or you're always late because you're out drinking with your friends."

JB, feeling defensive, fired back, "I'm out there busting my balls working, trying to put food on the table so we can have a roof over our heads and nice things for you and the girls."

"Gimme a break, JB. You completely ignore me and the girls. It's like you don't even have a family to come home to. Work, work, work is always your excuse," Marie exclaimed, her frustration evident. "I can't continue like this anymore."

Given past disagreements and near-miss incidents that nearly ended their marriage, JB stood his ground, declaring, "If this is what you want, then go ahead. Let's get a divorce. I'm done with this nonsense." JB added, "But Marie... This time will be the last time we go through this. I'm done putting up with your bullshit for good."

"I'm done with this, too," Marie replied. They agreed the girls should remain in their familiar home environment while Marie would move out in the fall. A date was set, and the remaining details would be worked out with their attorneys.

The memory of her mother leaving the house was forever etched deeply in Ally's mind. She was merely ten years old, returning from cheerleading practice with her friends. As their car pulled up to their house, Ally witnessed her mother stepping out and getting into her own car. Clutching a suitcase in one hand and a spice rack in the other, Marie drove away, leaving Ally standing silently on the sidewalk in front of their home.

That moment marked a turning point for Ally, as her once happy and outgoing demeanor faded, replaced by melancholy and introspection. Witnessing her parents' separation had a profound impact on Ally, for she loved her mother dearly. In the days that followed, she could often be found in the backyard, spending hours jumping on the big trampoline or lying there alone, gazing at the stars, lost in her thoughts. The trampoline became her refuge, a sanctuary from reality, school, people, and the turmoil of her parents' separation. It served as a meditative space, allowing her to process her emotions, thoughts, and the upheaval in her young life. As Ally bounced on the trampoline, her movements became a metaphor for the turbulence she felt inside. Each jump represented a moment of release, a chance to let go of the pain and confusion that weighed heavily on her heart.

Amidst the ups and downs on that trampoline, Ally found solace and a semblance of control. She could soar into the air, defying gravity for those fleeting moments, and for a brief instant, all her worries and troubles seemed to disappear. The rhythmic bouncing created a rhythm of resilience, a reminder that she had the strength to overcome the challenges before her.

Over time, Ally's sorrow transformed into strength. The trampoline became a symbol of resilience and self-discovery, a reminder that even in the face of adversity, she possessed the ability to bounce back and rise above. She carried that resilience with her as she navigated the complexities of her parents' divorce, school, and the ever-changing dynamics of her family.

The following summer, after enduring countless months of legal battles, the divorce of Ally's parents reached its final agreement. The judge would decide the custody of the girls based on the evidence presented. Ally's older sister, having no strong bond with their mother, made the choice to live with their dad. In order to keep the sisters together, the court ruled that Ally would also stay with their dad. JB was granted full custody, while Marie had the right to visit her girls whenever she wished.

Marie, struggling financially on a secretary's salary and feeling isolated without much family or friends in Gainesville for support, faced a heart-wrenching decision. Two months after the divorce, she made the agonizing choice to leave her daughters behind and return to her hometown in Illinois to live with her parents till she was able to get back on her feet. Financial realities loomed heavily for both parents, and JB had already prepared the girls for the likelihood of their mom moving far away. During the school year, Marie tried her best to visit her girls in Gainesville whenever she could afford it. But it was during the summer break that Ally and her sister traveled to Illinois, spending time with their mom and JB's family and cherished moments with their cousins.

The impact of the divorce weighed heavily on Ally's young heart. JB, thrust into the role of a single dad, had little understanding of the immense effort and care required of a mother. He struggled to fill both parental roles, seeking guidance from his female friends on how to navigate the challenges of raising two teenage girls. Ally's sister, now old enough to venture out and spend time with friends, often left Ally feeling lonely and left behind. This newfound solitude didn't sit well with Ally, prompting her to seek solace and a sense of normalcy in the company of JB's female friends. They became surrogate mothers to her, providing a listening ear and companionship during trips to the mall as she tried to establish a new equilibrium. Without a mother figure to turn to and a single dad still learning the ropes, Ally's older sister became the woman she often relied upon for guidance and support, seeking answers to the questions that arose on their shared journey.

In middle school, Ally's social circle expanded, and she maintained her position as a diligent student. She achieved Honor Roll status and stayed out of trouble, yet her self-esteem issues persisted. By the 7th grade, her friends noticed her thinning figure and became concerned about a potential eating disorder. Taking action, they reached out to a school counselor, prompting private counseling sessions to address her mental and emotional well-being, particularly in the aftermath of the divorce.

By the 8th grade, Ally's life started to improve. Her father gifted her a stylish pair of glasses, she finally got braces to enhance her smile, and her interest in fashion allowed her to develop a sense of style. Ally and Rose eagerly followed her older sister and her rebellious friends, aspiring to emulate their cool high school personas. They would even seek her sister's expertise to do their hair and makeup for picture day. With a touch of magic from a curling iron, a generous spritz of hairspray, and frosted pink lipstick, they felt confident and ready to conquer the world.

Just when Ally's life was beginning to come together, and her confidence was growing, her sister entered a serious relationship and decided to move away from Gainesville in order to be with her boyfriend and his family. The departure of her beloved sister left Ally feeling abandoned once again, forcing her to navigate her identity, life, and home on her own.

High school brought proms, parties, wild spring break adventures, and the typical teenage mischief. Now of driving age, Ally gravitated towards a group of girls who, like her, came from divorced families and shared rebellious and angsty attitudes. During one visit to a friend's house, where her older sister had become pregnant during high school, conversations revolved around partying and sex, common topics among wild young teenagers. This environment wasn't conducive to Ally's well-being, and she started experimenting with smoking dope, seeking an escape from her struggles.

On a Sunday afternoon, Ally made plans to attend a lakeside picnic with a friend. As the evening approached and suppertime drew near, JB paged Ally, concerned about her whereabouts. Despite multiple attempts, there was no response from her. Growing worried, JB decided to call the friend's mother to inquire if she had any information. Suspecting that the girls might be at an apartment where some guys resided, both parents embarked on an investigation. By 9 pm, they arrived at the apartment, where faint music emanated from within. Knocking on the door, they awaited a response, but no one answered. JB and the friend's mother agreed that if no one came to the door by 10 pm, they would involve the police.

Suddenly, the girls rolled up in a car accompanied by two boys who were clearly under the influence of marijuana. JB's anger surged as he approached Ally. "Ally, get out of the car. It's time to go home, young lady!"

Ally began to plead her case, desperately saying, "No, Dad. I don't want to go home. Please, Dad, please let me stay. I want to hang out with them a little longer."

JB's voice grew stern as he responded, "No, Ally. Let's go NOW! Or you are going to be in big trouble!"

"No!" Ally screamed back. "I don't want to go!"

"Get in the car, young lady. I'm not going to ask again," JB yelled as he advanced toward her. Finally, Ally reluctantly got into the car to go home. During the drive, she fretted over the abrupt departure and even threatened to get out of the car and run away. As they approached a traffic light, Ally impulsively opened the car door just as JB was making a turn. Reacting swiftly, he grabbed her by the neck and shoulders, preventing her from falling out. A nearby car witnessed the incident and began honking in alarm. JB glanced at Ally and asked if she recognized the driver. "No." Concerned for Ally's well-being, the witness immediately reported the incident to the local sheriff, suspecting a potential kidnapping.

Shortly after arriving home, two deputy sheriffs appeared at JB's doorstep, inquiring about the reported kidnapping incident. JB explained the misunderstanding and shared his account of what had transpired. One deputy noticed Ally slouched on the couch and decided to approach her. With a single glance, he recognized the signs of her being high—her bloodshot, red eyes. Ally, just seventeen, seemed distant and troubled. The deputy took a seat beside her and gently asked, "Allyson, your dad told me quite a story about what happened earlier today. Care to explain why it all unfolded?"

Ally let out a sigh and replied, "I just want to have fun, but I can't. I want to move out, but my dad won't let me."

The deputy responded, his tone empathetic yet firm, "Listen, I have a daughter too, and you need to understand something. At seventeen, you're not of legal age. You can't move out or make major decisions on your own. If you have the means to support yourself and your parents give their consent, then maybe it's possible. But right now, I'm seriously considering taking you down to the station and putting you in jail. I can see that you're high—your dilated eyes and the scent of smoke give it away. So, I know you've been smoking dope." Ally's eyes widened, realizing the gravity of her situation. The deputy continued, "You can reconcile with your dad, talk to him, or do whatever you want. You don't have to like it, but until you turn eighteen, young lady, you're somewhat stuck here. Once you're eighteen, he can't say anything about it. You can go wherever you want or wherever you can afford to live."

Ally listened attentively, nodding in understanding. "Yes, sir," she replied. The deputy's conversation saved JB from potential trouble that night and made Ally reflect on her actions. Before leaving, he clarified that the responsibility now rested in JB's hands, warning that any further issues would require legal intervention.

As Ally progressed through her senior year, her interests shifted away from teenage parties and social circles. She grew tired of the immaturity and what she perceived as a small-town mindset. Opting for dual enrollment, she left high school to pursue her GED at Santa Fe Community College. This choice allowed her to distance herself from things she no longer found fulfilling or wanted to be a part of. With JB's help, she secured a hostess position at a friend's restaurant, which was a popular college hangout near the University of Florida. Ally swiftly began earning a substantial income and moved out of the house as soon as she turned eighteen. She was determined to prove to herself that she could be independent and self-sufficient, just as the deputy had encouraged her.

Despite living separately, Ally and her dad remained incredibly close. On chilly winter evenings, she would visit, and they would build roaring fires in the fireplace. They shared their favorite meal, grilled cheese sandwiches and tomato soup, while snuggling under a pile of cozy quilts on the couch, indulging in old movies that brought them joy.

After high school, Ally embarked on a nomadic lifestyle, finding temporary homes with old friends, new acquaintances, coworkers, and even a romantic partner. These connections formed small, intimate circles where Ally felt safe. She cherished the one-on-one time spent with those closest to her and fiercely protected these bonds. Witnessing her parents' acrimonious divorce at a young age left Ally with deep-seated feelings of abandonment. The sudden departures of loved ones had made her vulnerable, forcing her to navigate life's challenges without much support or guidance.

The traditional path of attending a university didn't appeal to Ally. Instead, she continued her studies at the community college, allowing herself time to discover her true calling. However, the demands of bartending at The Swamp, coupled with the allure of money and meaningful relationships, caused her academic pursuits to take a backseat.

During her time at work, Ally encountered a new hire, a nervous, blue-eyed college student named Alli, whose name was spelled with an "I" instead of a "Y." Tasked with training her, Ally embraced her role and swiftly formed an unbreakable bond with Alli. They became inseparable, like two sisters on an exciting journey. Eventually, they moved into a cozy two-bedroom house situated behind a local Applebee. Their lives merged into a continuous celebration. They earned the moniker "the two Allies" or simply "the A's," distinguished by their last names, AB and AT. When people called, they playfully asked, "Do you want to speak to the brunette or the blonde?" Ally naturally assumed the role of the older sister, guiding AT through her school projects and ensuring she arrived punctually. Together, they hosted lively parties at their abode, creating a pocket of happiness. It felt like everything was finally falling into place for Ally. Once again, she became the vibrant soul, capturing attention wherever she went, just like the spirited little girl who was lovingly called "Little Miss Ally."

As time passed, Ally watched her closest friends graduate, secure well-paying jobs, acquire new cars and houses, and venture off to start their adult lives and families. From a young age, Ally understood people needed to move on, so she didn't hold any resentment towards this reality. She preferred focusing on the present and the people she loved, avoiding discussions about her past. However, as more friends departed, she felt like she was stagnating, stuck in the same place year after year. Ally never quite connected with the Florida lifestyle or its mindset. She believed her calling extended beyond what the small town of Gainesville had to offer. Her aspirations yearned for big cities, grand parties, and the allure of the fashion industry. Determined to pursue her dreams, she made the bold decision to study fashion design at the Art Institute in San Francisco, California. She desired to distance herself as far as possible, ensuring she wouldn't have to return home. It was her turn to leave behind the people she cherished and embark on a solo journey. Ally began revealing her plans to those who mattered most in her life.

Amid planning her own wedding after graduating from the University of Florida, Rose had asked Ally to be her maid of honor. Three months before the wedding, during a planning session, Ally gathered the courage to share her news. "Rose... I have something to tell you. I'm moving to San Francisco to study fashion design at the Art Institute. Eek!"

Rose stared at Ally, stunned, and exclaimed, "You're doing what?! San Francisco is so far away, and it's really expensive."

With determination, Ally replied, "Yeah, I know. I'm just tired of this situation. I don't want to live in this town anymore. It's stifling. I don't want to work in a bar forever. I simply want a fresh start."

Always supportive of Ally, Rose responded, "Hell yeah! Go for it."

The day before the wedding finally arrived, filled with a bridal luncheon, spa treatments, and a rehearsal dinner. It would be their final precious moments alone together. Caught up in the excitement, Rose and Ally lost track of time and ended up arriving at the church for the walkthrough approximately 45 minutes late. Their absence led everyone, including the groomsmen, flower girls, ushers, parents, pastor, and wedding planner, to speculate that Rose had pulled a "Thelma and Louise" and run off. Relief washed over them when the two friends finally made their appearance.

During the wedding, Ally dutifully held Rose's flowers and discreetly helped her navigate bathroom breaks in her dress. She fulfilled her maid of honor responsibilities with grace. Laughter, celebration, speeches, toasts, and tears filled the day and continued into the night. It was a flawless farewell, witnessing Ally's oldest and dearest friend marry the love of her life before Ally set out to pursue her own dreams. The date was July 1, 2002. The following Monday, just before the Fourth of July, Ally bid her final goodbyes and embarked on a journey westward to forge a new life—a poignant moment, occurring fourteen years after Marie had expressed her desire to leave as well.

CHAPTER 3

LEARNING ASIAN/AMERICAN

Once we arrived at the refugee camp, my dad wasted no time in reaching out to our sponsor. He made daily calls, determined to shorten our stay in the camps as much as possible. We eagerly awaited the opportunity to leave the crowded meager camps and begin our new life in Seattle, WA. During the war, my dad formed a friendship with an American soldier who had agreed to sponsor us. This soldier became our lifeline, taking care of us during our initial months in America. His support and kindness were a constant source of comfort as we navigated this unfamiliar territory. However, Seattle, with its big buildings, many cars, busy roads, and freeways, proved to be overwhelming for my parents. They were accustomed to the simplicity and slower pace of life in our small rural country. Realizing this, our sponsors sought a solution that would ease our transition. They discovered a group of compassionate Christian families in the quaint town of Lynden, about 100 miles north of Seattle. These kind-hearted families willingly took on the financial responsibilities of sponsoring our family and helping us adjust to our new surroundings. Their love and support became the pillars of our acclimation to the American way of life. In Lynden, we found a community that embraced us with open arms, providing the warmth and familiarity we craved in our new home.

Only fragments of memories from that time remained in my mind. I can recall visiting our American grandparents' warm and rustic home. It was adorned with Dutch antiques, hunting trophies, and a basement filled with a pool table and board games for us to play with their grandkids. Stories were shared about our first few months there. In those early days, my sister and I would run around, speaking in a foreign language, seeking comfort in each other and our mother. Whenever a loud noise echoed, we would scurry away and hide, gripped by fear and tears. Perhaps these reactions were triggered by subconscious recollections of the distant sounds of gunfire and bombs from the war. Looking back, I realize I was still too young to remember everything clearly. However, the fragments that have remained with me are the moments of joy. Swinging on the backyard set, savoring warm cookies fresh from the oven, and being embraced by our new extended family, who cared for and loved us dearly. Everything else that happened during that time must have been so distressing that my mind blocked those memories. I made the conscious decision to forget them rather than hold on to the pain they brought.

Over time, we all became proficient in English, allowing us to effectively express our desires, needs, happiness, concerns, and fears. My dad secured a job as a boiler engineer at a nearby oil refinery in a neighboring city. Eventually, we moved into our own home, embracing independence and adapting to the American way of life while holding onto our Vietnamese roots, language, and culture. While we occasionally indulged in American favorites like hot dogs, hamburgers, pizza, and fried chicken, our meals mainly consisted of traditional Vietnamese dishes and a generous amount of packaged ramen and rice.

Later on, we relocated to the larger nearby town of Bellingham, where we found ourselves among a predominantly Caucasian population of 30,000-40,000 people, with only a handful of Asian minorities, including our family. The town boasted a Chinese restaurant and a small Asian grocery store. We felt distinctively different from those around us. Making friends was a challenge, possibly because memories of the Vietnam War were still fresh in Americans' minds. However, we were fortunate to connect with one of the few other Vietnamese families in town. Despite being further from our sponsors, we felt more isolated from the world. Consequently, we kept mostly to ourselves during those early years, aside from occasional visits from our sponsor family. Thankfully, I had my sister by my side to talk to and play with. We were inseparable until my mother gave birth to my little brother, Billy. He was given an American name, inspired by my dad's love for Western movies and the infamous outlaw Billy the Kid.

As my brother grew older, my mother secured a job at a local seafood packing plant. With two incomes, we were able to upgrade to a larger house in a better neighborhood, surrounded by many other kids. My sister and I were enrolled in the YMCA Head Start program, where we learned the invaluable skills of socializing and playing with children our age. Attending church and Sunday school became a regular part of our weekends, and soon enough, we reached the age to start elementary school. Slowly but surely, we began to feel a sense of acceptance and belonging within the community. America was transforming into a place we could truly call home. The elementary school opened doors to new friendships. I found it easier to connect with others, and together with my newfound companions, we engaged in imaginative play. We built forts in the woods, created scenarios with cars and houses in the sandbox, and enjoyed swimming in the nearby creek. Team intramural soccer and basketball became thrilling activities we participated in. Life seemed uncomplicated during those days. We would wake up, tune in to our favorite cartoons, have cereal for breakfast, attend school, and return home eagerly, ready to spend hours outdoors until dinnertime. Exploring the world around us became our form of entertainment, and we reveled in the simple joys of childhood.

Growing up, we absorbed American culture through our beloved television shows like Happy Days, Three's Company, The Brady Bunch, Laverne and Shirley, and Mash. However, our parents made sure we stayed connected to our Vietnamese heritage by frequently speaking to us in Vietnamese, even though we responded in English. They pushed us to excel academically, insisting on being better than average. We were taught math and given extra homework before it was even taught in class. They emphasized that we had been given an opportunity for a better life, a gift that we must not squander. Respecting our elders and family was instilled in us, as our dad would often remind us, "Blood is thicker than water." We had each other to rely on, being one of the few Asian American families in our small town.

Being raised in an Asian American family already meant a strict upbringing, but having an Asian military father, especially a Green Beret, took it to another level. Fear and respect were the foundation of our relationship with our dad. We were expected to obey and respect our parents and elders, refraining from expressing our own opinions or talking back. Any misstep resulted in trouble and discipline. Kneeling against the wall or being whipped with a stick were common forms of punishment back then. I recall a time when I was in trouble for a mistake, as young kids often make. My dad instructed me to go outside and find a stick for my punishment. I searched for the most delicate branch I could find, hoping it would be less painful. However, my dad broke it instantly and sought a young, fresh branch to deliver a proper punishment. Just a couple of strikes on my bottom were enough to ensure I remembered never to repeat my wrongdoing again.

Within our household, there were instances of violence between my parents, as my father's expectations extended to my mother. Perhaps during that time, male dominance within American households was more prevalent. In Vietnamese culture, patriarchy was deeply ingrained, shaping the way of life in the motherland. American culture encouraged having an opinion, driving change, and fostering progress, while Vietnamese culture emphasized obedience, silence, and duty. Consequently, clashes between Eastern and Western cultures occurred intermittently in our home. We witnessed my mother being subjected to more violent physical abuse if she dared to disagree, speak out, or express opinions that differed from my father's. As the oldest, my sister often threw herself between the two of them, acting as a small human shield to protect our mother as she did her best to quell the violence. The opposite response of fear would consume me, leaving me paralyzed, unable to confront my father or intervene. All I could do was sit there, helpless, shedding tears in solitude.

Over time, the influence of our old customs and the practices of our past diminished as we gradually assimilated into American culture. In the Spring of 1981, we received our US citizenship, officially becoming Americans. However, despite our newfound status, the unmistakable differences remained, becoming more pronounced in my eyes. We were still Asian, visibly distinct from the people around us. I only felt a sense of normalcy when I was with my family and a few close friends in our neighborhood. Despite longing for acceptance from everyone, I developed feelings of low self-esteem, growing increasingly introverted and withdrawn. Transitioning from elementary to middle school exacerbated these struggles as I faced new pressures concerning girls, dances, dating, and the possibility of having a girlfriend.

Another significant influence on our young minds came from the iconic romantic comedy movies of the '80s. Films like Pretty in Pink, Sixteen Candles, Footloose, Fast Times at Ridgemont High, and many more taught us about popularity, what was considered cool, and what it meant to be in love or have a real girlfriend. We emulated the latest trends and modeled ourselves after the actors we idolized. However, my experience was slightly different. The only Asian character I had to compare myself to was Long Duk Dong from Sixteen Candles, a regrettable and stereotypical caricature who often faced ridicule due to his accent and being different from everyone else. It was a far cry from the Asian action movies of my early childhood featuring Barry Lee. The one thing that spared me from such stereotypes and mockery was that I didn't have an Asian accent and spoke English fluently. Had I possessed an accent or struggled with broken English, I, too, would have become the subject of jokes, joining my friends' laughter at the expense of the other ESL Asian kids in our school.

As my first Tolo dance approached, my insecurities reached their peak. When it came to girls and dating, a constant question plagued my mind: "Why would someone choose me when they could be with a white person?" With this self-doubt consuming me, I never even considered the possibility that any girl would show an interest in me. Instead, I opted for what I thought was the next best thing—trying to befriend everyone. To my surprise, a friend asked me to be her date, likely because she didn't have anyone else to go with or shared the same fear of asking someone to our first significant dance.

The desire to be well-liked had its advantages. Being associated with my popular older sister garnered me a certain level of favor among her friends. However, being liked by others eventually evolved into wanting someone to like me in a more romantic sense. Yet, whenever I was told that someone was interested in me, I would unconsciously sabotage any potential outcome. The idea that someone could genuinely like me seemed absurd and unimaginable. I spent the majority of my middle school years single and feeling isolated.

Growing up in a predominantly white community, my perception of beauty and desire aligned with what I was familiar with—my surroundings became the standard. If we had lived in a more culturally diverse neighborhood, beyond the handful of other Asian kids I knew, perhaps things would have been different. Late at night, lying in my bedroom, I would often find myself lost in thoughts, hopes, wishes, and dreams of finding my one true love, someone to whom I could give all my love and who would reciprocate it equally. Together, we would live a blissful, lifelong romance. In my mind's eye, I would imagine her appearance—a girl with flowing hair, sometimes black, sometimes brown, sometimes blond, but always with the most mesmerizing blue eyes I had ever seen.

As a teenager, high school brought about numerous transitions and challenges. The student body grew significantly, and with it came the emergence of various social groups: the jocks, the wavers, the preppies, the headbangers, and the nerds. Navigating through this complex landscape became even more challenging, especially since my social circle had diminished to my sister and a few friends from middle school. The desire to be associated with the "cool" kids remained strong. I befriended someone who seemed to have authority within the rebellious group of wavers and stylish preps. However, this friendship came at a price. I had to gradually distance myself from my old loyal friends from middle school in order to be accepted into this clique, all while playing the role of a subservient doormat, constantly taken advantage of. In return, I gained access to the company of the cool upperclassmen and received invitations to popular parties, fulfilling my deepest longing: to be popular, well-liked, and accepted.

While I continued to dream of the day I would meet my mystery blue-eyed love, my thoughts also shifted toward my future profession and what I could do for a living. I would lie in bed, gazing at my hands, and contemplate their potential. "If these hands possessed the power to heal any ailment with a single touch, like the miracles performed by Jesus in the Bible, I could heal the world of all diseases," I would think. However, such an idea seemed far-fetched. My thoughts then evolved into a wish to possess knowledge of everything, envisioning how I could use that knowledge to solve the world's problems, eradicate diseases, and even conquer cancer. But even that seemed like a lofty ambition. Being an average student who excelled mainly in art, I settled on the goal of attending a good college, hoping that, eventually, I would find a path that could lead to a prosperous future.

After graduating from high school, I received acceptance letters from several colleges and art schools. However, I decided to attend a local, smaller university. My parents offered to assist with the cost of my education on the condition that I lived at home. Their hopes and aspirations for a successful child were vested in my sister, who opted to attend a larger university in Seattle. She was the academically gifted one, while I was the average and somewhat lost middle child who still hadn't figured out what I wanted to pursue in life. With no clear major in mind, a college friend suggested that I join him in pre-med studies until I found my true calling. So, that's what I ended up doing.

As I grew older, I eagerly looked forward to turning 21 so that I could join my older college friends from high school in hanging out at bars, drinking, and partying. In the meantime, I settled for house parties with a small group of friends and coworkers I had met through a job I started after high school. Occasionally, we would venture across the border to Vancouver, where the legal drinking age was nineteen. There, we would dance to techno music until the early hours at clubs. Once I finally reached the legal drinking age of 21, I was able to visit local college dive bars. Tuesday nights were especially exciting because it was $0.25-pitcher night until 9 pm. We would strive to arrive early, beat the long lines, and purchase at least four pitchers of beer for a mere $1.00 before the discount ended. We were all taken aback when, the following year, the price doubled to $0.50 per pitcher. It caused quite a stir among us.

The college provided a slightly more diverse environment, but the ethnic representation remained limited. It was during this period that I experienced my first genuine relationship with someone who became my first girlfriend. Her eyes didn't possess the exact deep blue color I had often imagined during my late-night contemplations, but they were captivating, nonetheless. Depending on the lighting, they appeared to be blue, green, or even gray. She was slightly older than me, which felt normal considering my perpetual status as the youngest person around. Both of us lacked substantial relationship experience, so we embarked on a journey of learning and growth together, offering each other support and companionship. Our love for each other was profound, and I wholeheartedly believed that she was the one I would marry, destined for a lifetime of happiness together.

However, as time progressed, she completed her graduation while I still had more than a year remaining to finish college. Bellingham didn't hold promising opportunities for her in terms of a job or a career, so she made the difficult decision to move back to Seattle, where she could explore better prospects for both of us. I assisted her in packing her belongings, and she returned to her parent's home, marking the beginning of a long-distance relationship for us. Once again, I found myself in a state of solitude, channeling my energy into my studies and pursuing my pre-med courses.

During my college years, Al, an old friend from high school was also pursuing a pre-med track at the local community college, but with a focus on chiropractic medicine. His ambition was to attend graduate school at a Chiropractic College in the Bay Area. He extended an invitation for me to visit, explore the campus, and spend time together. Although the school itself was housed in a converted elementary school, lacking grandeur, something within me shifted when I found myself in that environment surrounded by fellow students. It became clear to me that this was where I belonged, prompting me to proceed with the admissions interview. Upon returning home, I redirected my efforts toward completing the necessary requirements to commence chiropractic school at the end of the following quarter. However, I faced the challenging task of breaking this news to my family and my girlfriend, who patiently awaited my return to Seattle.

Living as an adult in my family home, I was soon to embark on a journey to graduate school in California. Only my mother, younger brother, and I remained in the house. In recent years, my father had been frequently absent, traveling for his new profession as a professional poker player. With the change in ownership at the local oil refinery, he opted for early retirement, unwilling to adapt to new skills. Meanwhile, my mother immersed herself in the study of Buddhism, ultimately leading her to become a Buddhist nun after our high school education concluded. Guided by the teachings of detachment, she occasionally expressed to me, "Don't expect me to be saddened or shed tears when you depart for California."

I would simply respond with a smile, "There is no reason to be sad when I leave." Although my parents did not openly exhibit a great deal of affection while we were growing up, my mother and I shared a profound bond forged long ago when she nearly lost me during our time in Vietnam.

With my departure to chiropractic school in California imminent, my coworkers and friends organized a grand farewell party in my honor. Prior to my departure, my girlfriend made the journey to spend one last weekend together. The following days were filled with final preparations and gathering my belongings, readying myself for the journey ahead. As I finished loading my car, the moment arrived when my mother fulfilled her promise. She embraced me tightly and said, "Take good care of yourself, Vo. Drive safely," as she closed the door.

Before hitting the road, I made a stop at my younger brother's workplace, where he now attended the same university I once did. As

I walked up to his workplace, I saw him diligently straightening the products on the shelf. "Hey, Billy."

He looked up, a little surprised, and said, "Oh, hey, Vo."

"Well, I am all packed up and finally ready to head off to California. Just wanted to stop by to see you one last time before I leave." He smiled. "Hey, don't be sad, okay? Please take good care of yourself and take care of Mom while I am gone. And I will see you again soon."

He nodded and smiled, "Yeah, okay, I will." We reached in to give each other a brotherly embrace before he hurriedly retreated to the storage room, hoping to conceal the tears welling in his eyes.

As I embarked on the road toward my new life and adventure, an inexplicable feeling urged me to turn around and head back home. Trusting my instincts, I veered towards our house. As I stepped to the door and extended my hand to knock, the door immediately flew open. My mother stood there, her eyes soaked in tears, rushing to embrace me. We both stood there and wept uncontrollably. We found comfort in each other's arms as we held each other, never wanting to let go. After a long-extended embrace, she composed herself and uttered words that resonated deeply, "I am so proud of you. You will become the first doctor in our family. No matter where you are in this world, I will always be with you and love you very much."

With tears still glistening in my eyes, I mustered the strength to speak, assuring my mother, "I will always love you too, Mom. Please don't worry about me. I promise you will see me again soon." The month was March 1995, a pivotal moment marking my departure from the comforting embrace of home and embarking upon the uncharted journey of adulthood, venturing out into the world on my own for the very first time.

CHAPTER 4

MOROSE IS THE NEW BLACK

During the open house orientation at the Art Institute (AI), Ally crossed paths with an unforgettable character. He exuded confidence and style. He had an affinity for vintage fashion and adorned himself with dazzling accessories. Despite their contrasting personalities, Ally was drawn to him from the moment they met. They became instant best friends and partners in crime, embarking on adventures both on school days and weekends. Like spirited siblings, they often engaged in playful arguments, only to reconcile and embrace shortly thereafter. Barry became a trusted confidant, someone with whom Ally could share her deepest struggles. Acting as an older brother figure, he never hesitated to call her out on her past behaviors and push her toward growth.

As the next quarter began, Ally and Barry found themselves waiting in the hallway, eager for class to commence. Their attention was captivated by an exotic and elegantly dressed black woman who stood in the center of the hall. Without hesitation, Ally and Barry approached her, simultaneously grasping one of her ample breasts and exclaiming, "Oh, look at these fabulous boobs!" The trio erupted in laughter, forming an instant bond. The enigmatic newcomer introduced herself as Celeste, adding another unique and vibrant presence to their circle. The friends Ally made at AI were in their mid to late 20s, bringing prior schooling and degrees to the table compared to the fresh high school graduates.

Celeste was a remarkable fashion designer hailing from Israel. Celeste had already established herself as a successful and experienced designer, with her handmade garments garnering recognition in the industry. However, when she moved to the United States to be with her fiancée, her work experience didn't meet the requirements for the job she desired. Determined to continue pursuing her career goals, Celeste made the decision to return to school and pursue a degree in fashion. Despite her wild and fun-loving nature, she remained grounded and committed to her long-term relationship.

Ally also found solace and deep conversations with Celeste, often turning to her for comfort and guidance regarding life, her past, and the future. If Ally were to be completely honest with herself, she would acknowledge that she wasn't inherently suited for design school. Her friends often teased her, claiming that she charmed her way through her courses. She lacked artistic and creative abilities, struggling with tasks such as sewing or patternmaking. However, when it came to writing or delivering presentations, Ally truly shined and felt alive. To compensate for her shortcomings, she relied on her charm to partner up with friends who possessed the skills she lacked. She often joked, "I should have learned how to pattern from taking several pattern classes, but talking was much more fun."

Ally possessed a remarkable talent for transforming mundane topics into engaging conversations. While her classmates diligently worked on their tasks, she would captivate them with her stories and lively demeanor. There were moments when she collaborated with Celeste, who would playfully chide her, saying, "Girl, I have done five different patterns, and you haven't done anything."

In response, Ally would playfully retort, "I bring the wine, and I bring the entertainment girl!" Ally herself was a bundle of joy, always wearing a radiant smile and ready for new adventures. She had an infectious zest for life, adding a touch of fire and spice to every moment. Dullness was banished whenever Ally was around, and her laughter had a way of spreading to everyone. Her hugs were warm and encompassing, as if she never wanted to let go. With her sense of humor and love for dressing up, she always brought a vibrant energy to any gathering.

During Fashion Week in San Francisco, students were given the opportunity to participate in the show and be part of the team responsible for curating the event. Various roles were assigned to students, allowing them to contribute to this grand annual affair. Ally's strength lay in her vision and her ability to see the bigger picture. When it came to organizing and stylizing the shows, she had a keen eye for how design elements should look and how they should be presented. She yearned to pursue her dream, but she often found herself frustrated by the uncertainty of what that dream actually entailed. Ally seized the potential to curate and oversee an entire fashion show on her own if she desired. However, when assigned tasks that required responsibility without the opportunity for socializing or delegation, she found herself disinterested. While she excelled at generating innovative ideas, she struggled with the process of translating those ideas into tangible results. Instead, her true strengths shone through in her writing, modeling, directing, managing, and curating significant events and fashion shows. It took her a while to find clarity and determine her true passion in school.

When San Francisco's Fashion Week approached, Ally learned that the renowned shoe designer Manolo Blahnik would be in town for an event. She was thrilled and bought one of his books, getting it signed as a cherished memento. She couldn't wait to share the exciting news with her dad, JB. Hearing the name and the enthusiasm in Ally's voice, JB assumed Manolo Blahnik was a famous football or baseball player. Ally corrected him, explaining that he was a renowned shoe designer. During Fashion Week, Manolo Blahnik selected students to work behind the scenes with him, and Ally was among the chosen few. She immediately fell in love with the work and his exquisite shoes and felt a strong desire to switch gears and learn shoe design at AI. Unfortunately, the school didn't offer a program focused on shoe design and education. Ally took the opportunity to ask Manolo if his company had any apprenticeships available for students interested in learning shoe design. He informed her that such a program was still in the works and not yet realized, but he promised to contact her if and when it became a reality. Ally had to settle for pursuing a degree in fashion design and marketing unless a miracle occurred and the shoe design program became immediately available.

During their time in school, Celeste ventured into starting her own clothing line and secured rack space in a few consignment stores. Ally often accompanied her to help with filling racks and managing inventory drop-offs and pickups. One day, Celeste had to visit a store owner's house in the San Francisco hills, but she didn't feel comfortable driving in the city alone as she had recently learned how to drive. She asked Ally to come along to provide navigation assistance. As they drove, they passed by a small, concealed Eichler home nestled behind dense bushes. Although not the largest or most magnificent house, the architecture of the home moved Ally to tears. The sloping roof and the open glass walls at the front of the house allowed for a glimpse into its interior.

Celeste immediately pulled the car over. She was puzzled and confused by Ally's emotional reaction. Wondering what was going on in her head, Celeste put her arm around Ally's shoulder and asked, "What's going on, girl? Why are you crying?"

Ally replied, "This is how I see my life. I want to live in a house just like this. Drive my little car to go get groceries or coffee or hang out at a bookstore. This is all I want. If I don't have anyone right now, then how am I going to find someone so that we can get this?"

"Oh, Ally. Everything is going to be alright. We are going to graduate soon. You are going to get an awesome job. Meet a bunch of new people. And who knows… A fine-ass man will just show up when you least expect it. You just got to trust me, girl." Celeste gave Ally a great big hug as Ally nodded and tried to compose herself. From that moment on, every time they passed by the house, it evoked a strong emotional response in Ally because she saw herself living a life aligned with that vision.

Many of the deep conversations between Celeste and Ally revolved around Ally's longing for a family and a desire to be married. Among her past boyfriends, only one had treated her well, while the others were often flighty or treated her poorly. Over time, she grew accustomed to such treatment, believing it to be the norm. Deep down, she genuinely believed she would make a great wife. She enjoyed cooking, hosting and aspired to be a homemaker. Ally envisioned having a loving husband who would support her in staying at home, taking care of the household, and being a nurturing mother and wife.

Whenever Ally felt down or dissatisfied with her life, Celeste would take her to communities of Eichler houses in the East Bay. They would drive around, sipping Prosecco from their roadie cups, and admire these unique structures. Afterward, they would explore different stores, searching for items that resonated with Ally's vision. As she selected pieces, she would say, "I want this in my daughter's room" or "I want something like this in my living room." Ally had a clear vision of how she wanted her life to look. Her negativity didn't stem from a place of self-pity but rather from a sense of uncertainty about how to attain the things she desired. She genuinely felt clueless, especially when she witnessed others achieving their dreams. Thoughts plagued her: How do you meet a nice guy? How do you find a fulfilling job? What am I doing wrong that prevents me from attaining these things for myself? Many of their profound conversations always circled back to Ally's longing to be married and have a family she could call her own.

Ally often confided in Celeste about her past, her family, and the emotional strain caused by her parents' divorce. She rarely spoke about her mother except in passing comments, offering fragments of information about their distant relationship and what went wrong between them. Celeste didn't grasp the full picture because these conversations always ended with Ally in tears, so she never probed further. Ally also expressed envy towards her sister, who seemed to have a perfect life, always getting what she wanted, while Ally struggled to find a partner willing to marry her and start a family. She couldn't help but feel envious of friends who were living the life she yearned for.

After their discussions, Ally became even more motivated and focused on her studies, successfully completing her degree. She then collaborated with school recruiters to explore various employment opportunities, engaging in interviews with different companies. However, Ally often struggled with feelings of inadequacy, doubting her own intelligence for some of these jobs. Despite her passion for becoming a fashion designer, particularly in the field of shoe design, she couldn't wait indefinitely for the Manolo Blahnik internship to materialize. Instead, she contemplated starting her own shoe line. However, Ally faced challenges when it came to understanding numbers and business concepts. Rather than taking the time to learn these skills, she allowed her dream to fade into the background. During one of her interviews, Ally's enthusiasm got the best of her. She was meeting with a furniture design company recruiter who was impressed with her, considering her a good fit for the company and offering introductions to others. However, Ally's response—"Oh my God! If you do that, I will be all over you like shit on a stick!"—unfortunately ended any chance of progressing to the next round of interviews.

As part of the annual graduation ceremonies at AI, Goodwill Corporate participated with the hope of finding staff and trainees to support their Bay Area stores. Goodwill was renowned for providing assistance and training to individuals who were looking to turn their lives around, often hiring retired drug addicts or those who had experienced homelessness. Hiring a recent art school graduate like Ally would be advantageous—a young, eager, and teachable individual who could utilize their talent to advance into upper-level management. Goodwill was specifically seeking a Visual Aide Director to enhance the curb appeal of their San Francisco store and transform it into a more inviting space. Ally embraced the challenge and applied for the position, pitching her ideas and ultimately securing the opportunity to enhance the Goodwill brand in the San Francisco area.

Ally's successful project at Goodwill allowed her to share fresh ideas with the management team. She initiated pop-up stores featuring higher-end name-brand clothing donated to their warehouses. One of their first pop-ups, located in the Fillmore district, attracted many visitors interested in the new concept. However, being situated in a rough area of town, a significant amount of clothing was stolen by locals and the homeless, resulting in a substantial inventory loss. Goodwill reevaluated the concept and devised plans for better implementation of Ally's rebranding ideas while also reinforcing security measures.

Since leaving AI, notable developments have unfolded for her friends as well. Celeste's clothing line gained traction, and Barry continued to organize charity fashion shows while planning his own atelier shop. Meanwhile, Ally found a sense of fulfillment in her work at Goodwill, forging new friendships while maintaining her existing connections with different groups.

At work, Goodwill embarked on a project in collaboration with the creative director for Joe Boxer. Ally was thrilled to collaborate with a successful and renowned designer. The resulting store, named William Good, as a playful spin on the Goodwill brand, aimed to repurpose donated clothes by restructuring and redesigning them into new garments. Julian, a new hire for the William Good venture, was assigned to work alongside Ally on the project. On Julian's second day, the two of them conducted a photo shoot in an open storage closet in the basement of the old Coca-Cola building. Despite the space's cracked walls, chipped paint, and a makeshift setup with a used mannequin and a clothing rack, Ally's boundless energy propelled her to throw around ideas to Julian at full speed. During their hour of collaboration, they realized an instant connection and decided to become best friends. They celebrated their newfound friendship with happy hour and dinner, and from that point on, they never looked back. Ally affectionately referred to Julian as "Jules," and their shared dry sense of humor made them feel like they had known each other their entire lives.

Despite their project coming to an end, Jules remained employed as the manager of e-commerce at Goodwill, while Ally was assigned to the marketing department for store support. However, Ally felt creatively stifled within the company and believed her potential was not fully utilized. She found herself performing menial tasks instead of being able to exercise her creativity, which frustrated her. Lacking a business background, she encountered numerous barriers and was assigned tasks she didn't know how to complete, leading to ridicule from colleagues. These experiences gradually made Ally despise her work environment.

Throughout this period, Ally and Jules spent a significant amount of time together, meeting several times a week. Jules was going through a difficult breakup after living with his partner for nine years, discovering the partner's infidelity at the gym. In a typical San Francisco breakup scenario, they were unable to afford separate living arrangements but desired to avoid each other. Four months after meeting Ally, a room became available in her Victorian house, and she offered it to Jules. As best friends, they supported each other through tough times, waking up together, going to work together, and cooking dinner together. Their companionship was effortless and non-judgmental. They didn't need to explain themselves or feel guilty about their actions. In each other's company, they found solace and acceptance. They spent weekends shopping, visiting museums, and Jules even assisted Ally with her renowned brunches. Their friendship was built on mutual understanding and trust, where they could share their deepest thoughts and feelings without reservation.

Together, they brought out the best and worst in each other. Ally turned to drinking as a coping mechanism for her emotions, while Jules also indulged. They often found comfort in sharing a glass of wine, which sometimes escalated to consuming six to eight glasses. However, they never judged each other for their habits, even when it became apparent that Ally was developing a drinking problem. Despite the lows that followed these binge sessions, Ally became increasingly aware of her alcohol consumption and the need to address the issue.

Whenever Ally found herself in social settings and engaged with people, she would laugh, crack jokes, and bring lively energy to the conversation. However, once she returned home, she would question whether people genuinely liked her or found her funny. This self-doubt led her to over-analyze every detail of the evening, scrutinizing her behavior and second-guessing herself. She would think, "I should have done this differently," or "I shouldn't have said this or that." Ally worried about being perceived negatively and would go to great lengths to avoid judgment. She felt the need to hold back, which prevented her from fully expressing her true self. She only shared her positive experiences, withholding the downsides to evade criticism. This pattern of behavior led to manic episodes a couple of times a week, causing concern for Jules, who was vigilant for any signs of Ally spiraling out of control. He even considered sleeping in her room to ensure her well-being.

Despite seeking help through therapy, Ally didn't feel that she was making progress or being understood by her therapist. She desired autonomy in making her own decisions and resisted feeling criticized or guided in her actions and emotions. Going out served as an escape from the internal turmoil she experienced, allowing her to break free from the oppressive weight of her own morose thoughts. Ally yearned to be the bold girl who could rap LL Cool J lyrics, the fearless Floridian, and the person who could effortlessly connect with anyone at any party. However, recently, she no longer felt that same sense of self-assuredness and confidence.

Instead of confiding in her therapist, Ally found consolation in opening up to Jules about her struggles. He provided support when she experienced asthma attacks in the morning, showing his care and understanding. Ally had a tendency to hold on to stress and compartmentalize it, allowing it to accumulate over time. She carried anxiety about her work and her roommates, and her upbringing had made her defensive. Any feedback or constructive criticism, even from friends, was taken personally and caused her anxiety. She felt alone, believing that no one truly cared about her. During bouts of depression, she preferred to be alone, afraid of being monitored or having others impose their solutions on her. She would pretend that everything was fine until it inevitably reached a breaking point, leaving her with mounting anxiety and the anticipation of the next crisis.

Ally shared with Jules that she grew up feeling unsafe, lacking the love and support from her parents that others often took for granted. Her sister became a mother figure after their mother left, but she longed for a sister with whom she could share laughter and commonalities rather than another authority figure dictating her behavior and identity. As a creative person, she felt stifled and unable to become the person she wanted to be under those circumstances. She held herself to high standards and had regrets about her early years. The relationship with her parents, even as an adult, never brought her happiness. The dynamics with her parents remained a significant stressor, leaving her feeling unsupported by the very individuals she expected to rely on the most. Ally longed for the idealized version of parents she thought she should have, but she couldn't find the support she sought from her own family. She felt a sense of family was missing from her life.

Chapter 5

New Beginnings

A mix of nervousness and excitement coursed through my veins as I stood there, finally on my own. The San Francisco Bay Area beckoned me with its vibrant energy, promising a world of new experiences. It felt like stepping into a real city that dwarfed the familiar towns of Bellingham and even Seattle. Thankfully, my friend played the role of a guiding star in this vast universe. He introduced me to Dean, another friend from school, who rented out rooms in a big, beautiful, gated house. Nestled in the heart of a not-so-nice part of town, Hayward, CA. In the weeks leading up to my arrival, I had spoken to Dean on the phone, building a connection and confirming that he had a vacant room available for rent. After an exhaustingly long day of driving, I finally arrived at the address. I hesitated for a moment, gathering my courage, and then I knocked.

The door swung open, revealing Dean, a tall figure with a rugged, white-red neck appearance that instantly caught my attention. His voice boomed with a hint of his Oklahoma origins as he asked, "What can I help you with?"

I replied, "I am here for the room."

At that moment, his eyebrows furrowed in confusion, and he uttered, "Nope. I think you got the wrong place." He swiftly closed the door, leaving me standing there, bewildered. The pang of rejection mingled with my perplexity, creating a knot in my stomach. Determined not to let this setback define my journey, I reached for my phone and dialed the number of the friend who had referred me to Dean. I recounted the incident that had just unfolded. Hoping that he could bridge the gap between Dean and me. As my friend dialed Dean's number, a sense of uncertainty hung in the air as I waited patiently in front of the door. What would transpire during this conversation? Would Dean be willing to reconsider? The answers remained elusive as the phone rang on the other end.

Finally, the connection was established, and my friend unraveled the misunderstanding. Dean, it seemed, had been awaiting the arrival of his new roommate, "Bo." However, with no knowledge of my identity or appearance, he had assumed that "Bo" hailed from the same small town of Bellingham, a white redneck like himself. With patience and clarity, my friend set the record straight. "Bo" was actually called "Vo"; it was a misinterpretation. I was the Asian guy standing outside Dean's door.

A few minutes passed, and suddenly Dean swung the door wide open. To my surprise, a wide grin spread across his face. With enthusiasm, he exclaimed, "Oh my God! I just got a call from Al. I was waiting for some white guy named Bo!" I kind of smiled. Dean motioned for me to follow him, leading the way to my room. It was a cozy space, complete with an adjoining bathroom that added a touch of convenience to the arrangement.

With a genuine desire to make me feel welcome, Dean lent a helping hand in unloading my car. Once the practical matters were taken care of, Dean took on the role of a hospitable host, setting down a few ground rules to establish a harmonious living environment. Then, with a glint in his eye, he posed a question, "You want a beer?"

"Of course," I replied. We continued to bond over polishing off a case of beers together and quickly became friends. Being a 3rd generation chiropractor, he took me under his wing and taught me early on how to adjust by practicing and wailing on each other, the ways of chiropractic student life, where to find the best cheap eats, and how to have fun and survive in the big city.

The transition from University, where I took 12-18 credits per quarter, to Chiropractic College, where I was suddenly facing 30-36 credits per quarter, was a seismic shift in terms of class time and academic demands. Gone were the days of managing 3-5 classes; now, I found myself juggling an overwhelming load of 10-15 courses. I had chosen the accelerated track, a 12-quarter program with summer school included, determined to complete the 4-year curriculum in a mere three years. As I delved into the depths of graduate school life, it became abundantly clear that my existence revolved around three pillars: studying hard, playing hard, and, on occasion, partying even harder. Survival in this rigorous environment demanded unwavering dedication. The school's mission statement, encapsulated in the phrase "Lasting Purpose (LP)," carried a weighty significance. Basically, we had to keep a "Low Profile" to make it through the program.

I was confronted with the complications of a long-distance relationship. What was already a challenge when we lived an hour apart became nearly impossible as I found myself in a different state, consumed by the demands of my heavy school load. The strain took its toll, and with a heavy heart, I had to make the painful decision to let go of my first love, abandoning the dream of a future together. It was a sacrifice we both had to make, allowing us to forge ahead on our individual paths, pursuing our respective careers. The personal aspects of my life, for the most part, had to be put on hold as I prepared myself for what I anticipated to be a grueling three-year journey of academic pursuits.

The first two years of school consumed a lot of time, but surprisingly, it wasn't as difficult as I expected. Somehow, things fell into place effortlessly. Though there were countless classes, endless studying, and an overwhelming number of exams, I felt like I had finally found my purpose in life. It was a transformation from a sickly child in Vietnam to someone capable of making a positive impact on others' lives. I saw it as my way of repaying the gift of life I had received when I hovered on the brink of death in that hospital bed. This deep-rooted passion for giving back made the heavy workload more manageable. I excelled in my studies, chiropractic skills, and clinical internship. In March of 1998, I proudly walked across the stage, receiving my Doctorate in Chiropractic. The time had come to bid farewell to San Francisco and the Bay Area, my cherished home away from home, and return to Washington.

During my time away in grad school, a lot of changes unfolded within my family. My sister found love and got married, eagerly awaiting the arrival of her first child after my graduation. Meanwhile, my parents decided to part ways, leading to the sale of our cherished house in Bellingham. My mother and brother relocated to Seattle as he pursued his studies at the University of Washington. In the midst of this, my mother, on the verge of embracing her chosen path as a Buddhist nun, needed to sever her legal marriage ties with my father in order to embark on her spiritual journey under the guidance of her chosen teacher. I recall returning home for an extended winter break during the joyous holiday season. A pivotal conversation unfolded as I sat at the computer in my mother's and brother's cozy two-bedroom apartment. My mother turned to me and gently revealed, "You know, your dad and I are divorced now." The words hung in the air, and I paused. With utmost sincerity, I replied, "As long as both of you are happy, then I am happy for you." As an adult, I understood that this was the best course of action for them, considering the challenges they faced in the later years of their marriage. They had remained together solely for the sake of ensuring our stability and allowing us to mature into responsible adults. They shielded us from the psychological and emotional impact of a fractured relationship during our formative years, prioritizing our well-being above all else. Their selfless act served as a testament to their love for us, fostering an environment of strength and resilience.

Now, I found myself back in what I considered home, residing in a modest two-bedroom apartment with my mother and my brother in the same complex where my sister and her husband, Alex, lived. Seattle was still new to me, and my social circle consisted primarily of family and a handful of friends from high school and college. However, it was my sister and brother who opened the doors to a world I had yet to discover. Immersed in the Asian Christian church community, I witnessed firsthand the deep-rooted connections they had formed with a vibrant congregation of fellow Christian Asians. It was as if I had stumbled upon an instant community. I found solace in their presence. Finally, I discovered what had been missing throughout my childhood. Growing up in Bellingham, my interactions were predominantly with white individuals. In order to fit in and avoid feeling like an outcast, I resorted to adapting my behavior, attempting to mimic and assimilate into the white culture that surrounded me. But now, within this new community, surrounded by people who shared my struggles, insecurities, and experiences as an Asian in a predominantly non-Asian environment, I no longer had to pretend. I could be authentically myself, finding comfort in the knowledge that I was accepted and understood for who I truly was.

On that fateful day of my return to Seattle, an invitation to a church picnic led me to meet Bobby, my sister's best friend's husband, a Korean man brimming with warmth and kindness. Bobby graciously introduced me to his circle of friends, expanding my social horizons in an instant. Among the newfound connections, one stood out—Leo, a compact yet sturdy Chinese guy, a stark contrast to my taller stature. Our paths intertwined during my inaugural Christian retreat, where our shared ineptitude in basketball brought us together. As the only two guys who could hardly make a shot, we dashed around aimlessly, our attempts ending in air balls. Our lack of rhythm extended beyond the court as we struggled to clap in sync with the church songs. Though I made a valiant effort, Leo would simply tuck his hands in his pockets, skillfully evading any missteps in the rhythmic pattern. Weekends became one and the same with our prospering friendship as we ventured into the vibrant city scene, exploring bars and dance clubs like any young, single individuals of our age. Leo once shared a profound insight with me, proclaiming, "A roller can always spot another roller in a crowd, even if it is at church." In the realm of nightlife, Leo often played the role of the mentor, cautioning me to remain silent. "Just stand there and look pretty," as he would roll up on a table of girls to introduce us as he weaved his stories to the females who would just sit there and laugh. We became the duo humorously likened to the characters from "Night at the Roxbury," as Bobby would often call us, adding a playful touch to our escapades. And yet, the Sundays that followed saw us seeking solace within the walls of the church, repenting for our weekend indulgences, a ritual to accommodate our sins of debauchery.

During my second Christian retreat, a serendipitous encounter occurred, forever altering the course of my romantic journey. It all began within the walls of the church, where I caught sight of a mesmerizing presence—the way she styled her hair, kind of like Chun Li, the iconic character from the video game Street Fighter. Fate seemed to conspire in my favor, positioning me right in front of her during a horseback riding experience at the retreat. Throughout the ride, my attention was entirely consumed. My body instinctively turned towards her as I strived to engage in conversation. The horseback ride became an unforgettable memory, not for the scenery or the physical experience, but solely for the captivating connection that prospered between us.

As the summer drew to a close, I conquered the formidable national and state board exams. The long-awaited moment arrived when I held in my hands the precious document—the license granting me the privilege to practice chiropractic in the State of Washington. A classmate extended a referral that led me to my first job opportunity. Thus, I embarked on my professional journey as an associate chiropractor, joining forces with a seasoned practitioner who already had another associate. Together, we formed a formidable team, operating from a clinic nestled within the prestigious Medical Dental Building, a prominent landmark in downtown Seattle. The initial salary offered to me—a modest $2000 per month—served as a stark reminder that the road to financial prosperity was still on a distant horizon. Survival on this pay grade proved challenging, but the generosity of my mother and brother came to my rescue as they graciously offered me free rent within their apartment. It was a sanctuary that helped me navigate my profession's early stages, made me stronger, and pushed me toward a brighter future.

Following my first year as an associate, the owner of the clinic approached me with an unexpected proposition—to sell me the practice.

This wasn't a thriving establishment, nor did it boast remarkable success. Nestled on the top floor of a towering office building in downtown Seattle, lacking foot traffic or any tangible means for people to discover its existence. Its limited visibility relied solely on the whispers of satisfied patients and its presence on insurance provider lists. The chance to assume ownership and wield authority over the business. It was an opportunity to manifest my vision and shape my future. This decision weighed heavily upon me, demanding profound contemplation and an outpouring of heartfelt prayers. Ultimately, I mustered the courage to seize the moment, propelled by a $150,000 loan. This bold move made my student loan debt even bigger, but it could help me achieve my dreams.

The first five years of my practice were extremely stressful. I felt a heavy burden of responsibility as I tried to manage my chiropractic clinic and navigate the world of small business. I often felt inadequate and unsure of how to keep things running smoothly. Every day, I had a flood of worries. How would I find enough money to pay the rent, cover expenses, and give my employee a paycheck? I also wondered if I would have enough left over to support myself. Sometimes, I think I used these worries as an excuse to engage in self-destructive behavior. To escape the pressure, I turned to weekends as a way to let loose and forget about my financial troubles. I sought comfort in drinking and partying, hoping it would ease my anxieties. My friend Bobby was always there to cheer me up, treating me to drinks and making me laugh. He had catchy phrases like "Let's get it on like Donkey Kong" or "Do you want to party like a rock star or a pop star?" that set the tone for our wild weekends. It was a temporary escape from my money worries, and it allowed me to enjoy carefree moments.

In the midst of my messy journey, there were a few lifelines that kept me grounded and preserved my sanity. Every week, I sought support in my business coach calls and in my self-help audiotapes, found consolation in the embrace of my church, and offered countless prayers for guidance and strength. As a person of Christian faith, my coach often posed a poignant question that stirred my soul. "Do you believe in God?" he asked, his voice filled with earnestness.

I responded without hesitation, "Yes, without a doubt."

In a gentle yet profound tone, he offered a reassuring perspective, "Do you think God would burden you with challenges that you are incapable of overcoming?" His words resonated deeply within me, stirring a wellspring of faith and hope.

The weight of his questions left me grappling with their profound implications. If I were to confront my innermost truth, a different reality emerged—a reality where I clung to the edge of my tolerance, stumbling on the cliff of despair. Week after week, the daunting specter of failure loomed ominously, threatening to swallow me whole. As the pendulum swung closer to what I believed was the end, I trudged wearily to my girlfriend's apartment after another grueling day at work. Collapsing onto her worn futon, I curled up in a fetal position, my eyes tightly shut, seeking comfort in the darkness. I was drained in every sense of the word—mentally, emotionally, and beyond. Sensing the weight of my burden, she moved beside me, perching on the floor with tender compassion. Her gentle touch caressed my hair as she whispered softly, "Is everything okay?"

"I'm alright. Just a bit exhausted and in need of some rest," I managed to respond, although deep down, I battled against a torrent of emotions, desperately fighting back the tears of defeat threatening to escape.

Her eyes still harboring concern, she spoke with gentle reassurance, "Everything will be ok. I am here for you when you want to talk about it, but I will leave you alone for now so that you can rest." Leaning in, she brushed her lips against my forehead in a tender gesture imbued with unwavering support before gracefully rising to attend to her unfinished tasks.

Lying there motionless, as if trapped in a state of numbness, I closed my eyes tightly, almost believing that shutting out the world would dissolve my troubles into thin air. Then, in a moment of surreal clarity, a calm and comforting feminine voice whispered in my ears, "Don't give up." It resonated with such certainty that it felt as though someone sat beside me, offering guidance. Was it God? An angel? Or perhaps a benevolent spirit guide reaching out to me? I couldn't discern the source, but those words penetrated my being, causing my stress and fears to dissolve like ice melting under the sun. In an instant, a surge of newfound strength, courage, and inspiration coursed through my nerves. I sat up, determined to continue the battle and fulfill my life's purpose. That voice, those words, injected me with an invigorating energy and unwavering motivation to forge ahead, undeterred by the challenges ahead. A sense of assurance washed over me, an unexplainable knowing that everything would somehow be alright, even in the face of uncertainty.

CHAPTER 6

A LEAP OF FAITH

In my fourth year of practice, I stumbled upon an audiotape by the visionary behind Network Chiropractic. Something he said resonated deeply within me. He posed a thought-provoking question to himself: Could the person he was today accomplish all the aspirations he held for the future? The answer was a resounding no. It struck a chord, and I realized that I, too, needed to grow and transform on all levels: mentally, physically, and spiritually. With newfound determination, I embarked on a journey of self-improvement. I prioritized my physical well-being by adopting healthier habits, engaging in regular exercise, nourishing my body with vital nutrients, and seeking out holistic therapies such as chiropractic, massages, and acupuncture. To nurture my mental and spiritual well-being, I delved into the Bible and other spiritual literature, immersing myself in audiotapes that fueled my growth. I found peace and community in attending church, participating in Bible studies, and, of course, dedicating myself to daily prayer.

Another profound revelation came to me through an audio sermon delivered by a renowned Southern Christian minister. His words struck a chord within me as he pointed out how people often approach God with their demands: God...? I need a new job, a new girlfriend, a new car, etc. But he emphasized the importance of listening to God, a practice often overlooked. Inspired by his example, he shared his morning routine of reading a passage from Scripture, seeking guidance on how to be a faithful servant and fulfill God's will. Afterward, he would sit in quiet reflection, attuning his ears to listen. Intrigued by this concept, I decided to incorporate it into my daily routine before heading to work. For three or four months, I faithfully practiced this ritual, consciously choosing to evolve myself. And to my amazement, I began to witness a shift. My chiropractic practice started to attract more patients, and a steady stream of income flowed in. I experienced what some might call "synchronicity" – a remarkable alignment with the divine, spirit, or purpose. It was as if my life orchestrated encounters with the right individuals, placed me in opportune situations, and guided me to take the necessary steps toward fulfilling my intentions and higher calling. With my practice flourishing, I continued to focus on personal growth and evolution, knowing that aligning myself with a higher purpose brought forth abundant blessings.

On my synchronistic journey, I found myself meeting friends for happy hour at a quaint old Japanese restaurant nestled in the heart of Chinatown. As the sun set, this unassuming place would transform into a lively karaoke bar, attracting college kids and locals alike. Being someone who valued punctuality, I arrived a little early and settled in at the bar, eager to quench my thirst with a drink. Behind the counter stood an older woman, her stature robust and her long curly brown hair flowing freely. She donned enchanting, dark, and billowy attire reminiscent of a gypsy's garb. Sipping my beer, biding my time until my friends joined me, the woman turned to me and spoke with a gentle smile, "You have nice energy. What do you do for a living?"

"I am a chiropractor," I replied.

"Oh, I am in the healing profession as well," she said.

I looked at her curiously and asked, "What do you do?"

"I am a Reiki practitioner," she said.

"What is Reiki?" I asked.

She paused for a moment, contemplating the best way to convey the essence of Reiki. After a brief reflection, she shared, "It's kind of like what Jesus did when he would lay his hands on people to heal them." As a Christian and a healthcare practitioner, her words ignited a spark of curiosity within me. Sensing my interest, she posed the question, "Would you like to try a session?" Though her description left me somewhat uncertain, I embraced the mindset of openness and willingness to try new things, especially when it involved healing and the connection to Jesus. Considering that I had a massage room in my practice, I proposed the idea of her visiting my office for a session. To my delight, she accepted the invitation, and we scheduled an appointment for the following weekend. I reasoned that, at worst, I would be out $60, and life would simply move forward.

During my inaugural Reiki session, I laid on my back, fully clothed, with closed eyes, resting on a massage table. The practitioner gently touched various points on my body and traced symbols in the air with her hands. My natural curiosity prompted me to share the sights and sensations that arose within me. As I voiced my experiences, she maintained a serene presence, diligently continuing her work. I vividly described vibrant purple and cobalt-blue clouds, resembling ethereal swirls, manifesting in my field of vision. These mesmerizing formations seemed to revolve around a recurring black silhouette that intermittently emerged. I eagerly shared this imagery with her, expecting a response. She acknowledged the colors as representative of the chakras but omitted the enigmatic silhouette that captivated my attention.

As my session neared its conclusion, a new vision materialized before me. In this vision, I observed a familiar woman leaning in to whisper into the ear of another girl, who was adorned in a delightful pink fairy costume. They merrily skipped along the sidewalk, exchanging laughter over their shared secret. However, in a startling turn, the scene abruptly transformed, akin to a magician unveiling a trick. The image of the enigmatic black silhouette reappeared, and this time, it embodied me.

The swirling purple and blue clouds, which had previously captivated my senses, now felt like a surge of electric current coursing through my being. In this transformative moment, my body seemed to convulse as if caught in the throes of an uncontrollable force. It was an intense experience, lasting for what felt like a significant duration. As soon as this episode subsided, I promptly sat up on the table, overcome with confusion and concern. I urgently questioned, "What just happened? I felt like I was being electrocuted."

She glanced at me with an air of indifference and casually responded, "Nothing, really. You were lying still for the most part. Maybe your big toe twitched a little bit as I was working down by your feet." I proceeded to recount in detail the profound sensations and emotions that had enveloped me. In response, she closed her eyes, her face turned upward, and she entered a momentary pause, seemingly attuned to some internal spiritual guidance or affirmation. Afterward, she directed her gaze toward me and uttered, "You were touched by the archangel Michael." Despite the seemingly outlandish nature of her statement, I found myself inexplicably intrigued by the physical and emotional encounter I had just undergone. This intrigue prompted me to embark on a series of additional reiki sessions, eager to unravel the mysteries that lay ahead.

With each subsequent reiki session, a new chapter of physical and spiritual exploration unfolded before me. The second session proved to be rather discomforting, as if I had outgrown my body, constantly yearning to stretch and release the tightness and aches that consumed me. It was as if I were being compressed, shedding old layers to create space for the new to flourish, akin to decluttering a neglected drawer. By the end of the third session, a remarkable clarity washed over my mind, accompanied by a buzzing sensation within my head. Such a state of heightened awareness was entirely foreign to me, compelling me to venture further down the rabbit hole. Thus, I eagerly booked additional sessions, ready to embrace the unknown. During my fourth session, an extraordinary occurrence transpired. Amid the session, my body unexpectedly sat upright, spontaneously performing intricate hand mudra motions that I had never encountered or witnessed before in my entire life. The initial shock soon gave way to a sense of curiosity, for despite the inexplicable nature of these manifestations, they posed no harm or threat. Thus, I resolved to surrender to the enigmatic journey, eager to unravel its mysteries. These newfound mudras soon became an integral part of my daily spiritual practice. They would materialize during my morning and evening prayer sessions, gradually transforming those moments into prolonged periods of meditative contemplation rather than traditional prayer.

A month had elapsed since I embarked on my regular mudra meditations, and on one particular evening, a profound shift occurred. As I gazed upward, a deep inhalation filled my lungs, followed by a resounding "Ommmm" that reverberated through the very core of my being. In that transcendent moment, an overwhelming wave of indescribable, boundless love washed over me, evoking tears of pure joy that streamed down my cheeks. It was as if I had forged an unbreakable connection with the divine, a sacred union with God Himself. Encouraged by this extraordinary experience, I persisted in my newfound practice for several more months. And then, one fateful day, I underwent a momentous event—a complete awakening of my kundalini energy. From that transformative juncture, my perception of life underwent a profound shift. I had ascended to a higher plane of knowledge and awareness, forever altering the course of my existence.

I embraced my personal understanding of God, as countless individuals do, and adhered to the principles I had gathered throughout my journey: "Do good things and not bad." "This too shall pass." These adages resonated across various faiths and philosophies, gradually shaping my own mantra: "Why you gotta be like that?" I concluded that giving my best effort was the pinnacle of achievement, rather than fretting over others' opinions or judgments. If someone couldn't accept or appreciate me for who I truly was, then their presence in my life was unnecessary. I made a conscious choice to surround myself with individuals who genuinely loved and supported me, shedding the weight of others' negativity and burdens. And whenever I faltered in following my advice, Leo would kindly remind me, "Don't worry about it."

With this heightened level of consciousness and awareness, a thirst for knowledge and understanding consumed me. It brought to mind a moment from my high school days when I stumbled upon a plain blue book titled "Telepathy" by Alice Bailey at a garage sale. Although the words within seemed elusive and difficult to grasp, I felt compelled to purchase it, believing that one day its wisdom would be within my reach. From a young age, I had been captivated by science fiction, fantasy, and the unexplained. Movies like *The Hobbit, The Dark Crystal,* and *Star Wars* enchanted me, while the writings of J.R.R. Tolkien, C.S. Lewis, and Michael Moorcock fueled my imagination. Occasionally, I would seek out the counsel of psychics, eager to explore different versions of my life, to understand who I was, who I am, and who I would become. At first, I found amusement in their insights, but as some of their predictions manifested in reality, I began to ponder. Perhaps deep within my subconscious, I had been primed for the experiences that accompanied my newfound state of being – to confront the mysteries of the unknown and persevere, even if my beliefs diverged from the prevailing social norms of the world.

Driven by a thirst for deeper understanding, I embarked on a quest to find additional mentors and explore diverse realms of energy work and healing. I sought practitioners who could guide me in unlocking the vast knowledge that lay within. These encounters inspired me to venture into uncharted territory, developing my unique approach to energy work and offering it to open-minded individuals seeking enlightenment. Past-life regression, inner-child healing, drumming circles, and shamanic journeying became integral parts of my spiritual exploration. In my relentless pursuit of spiritual evolution, I embraced new methods and practices, driven by a desire to expand my consciousness and heighten my awareness.

In my quest for a profound spiritual experience, I found myself introduced to ayahuasca by a Peruvian shaman who hosted a retreat in Seattle. Ayahuasca, a brew derived from specific plants found in the Amazon jungle, contains Dimethyltryptamine (DMT), a powerful hallucinogen. Unlike other forms of DMT, ayahuasca is renowned for its ability to facilitate a deep spiritual journey, unraveling the layers of human consciousness and providing access to the realms beyond. It was believed that this sacred drink allowed communication and collaboration with spirit guides, enabling profound healing on spiritual, physical, mental, and emotional levels. However, during the retreat, the limited availability of the medicine meant that my personal encounter with ayahuasca did not differ from what I could achieve through my meditation practice. Ultimately, I returned to my meditative reflections to gain insight, introspect, and address the temporary challenges life presented along my path. Each individual must embark on their own journey, seeking their own understanding and forging their unique path toward self-realization.

This experience brought to mind the time when my brother and I were entrusted with accompanying my mother's revered Zen Buddhist master on a journey back to Vietnam. In the Vietnamese Buddhist tradition, it was customary for male monks to be accompanied by other males versus female nuns during travels. Hence, my mother requested my brother and me to serve as escorts for her master's return. It was my first visit to my homeland since I had left as a child. During the lengthy plane ride, I had the privilege of sitting next to the Zen master. Intrigued by his wisdom, I posed some questions. I asked, "What do you see in meditation?" To which he replied, "You see yourself." Curiosity still piqued, I asked him, "How do you know you are enlightened?" He smiled and calmly responded, "It is like riding a bicycle. You just know." Although these statements may seem simple, the attainment of such profound understanding and realization transcends the capabilities of most individuals. Merely striving to be one's true self can prove challenging enough. However, for those who persistently tread this path, there is a possibility of experiencing and comprehending what the great masters and teachers discovered within themselves as they traversed the earth, fully transcendent, realized, and enlightened. This transformative encounter eventually inspired me to write several books on spiritual development, capturing the invaluable lessons I had learned along my own journey.

As the monotony of everyday life lost its allure, my girlfriend intelligently observed my interest and shared her own perspective, saying, "The only time I ever got excited about anything was when I was teaching or working with students or patients on spiritual development." Her words resonated deeply with me. Witnessing individuals who were eager to learn and develop, much like I had been at the start of my journey, filled me with a renewed sense of purpose. The prospect of becoming a successful young author and potentially a spiritual teacher ignited a passionate fire within me. Increasingly, the idea of leaving behind my chiropractic practice for a new life and career grew more enticing. The demands of the practice had taken their toll, leaving me feeling drained and devoid of any desire to continue down the path of chiropractic care. Embarking on a fresh journey, one where I could share my insights and guide others along their spiritual paths, became increasingly appealing.

As the choice to leave behind my practice and my life in Seattle was solidified, the universe seemed to cooperate in my favor. Significant events unfolded, and it became evident that a new chapter was about to unravel, much like when I initially departed from Bellingham to pursue chiropractic school. However, this time, my aspirations had transformed, and a new dream had taken root within me—to become a spiritual teacher and touch the lives of a broader audience. In the spring of 2008, I embarked on a transformative journey, symbolized by downsizing my belongings to fit into an SUV. With the weight of material possessions lifted, I set my sights on southern California, where my new dreams patiently awaited me. The open road stretched out before me, beckoning me toward a future filled with endless possibilities and the fulfillment of my purpose.

When I finally arrived in Los Angeles, CA, I wasn't greeted by a big audience waiting with bated breath to hear wise words fall from my lips. I didn't have book signings, let alone a book tour that would promote me around the world, with thousands of followers waiting for me to sign my books. Instead, what waited for me was a couch at my good friend JR's place in his one-bedroom loft in downtown L.A.

JR and I had forged a strong connection in Seattle, united by our shared interests in metaphysics, meditation, and higher consciousness. He wholeheartedly supported my decision to move and graciously provided me with a place to stay while I navigated this new chapter of my life. For the following month, I resided on that couch, embracing the simplicity of my surroundings as I searched for a place to call my own. It struck me as ironic that the self-help book industry predominantly featured either already successful and well-known individuals or authors who secured endorsements from famous celebrities, leveraging their vast followings to spread the word. In my case, my agent made it clear that the responsibility of promoting my book and ensuring its success rested squarely on my shoulders.

After securing a place to live in Santa Monica, my focus remained on self-evolution, as it had been the driving force behind my journey thus far. I maintained a daily routine of exercise and meditation, all while trying to navigate the intricacies of self-promoting my book. During my free time, I cherished the company of JR, with whom I continued engaging in profound discussions about reaching higher states of consciousness. One particular topic of conversation revolved around my previous encounter with ayahuasca, a plant-based hallucinogen known for its potential to facilitate spiritual experiences. However, I felt that my initial experience with it hadn't fully tapped into its transformative potential. Intrigued by our discussions, JR delved into his own research on ayahuasca—how to prepare it and what to expect during the journey. He even purchased the necessary ingredients, including the bark and leaves, from an online source. We decided to make our own brew, following the instructions we had gathered from our research. Boiling the dried bark and leaves in water for several hours, we meticulously crafted our concoction in a large pot at my Santa Monica residence. We knew from our readings that it was advised not to consume ayahuasca alone, so we embarked on this journey together. To ensure maximum absorption and potency, we adhered to the guidance of fasting on the day of our ayahuasca experience. As dusk approached, we positioned ourselves in the center of my living room, each with a blanket for comfort and a bowl by our side just in case we had to vomit, as described in our research on taking medicine. With a sense of anticipation and camaraderie, we cheered each other on and consumed a cup of the bitter and pungent brew we had prepared. We pulled our blankets over ourselves, enveloping the space in darkness, as suggested, for a more immersive experience. Time passed, and after thirty minutes without any noticeable effects, I turned to JR and asked, "Do you feel anything yet?"

JR responded, "Nope. Maybe we didn't drink enough." We agreed to try another cup. We poured ourselves another serving of the potent brew, hoping that an increased dosage would elicit the desired effects. Another hour slipped by, and a sense of restlessness began to overshadow our anticipation. I removed my blanket and turned to JR, asking, "Did you feel or experience anything yet?"

JR ripped off his blanket and said, "Nah…I am starving. You want to go get some Carl's Jr?"

"Hell yeah!" We both hadn't eaten all day, so off we went to reward ourselves with our favorite double western bacon cheeseburgers, a side of onion rings, and a Coke to wash it all down.

Each day, I hit the road, determined to find opportunities to connect with others and spread my message. My mission was clear: to find venues willing to host small talks, teach classes, or even just display a few complimentary copies of my book in local bookstores. I reached out to a recommended spiritual book publisher, entrusting them with a batch of copies to help promote and distribute to other bookstores across the nation. I traveled from city to city; I faced a mixed bag of experiences. Some venues graciously welcomed me, allowing me to deliver talks that resonated with those seeking spiritual guidance. Despite my best efforts, progress proved elusive. Many bookstores, while appreciative of the offer, hesitated to take on additional inventory or showcase unfamiliar works. The path to becoming the spiritual teacher I had envisioned seemed arduous, and the road ahead was uncertain.

My friends from Seattle asked if they could stay with me. They were excited about a motivational seminar happening that weekend and had an extra ticket for me. I was feeling a little lost and unsure of my path, so I reluctantly agreed to join them. As the days passed and the event drew closer, a strange feeling tugged at my heart, urging me to return to Seattle. I tried expressing my inner turmoil, saying, "I have this strong feeling that I need to be back in Seattle this weekend." But they reassured me that the seminar would be beneficial and convinced me to stay. Though hesitant, I finally gave in to their persuasion.

During the seminar, my phone buzzed with an incoming call from my dear friend Bobby. He reminded me that his birthday was coming up, and he couldn't contain his excitement about visiting me. We hadn't seen each other since I left, and we had big plans to have an unforgettable celebration, just like the old days in Seattle. As we bid farewell on the phone, we exchanged heartfelt words, "I love you, man," reminiscent of a comedy movie we both enjoyed. The seminar turned out to be exactly what I needed. It breathed new life into my weary soul, recharging my spirits and reigniting my drive. As we shared a satisfying meal together, my friends echoed my thoughts, affirming that attending the seminar was indeed a worthwhile endeavor. And with the added news of Bobby's upcoming visit, it felt like a perfect win-win situation.

The following morning, a surge of newfound energy coursed through my veins after the invigorating seminar. Determined to capitalize on this revitalization, I laced up my running shoes and embarked on a brisk two-mile jog toward the beach. With my trusty iPod in hand, I selected an empowering playlist that fueled my resolve, making me feel resilient, motivated, and unstoppable. Upon my return home, I glanced at my phone, only to discover a startling sight: a slew of missed calls from numerous friends in Seattle. Intrigued by this unusual influx of notifications, I snatched up my phone from the table, ready to unravel the mystery within the voicemail messages. Each one bore an urgent tone, conveying distressing news about Bobby: "Bobby got into an accident," "Bobby got hurt," "Something happened to Bobby," "Call me back ASAP." Though a tinge of concern pricked at my consciousness, I refused to succumb to panic. After all, Bobby was the epitome of strength and fearlessness, a veritable force of nature. In my mind, he resembled a real-life Superman, capable of shrugging off any misfortune with nothing more than a minor scratch or bruise. Yet, my curiosity was piqued, fueled by the multitude of messages that flooded my inbox. Just as I was about to dial the first person on my lengthy call log, the phone rang, and a familiar voice pierced through the chaos—a former girlfriend, her tone tinged with hysteria as she exclaimed, "Did you hear about what happened to Bobby?!"

I casually replied, "Yeah, I heard that he got into some kind of accident. It's not a big deal. I am sure he is fine."

After a long pause, she said in a calm voice, "No…he is dead."

In disbelief, I shouted, "What are you talking about? That is impossible! He is supposed to be here next weekend to hang out!"

Her words reverberated in my ears, but their weight crushed my soul. "No, he is dead. I'm so sorry," she calmly repeated. As the reality of her message sank in, my legs gave way, collapsing beneath me, and I crumpled to the floor. Tears welled up in my eyes, escaping in rivulets down my cheeks. Through the haze of sorrow, I mustered the strength to express my gratitude for sharing the painful truth before ending the call, my heart heavy with grief.

Conversations with other friends who had attempted to reach me filled in the chilling details of Bobby's final moments. Borrowing a friend's motorcycle due to a car breakdown, he found himself hurtling down the freeway. In a tragic instant, control slipped through his grasp, and his body collided with the unyielding guardrail, severing his life with a merciless snap of his neck and shredding his being upon the unforgiving pavement. Overwhelmed by guilt, I mercilessly questioned myself, haunted by the persistent query, "Why didn't I listen to my intuition?" If only I had returned to Seattle, perhaps I could have averted this tragic fate. Numbness engulfed me, leaving me adrift in a sea of shock for the remainder of the day. That night, seeking solace amidst the deluge of pain and emotions threatening to consume me, I sought refuge in meditation. As I sat, tears streaming down my face, Bobby materialized before me in a vision. His presence stirred a floodgate of questions, and I implored, "Why did this happen? Why did you have to leave?" With a serene smile, he replied, "It was simply my time, Bro. You, above all, should understand." And just like that, he vanished, leaving me to grapple with the bittersweet acceptance of his words. In the wake of our ethereal encounter, I embarked on a solemn journey back to Seattle, where I would deliver Bobby's eulogy at his memorial service. Among his friends, I stood alone, granted the painful privilege of viewing his ravaged body one last time before the cremation. In that solemn room, I stood in solitude, fixated on the remnants of his lifeless form. Placing my hand where his heart once beat, I uttered heartfelt gratitude for his presence in my life and the profound impact he had on me. Through tear-stained words, I vowed that one day. We would reunite, destined to meet again.

Death had made its presence known to me before. As my time in Seattle drew to a close, a fellow endodontist on our floor was struck by a relentless adversary: colon cancer. Despite the weight of his diagnosis, he remained a towering figure of positivity, radiating kindness and love to all he encountered. He cherished his life, his family, and his work, epitomizing the creed to "Love more and judge less." When news of his battle spread through our professional realm, hope swelled within us, convinced that he would emerge victorious from this daunting trial. Week after week, he would grace my office, sharing updates on his health with an unwavering smile etched upon his face. But then came the day when his absence lingered, stretching into weeks. The cancer's insidious grip tightened, siphoning away his vitality, impairing his ability to fulfill his professional duties. In the months that followed, I caught fleeting glimpses of him, a mere shadow of his former self, as the disease waged its ruthless war. The inevitable moment arrived, and he left this world behind, escaping the clutches of suffering. Standing before his open casket at the memorial, I struggled to recognize the figure of the man I once knew lying before me. The cancer had reduced his once robust frame to a frail shell, a mere fragment of the man he once was. Yet, despite the ravages inflicted upon him, he exuded an undeniable serenity. In that solemn moment, death's cold touch became palpable, searing an indelible imprint upon my consciousness.

As the final reverberations of Bobby's memorial faded away, my world also seemed to descend into a slow-motion disintegration, crumbling like a fragile sandcastle slipping through my fingers. The sands of fortune were shifting, and I teetered on the precipice of financial ruin with my pursuit of becoming a spiritual teacher. Anger, like a wild tempest, brewed within me, fueling the bitterness that consumed my being. The realization of my self-imposed predicament gnawed at my soul, leaving a bitter aftertaste of regret. The path I had chosen with unwavering conviction, believing it to be guided by spiritual forces, now lay shattered before me. Mockingly, I scoffed at the notion of spiritual guidance, dismissing it as a mere illusion. The promises of synchronicity and higher purpose, once held in high regard, now seemed like hollow, empty rhetoric. Defiantly, I spat out my disdain, uttering a resounding "FUCK YOU" to the very ideals that had led me down this unforeseen path. Desperate to regain my footing, I sought refuge in the familiarity of chiropractic, hoping it would salvage what little remained of my shattered dreams. Yet, as the days turned into weeks and the weeks into months, it became painfully evident that my return to familiar terrain offered no respite.

My journey to obtain a chiropractic license in California became an agonizing journey, fraught with bureaucratic hurdles and relentless setbacks. In my pursuit of this seemingly simple goal, I encountered unforeseen obstacles and little to no cooperation. With hopeful anticipation, I diligently submitted what I believed to be the necessary documents, only to be met with an agonizing silence that stretched on for many months. I made the decision to reach out to the authorities, seeking answers to the mounting questions that plagued my mind. A voice on the other end of the line finally answered and promised a swift resolution, instilling a renewed sense of optimism within me. Time continued to pass with agonizing slowness, dragging on for several more months. Determined to grasp the elusive license that had eluded me for so long, I contacted the same individual who had offered her help. To my dismay, I discovered that my application still languished on the desk of the very woman who held the power to grant my approval. A year had come and gone. Stunned by this revelation, she gaped at the lack of service displayed by her colleague. Sensing my desperation, the compassionate woman vowed to rectify the situation, assuring me that my California license would be secured within the coming month. However, by this time, life had propelled me to move to San Francisco.

Months prior to my move, unable to practice chiropractic legally in California, Leo proposed a solution—I should relocate to San Francisco. Generously, he offered me a place to stay with his family as I sought employment and a new home. In the autumn of 2009, I packed my belongings and embarked on a northward journey. After months of job hunting, a disheartening truth emerged. I discovered that my chiropractic degree held limited value in the Bay Area's tech-heavy job market. Overqualified or under-skilled, I encountered closed doors at every turn. With the holiday season fast approaching, Nordstrom sought additional staff, providing an opportunity for temporary employment. With little remaining funds, I simplified my resume and applied for a retail position reminiscent of my undergraduate days. It wasn't ideal, but it brought much-needed income and matched my qualifications. Thriving in sales, I earned praise and was asked to stay beyond the holidays. The job demanded a lot of my time, but it offered stability—for now. Though my chiropractic license remained pending with the State, I felt at peace about my return to San Francisco. It felt like a semblance of stability and a place to call home once again.

CHAPTER 7

BOTTOMS UP!

I secured a rented attic space in a grand Victorian house, sharing it with four roommates and a dog. The house sat on the border of Noe Valley and the Castro, San Francisco's renowned gay district. This was a new experience for me since I had never lived with roommates since leaving my brother's place in Seattle. Despite the adjustment, I felt grateful that I wasn't couch surfing or imposing on a friend's hospitality. Finally, I was able to support myself financially, which was a significant relief. Before my move to San Francisco, I recall strolling through Costco with my father during one of his visits to LA. With limited funds in my bank account, I couldn't indulge in impulsive purchases. At that moment, I silently vowed to remember this experience as a reminder of gratitude, acknowledging that there was a time when I possessed very little.

Coming from a small town, my knowledge of the gay community was limited to a college friend who came out after I had left Seattle. We maintained contact over the years, occasionally visiting each other post-graduation. Now, as a routine, I traversed the Castro district daily to catch the Muni train for work at Nordstrom downtown. While awaiting approval for my chiropractic license, I often met up with fellow gay friends from chiropractic school for a few drinks in one of the gay bars in the Castro. These outings differed significantly from my previous encounters with gay bars.

My initial experience at a gay bar, aside from attending a drag show dinner at Asia SF, took place in grad school when my friend Dre convinced me to join him at a random gay club. As I entered, my eyes beheld two muscular men in neon-colored speedos dancing to Britney Spears' "Hit Me Baby One More Time." Onlookers gazed at them, evaluating their physiques and strategically placing dollar bills in their waistbands. Whether I was seen as fresh meat or unknowingly the subject of an Asian fetish among gay men, numerous individuals in the club instantly focused their attention on me. They attempted to encircle me, invading my personal space, offering drinks while testing out pickup lines. To establish a boundary and seek safety from unwanted advances, I promptly latched onto Dre and declared, "I'm with him." It didn't take long for me to convince Dre to switch to a more heteronormative venue where I could blend in as an average-looking guy among the crowd. Apparently, at that time, I possessed a particular allure for gay men, akin to a gay man's kryptonite. Interestingly, the only women who typically found me attractive were older Asian women and grandmothers who expressed admiration after introductions from my parents.

During my early adventures in Seattle after grad school, I met Leo and his girlfriend at Man Ray in Capitol Hill for my second gay bar experience. Curiosity led me to question Leo's choice of venue, to which he imparted his wisdom, praising the strength of a "Gay Strong pour." This concoction primarily consisted of alcohol with a hint of mixer. Inspired by this philosophy, we crafted our own pre-funk drinks before hitting the clubs to dance to hit on with girls. Our signature drink involved filling a large red Solo cup with ice and pouring equal parts vodka and

Red Bull. To get ourselves hyped, we'd blast "Sandstorm" by Darude before venturing out. Bobby playfully labeled our potent drink pours as "Vo Strong," even though Leo's 1:1 liquor-to-mixer ratio was the true recipe for maximum intoxication. We created a drink hierarchy: Strong, Gay Strong, and Vo Strong.

While San Francisco was renowned for its high cost of living, it surprisingly offered affordable drinking options. This was particularly true in the Castro, where Happy Hour consisted of two-for-one drinks from noon to 9 pm in most bars every day of the week. For a mere $10, you could enjoy two Gay Strong Kettle One and Sodas and feel quite content. Doubling the amount to $20 would secure four drinks, bringing a sense of happiness and slight intoxication. Anything beyond that, I jokingly claimed, would result in waking up the next day from a blackout with your boxer shorts on backward. This appealed to my cheap Asian side, especially since my income in San Francisco was considerably lower than what I had acquainted in Seattle.

After residing in SF for approximately six months, I finally received my eagerly awaited chiropractic license. I reached an agreement to rent shared space at Dre's clinic in Lower Haight, where I started seeing a mix of chiropractic and energy medicine patients on my days off from Nordstrom. One day, a female shaman visited the office and showed interest in my book and energy work. After a few months of conversations, she requested a complimentary energy session from me so she could understand my work and potentially refer others to me. I agreed. Following our session, she expressed a remarkable sense of well-being and departed with enhanced connection and clarity. She then asked if there was anything she could do for me. Recognizing her shamanic background, I inquired if she knew any practitioners who worked with ayahuasca, as I had yet to experience the true profound journey others had described. It felt like hearing about an elusive unicorn that everyone else had encountered except for me. A week later, I received an email from her informing me that she had found a group I could contact to embark on the sacred ayahuasca ceremony. Finally, I discovered what I had been seeking for years. Overjoyed, I immediately contacted JR to share the news and ensure we could both sign up and experience this transformative encounter together for the first time.

In the weeks leading up to the ayahuasca ceremony, we received a detailed set of instructions: bringing a pillow and sleeping bag for the overnight stay, abstaining from alcohol and drugs, avoiding violent movies or TV shows, refraining from sexual activity, and following specific dietary restrictions for three days prior to the ceremony. Additionally, we were instructed to set intentions for what we wanted to accomplish or heal during the journey. For me, it was evident that I carried lingering anger from the disappointment of my book's failure. My heart remained closed and numb due to trust issues arising from past experiences of being lied to and cheated on by ex-girlfriends. The words of one particular ex resonated deeply with me: "People are going to do whatever they want to do in life, no matter who is involved." It felt as though her statement foreshadowed events yet to come. I felt adrift, lacking a clear path or direction. I resumed meditation and focused on three intentions: Why is my heart closed, and how can I open it again? What hidden wounds do I still need to heal? What is holding me back and preventing progress in my life?

Finally, the day of the ceremony arrived. JR and I met up and carpooled to the undisclosed location. We joined the shamans, assistants, and a diverse group of about a dozen others who had gathered for the same purpose. We settled into our designated spaces for the night, changing into comfortable attire. In between moments of rest, we engaged in conversations with fellow participants until darkness fell, signaling the beginning of the ceremony. JR and I were the newcomers that night, while others had experienced the medicine before. We sought advice from those more experienced, inquiring about what to expect throughout the entire journey. They provided a range of responses, including warnings about the unpleasant taste of the medicine, the need to keep a bucket nearby due to potential vomiting, and the likelihood of seeing geometric shapes. They emphasized not disturbing others' journeys and the difficulty in explaining the experience. Each person's journey would be unique, depending on their level of awareness and the specific healing or work they had chosen to focus on. The key advice shared was that if the medicine became overwhelming, to repeat the mantra "I surrender" and take deep breaths to navigate the healing process. Essentially, we were told to wait, observe, and trust that we would understand as the journey unfolded. They all seemed to chuckle or smile as if they held a secret they couldn't reveal, knowing that both JR and I were virgins of the sacred ceremony and were both in for an extraordinary and transformative experience.

As night fell, we settled into our designated spots. JR was seated next to me, and we had jokingly discussed the possibility of meeting in another dimension during our journey, even though we knew it was far-fetched. We exchanged a high-five, and JR flashed his signature phrase, "See you on the other side!" The ceremony commenced with prayers and rituals, and then one by one, we approached the shaman at the altar. When it was my turn, he looked at me and asked, "How far down the rabbit hole do you want to go?" In life, my philosophy had always been to go all-in or not at all, so I responded with a smile, "All the way, of course."

Instead of presenting a blue or red pill, the shaman poured a thick brown liquid into what appeared to be a shot glass. He said a prayer and blew tobacco smoke into a cup, blessing it before handing it to me. The cup was filled to a level that he believed would suit my comfort and experience. I took the cup, offered a prayer of gratitude, and whispered, "Thank you," as I bowed. Holding this mysterious dark-brown liquid in my hands, I thought to myself, "This is it. Bottoms up!" I quickly consumed the unappealing, putrid-looking liquid, grabbed a small piece of ginger in a feeble attempt to counteract the taste, and returned to my seat. We all sat in the dark silence, waiting for the unknown to unfold. All I could discern was that the medicine tasted repugnant, and the taste alone made me want to vomit. Perhaps that's what others had warned me about. Thirty minutes passed, and nothing happened. I began to doubt myself, thinking, "Damn, maybe I didn't take enough. Maybe this is a complete waste of time, like when JR and I tried it ourselves back in L.A." Despite my reservations, I persisted and remained seated, focusing on my three intentions while meditating.

Approximately fifteen more minutes passed when suddenly, I heard a soothing voice in my head ask, "Are you ready?" Going with the flow,

I replied, "Yes, I am ready." The voice returned, questioning, "Are you sure you are ready?" Confused and frustrated, I thought to myself, "What the hell! Yes, I'm ready! Let's do this!" Then, I began to perceive small cobalt-blue geometric patterns forming within my vision, confirming that this was the geometric jungle I had read about. The patterns multiplied and took on the shape of an Amazonian goddess being, beckoning me with her finger to enter her psychic dimension. I heard the word "Welcome."

Houston, we have lift-off. Suddenly, everything intensified, and BLAHH... Oh no! I was the first one to vomit into my bucket, and soon others joined in, creating a symphony of retching that filled the room and all the buckets. After finally emptying my stomach, I was immediately shown visions of specific individuals and events from my past that I held deep emotional anger towards. The medicine surged through me like wildfire, aiding in the release of all the negative energy surrounding each experience, one after the other. I cried out, "I surrender! I surrender! I fucking SURRENDER!!!" With each release, intense anger, guilt, pain, and sadness poured out, encompassing each experience. The medicine refused to relent until I had let go of every last drop of emotion, leaving me still and utterly exhausted. Or so I thought. I only had a brief moment of respite before the next wave of intentions began.

Then, I heard the words, "Do you want to go higher?" Never one to shy away from accelerated learning or confronting challenges head-on, I thought, *Fuck it. I'm already on this spiritual yellow submarine joy ride. Let's do this.* "Yes," I responded. Just then, the head shaman offered a second cup to those who wanted a deeper experience. I managed to crawl up to the altar slowly, resembling a drunk person and informed him that I was instructed to take another cup. He looked at me, smiled, and handed me another half-shot of... BLAH. I downed it and returned to my spot, eagerly waiting to see what would unfold next. Shortly after, I felt a surge of energy coursing through my body, propelling me through different dimensions—the red planet, the blue planet, the crystal city—places that woo-woo metaphysical enthusiasts discuss in their books and on websites dedicated to higher dimensions. Higher and higher, I ascended until I passed through a brilliant white star, standing before the Council of Light. Supposedly, they were the highest spiritual council in metaphysical terms. There, I screamed at them, "You abandoned me! You lied to me! You let me fall!" while these luminous beings sat in stoic silence. Waves of tears and emotions flooded my body until I once again lay still as the medicinal effects gradually subsided for the night.

Five or six hours must have passed before the head shaman commenced the closing rituals and prayers. I checked my phone, and it confirmed the time had elapsed from the start to the finish. Some of us quietly rose from our spots and made our way outside, where hot cups of tea awaited. We gathered together and shared our incredible adventures. JR recounted some of his experiences and mentioned that he had attempted to reach out and give me a hug but was stopped by the shaman to avoid disrupting my journey. We had to maintain a hushed tone as a few individuals were still deeply immersed in their own experiences. Others opted for the comfort of their sleeping bags, seeking rest after the exhaustion or perhaps due to the fact that it was around four in the morning by the time we concluded.

I believed I had accomplished a great deal in my years of expanding my consciousness, but that night, I learned and experienced so much more. My body underwent a significant shift that eluded precise explanation. I deemed it one of the most transformative psychic and spiritual encounters I had ever encountered and returned home to ponder how it would manifest in my life. We were advised to continue following the pre-ayahuasca instructions for the next three days, to be gentle with ourselves, and to remain open to receiving further messages from the medicine within us. True to our rebellious nature, JR and I contemplated going out to party in San Francisco before he departed for Los Angeles the following day. However, we opted to play it cool and watched a horror movie instead; so much for following the rules.

CHAPTER 8

THE GIRL WITH BLUE EYES

    I found myself back at work, immersed in the daily grind of San Francisco. As one of the top tourist destinations in the US, there was always something happening every day of the week. When the sun was shining, people flocked to Dolores Park, known as the Gay Beach, where members of the LGBTQ+ community basked in the sun while friends and families with children gathered on the grass with blankets, enjoying wine, beer, or other delightful libations. "Sunday Funday" became the anthem for going out to brunch and indulging in bottomless mimosas or a few too many cocktails. And every once in a while, you may catch a glimpse of a few bottomless chaps. In reality, there was never a genuine need for an excuse like it being the weekend or someone's birthday to party and have a few drinks. It could be as simple as visiting Costco and purchasing a massive 1.75-liter bottle of vodka to invite people over and share it. If one was feeling bored, going out for drinks was usually everyone's go-to option.

I once accompanied Leo to a medical consultation as his designated driver, always picking him up after whichever procedure he underwent. He often couldn't drive himself because of the lingering effects of Valium or pain medication. It had become a tradition for us to grab dim sum together afterward. During one such consultation, the doctor went through the usual list of questions. When the doctor asked Leo how many drinks he typically had in a week, he added, "Well, I probably drink more than you anyway, so you're probably fine." The doctor smirked, well aware that most patients downplay their alcohol consumption, claiming to have only one or two drinks a week or a month, and always with dinner, of course. Leo was never one to shy away from answering such questions honestly. In fact, he once shockingly informed a doctor that he had 8 to 10 drinks when he went out partying on weekends. On this occasion, we all chuckled, knowing the truth behind his response.

While at work, I unexpectedly ran into an old friend from Seattle who happened to be of Asian descent. Seeking an escape from the drama in Seattle, he secured a job with one of the prominent banks in San Francisco after completing college. Being half-Filipino and half-Chinese, he often delighted in cracking jokes using Asian slang. He would playfully ask, "What da pho doo?" instead of "What's up?" or respond with "Ayaaa" instead of a simple "yes," while expressing gratitude by saying "M goi" instead of "Thank you." We happened to meet at a gym where I had established professional connections as a chiropractor while he worked as a personal trainer while attending university. After our respective workdays, Bobby and I would often engage in intense sweat-inducing workouts together. Spotting him sitting on the shoe bench, engrossed in reading a newspaper as his shoes were being polished at Nordstrom, I approached him and called out, "Hey, Lee!"

"Well... Well... Well... If it isn't the DMV!" he exclaimed, clearly surprised by our chance encounter. "What brings you to SF?"

Feeling a bit self-conscious about the fact that our last conversation took place years ago back in Seattle, I couldn't help but wear a sheepish smile as I revealed, "I'm working here at Nordstrom, waiting for my chiropractic license to be approved by the state."

It was evident that Lee was taken aback by this unexpected turn of events. To him, I was still the successful chiropractor living it up in Seattle. However, he swiftly recovered from the surprise and flashed a genuine smile. It was clear that he was delighted to see me and said, "If you don't have any plans this weekend, let's go grab dinner and a few drinks. I just started dating this girl. Maybe she can introduce you to some of her friends."

"Sounds great, Lee!" I replied enthusiastically, sensing that this would provide me with another straight friend to hang out with. While Leo, being married with a new baby, had taken on more adult responsibilities, meeting Lee meant I had another companion for various activities. As a newcomer to the city, my options for socializing were somewhat limited, with most of my friends being gay and frequenting gay bars, which didn't offer many opportunities to meet straight women.

On that weekend, Lee and his girlfriend picked me up, and we embarked on a night out. Given the proximity to the Castro, I suggested stopping by for a few inexpensive drinks during Happy Hour. Although initially hesitant, considering it would be their first experience at a gay bar, I assured them we would only stay for a brief moment before moving on to grab some food. Toad Hall seemed like a suitable choice, and I invited Dre, whom Lee also knew, to join us and create a more comfortable atmosphere. Arriving early, we found a booth for the four of us and ordered our first round of drinks. I swiftly finished my first two and made my way back to the bar to order two more before Happy Hour ended.

As I approached the bar, my attention was immediately captivated by a girl seated with her back toward me. She wore a simple white V-neck t-shirt and a pair of jeans, her long brown hair carelessly tied up in a bun with what appeared to be a pen. Engaged in conversation with a guy, who I assumed was gay considering our location in the Castro, she seemed engrossed in the discussion. Emboldened by the slight buzz from the drinks, I couldn't help but try to catch her attention. Perhaps prompted by a gesture from her friend or simply sensing my gaze, she turned to look in my direction, revealing her striking blue eyes. I couldn't resist but express, "You have the most beautiful blue eyes that I have ever seen."

As she swiftly responded, "I am a lesbian," I couldn't help but burst into laughter at her remark. There was something about her demeanor that made me doubt her words, and I playfully retorted, "No, you're not."

Maintaining a serious expression, she turned to her friend seated beside her and called out, "Jules?" With a smirk on his face, he took a sip of his drink and gave an approving nod, confirming the truth behind her statement.

Maintaining my smile, I responded, "Sure you are. Well, at least can I buy you a drink?"

She swiftly replied, "Sorry, but I'm just here to catch up and have a drink with a friend after work." With that, she turned away from me, giving me the cold shoulder. Taking the hint that she wasn't interested, or perhaps considering the possibility that she truly wasn't interested in men, I proceeded to order my drinks from the bartender, ready to move on to dinner. As I turned to walk away, I suddenly felt a tap on my shoulder. I spun around to find her standing there behind me, and she confessed, "You're right. I'm not a lesbian."

I replied, "Obviously…"

"But I really am here to catch up with my friend Jules. Maybe we can chat another time?" she replied. We exchanged phone numbers, and as the night progressed and the Gay Strong drinks flowed, the details started to blur. I woke up the next morning with a faint memory of the night but a clear recollection that Lee and his girlfriend had left me at the bar, likely recognizing my interest in the girl and wanting to give me space to pursue it.

I found myself still fully clothed, sprawled on my bed. As I reached into my pocket, I pulled out a crumpled napkin with a phone number on it. Slightly unsure of the name she had mentioned, I decided to play it cool and texted, "Hey you," hoping for a response. I hoped I hadn't made a fool of myself, considering the possibility that she might be nursing a hangover as well.

A few minutes later, she replied, "I probably feel better than you. Do you even remember what happened last night?" with a playful look plastered on her face.

Trying to maintain my composure, I responded, "It's a little hazy, but yeah, I remember." Internally, I chuckled at the thought of what might have transpired. Gathering my courage, I decided to take the next step and asked, "Do you want to hang out again soon?"

She responded, "I'm leaving for Arizona to meet up with a friend and watch some PGA tour this coming weekend. So, I won't be available for a few weeks. Hit me up another time."

"Ok... Cool," I replied, trying to hide my disappointment. Strike one, I thought to myself. I still couldn't fully piece together what had happened the previous night. Dre later informed me that we were dancing together after her friend convinced her to join in. Or perhaps I had interrupted their dance. Supposedly, we even shared a kiss. I decided to save her number on my phone as "Toad Hall Girl" to avoid the embarrassment of asking for her name again.

Three or four weeks had passed before I mustered up the courage to reach out again. I texted her, "What's going on this weekend?"

She replied, "Sorry, I already have dinner plans with a friend this weekend. Hit me up again later."

Strike two. Being rejected twice now would typically lead me to categorize her number as "Reach out if I had nothing better to do." I was content with my casual, unattached lifestyle and had no intention of pursuing her further.

San Francisco was experiencing an extraordinary winter with no rain and several warm days of sunshine. At work, the holiday rush had finally subsided, and the once bustling retail scene had transformed into a ghost town. With salesmen outnumbering customers, our manager asked if anyone wanted to go home early. I decided to take a chance and texted "Toad Hall Girl," asking if she wanted to meet up for a drink. Surprisingly, she responded with a "Yes. How about Absinthe in Hayes Valley?" I quickly volunteered to leave work and hurried home to change, excited about the possibility of meeting her. She instructed me to look for a girl wearing a hat and a long white dress at the bar.

She proceeded to call up her friend Jules and asked, "Hey Jules. That dude from Toad Hall texted me and asked if I wanted to meet up for a drink. It's been a while since we first met. What does he look like?"

The first thing out of Jules' mouth was, "You know he is Asian, right?"

With a snarky reply, she said, "Well, no shit, Sherlock. I remembered that much."

Jules then said, "Well, that's easy. When you see a really good-looking Asian man walk through the door at the time you are supposed to meet, that will be him." Gay kryptonite strikes again!

As I walked into the bustling French-Mediterranean Brasserie, I immediately saw a girl with long, dark hair sitting there. She wore a straw fedora and a long white summer dress, sipping her glass of Prosecco. Originally, I thought she had dirty-blonde hair, but in the dim lighting and with a few drinks in me, hair color could be deceptive. However, when she turned around and those blue eyes met mine, I knew without a doubt that she was the same girl I had met several months ago. A smile spread across her face as she greeted me with a big warm hug. Finally, I didn't have to refer to her as "Toad Hall Girl" anymore—I had heard the bartender call her Ally.

Our conversation flowed effortlessly, and time flew by as we sat there, enjoying each other's company. Ally called up Jules and invited him to join us at Toad Hall as if we were recreating the night we first met. Jules arrived with his usual impeccable fashion sense, dressed to attract attention. I ordered a round of drinks and splurged on special vodka shots with neon plastic shot glasses and shark gummies. In the midst of the festivities, as Julian attempted to devour his gummy, it somehow escaped his grasp and found its way into the coat pocket of his white jean jacket, leaving a noticeable blue stain on the next day. I reached out to some friends in the neighborhood, inviting them to join us and add to the celebratory atmosphere. Everything seemed to be going wonderfully until Jules suddenly pulled Ally aside and hurriedly escorted her out of the bar. Their private exchange left me confused and questioning what had just happened. Perhaps something I said had triggered Jules' protective instincts, or he was concerned about Ally reliving the events of our first meeting. I immediately tried calling and texting Ally, seeking answers and making sure everything was alright but received no response. It wasn't until the following morning that I finally heard from her. She explained that Jules had been overly protective and didn't want her to get too intoxicated.

Despite the abrupt departure, our connection remained strong, and we continued to see each other whenever our schedules aligned. Our primary mode of communication became talking and texting as we bonded over long conversations, our shared love for horror movies, and our mutual appreciation for good food and wine. Ally, known for her impressive cheese plates, wanted to demonstrate her culinary skills and offered to cook dinner for me. While she was shopping at the local Safeway grocery store, she called to ask what I wanted. Recalling Leo's advice, I replied, "Buy whatever is on sale."

Ally was initially perplexed by my response, as the idea of buying random sale items didn't seem like the most impressive choice for a first meal. Curiosity got the best of her, and she inquired further to understand the logic behind my statement. With a smile, I shared the wisdom bestowed upon me by Leo: Buy what's on sale for the day because the food items are essentially the same every day of the week. So, why not save a little money and opt for whatever is on sale? Ally chuckled in response, unable to argue with the logic that made perfect sense. At that moment, she was initiated into the world of being "Asian cheap," or, as Leo and I referred to it, being "smart" with our choices.

Despite Ally's occasional guardedness, our relationship continued to progress positively. Within the first month, as we basked in the sun at Dolores Park, I turned to her to express my deep affection for her, "I adore you." She smiled and reached over to give me a kiss.

We mutually agreed that the past should remain in the past, and there was no need to discuss it further. Judgments and explanations were unnecessary; instead, we embraced and accepted each other for who we were in our relationship. This was a refreshing change from my previous experiences, where girlfriends often tried to dictate my actions and behaviors or shape me into someone I wasn't. Dating me had felt like a constant battle of conforming, and I had no intention of being with anyone who couldn't fully accept me for who I was. It crossed my mind that perhaps there was some truth to the transformative power of ayahuasca, as my heart was once again open to love. I was rapidly falling for Ally, and it felt like a beautiful journey.

After two months had passed, I headed to LA to surprise a mutual friend for his birthday, accompanied by the newfound feelings of love for Ally. Unable to contain my emotions, I called her from the road and blurted out, "I think we should be exclusive, like boyfriend and girlfriend." To my surprise, Ally questioned the need to define ourselves, especially when things were going so well. She believed that happiness didn't require labels and expressed her intention to think about my proposition while I was away. Her hesitation triggered a wave of thoughts, causing my mind to wander and worry about the possibility of her rejecting my offer. Upon my return, Ally opened up to me about her previous toxic relationship, which had deeply affected her mental well-being. It had led to severe depression and left her with intense insecurities, making it challenging for her to find happiness in life and embrace her singularity. After much contemplation, Ally decided to take a chance on us, willing to see where our relationship would lead.

Following our heartfelt conversation, everything seemed to fall into place. We cherished our shared days off, embarking on little adventures together. Whether it was spending the day at the museum, enjoying the park, or taking trips to Napa or Sonoma for wine tasting with friends, our time was filled with joy. In the evenings, we cooked dinner together and snuggled up in bed, MacBook resting between us, while we sipped wine and indulged in the latest action movies, comedies, and, of course, the newest horror films. It often felt like Ally's life itself was a dark comedy, with strange incidents occurring from time to time. For instance, she accidentally set my duvet on fire while playfully reenacting a dramatic scene, causing it to fall onto a candle's open flame. The smell of smoke filled the air as we wondered where it was coming from. Another instance involved a horror movie jump scare that made Ally startle, resulting in her spilling a full glass of wine onto my MacBook, rendering it unusable for the rest of the film. Thankfully, I had learned the art of non-reaction and letting go, regardless of the situation's magnitude. Even though Ally would often freak out, feeling guilty for these mishaps, I assured her that everything was fine and there was no need to worry.

With my chiropractic license finally granted, along with my job at Nordstrom creating an increase in income, I decided it was time to leave the dark and dingy attic behind. I rented a room in a charming townhouse in Lower Haight, sharing the space with two gay men and a straight guy. Devon, the owner of the flat, stood out with his svelte figure, attractive appearance, and white hair. He had a passion for singing old Judy Garland show tunes and was locally known for his role as an extra in a famous Stanley Kubrick movie. During the walk-through of the flat, Devon showed me the room I would be renting. Being unfamiliar with living with gay individuals because of my sheltered small-town upbringing, I let my naivety get the best of me and asked, "Does this door have a lock on it?"

Devon looked at me, a mix of shock and amusement on his face, and sarcastically responded, "What? You think you're going to get raped by a gay man in the middle of the night?" We both burst into laughter, acknowledging the absurdity of my question. After signing the lease, we headed to a nearby café to celebrate with a beer, where Devon laid down the house rules: pay rent on time, be considerate and respectful towards roommates, no late-night parties or disturbances after 10 pm, and limit sleepovers to no more than twice a week. As I settled into the new living arrangement, I soon discovered that sleepovers were not a necessity for gay men, as they could easily arrange quick encounters through dating apps like Grinder during the day.

After Ally's return from her trip to London and Croatia with Jules, things took an unexpected turn. They had attended a Kylie Minogue concert in London, and whatever had transpired during their travels seemed to have sparked doubts and insecurities in Ally's mind. Out of the blue, she called me and expressed her belief that it would be best if we ended our relationship. She felt that she wasn't suited for relationships and thought we would both be better off remaining single. I asked if there was something specific I had done to lead her to this decision, but she assured me that it wasn't my fault. It was simply what she believed was best for her. With little say in the matter, I wished her well and reached out to a friend to help distract me and ease my sorrows for the evening.

The following day, I awoke to multiple missed calls and voicemails from Ally, urgently asking me to call her back. She confessed that she had made a mistake. Ending things triggered overwhelming panic attacks, anxiety, and regret. Ally realized that what we had together had been special and that her fears and past relationship experiences had clouded her judgment. She didn't want to sabotage our connection out of fear. In response, I expressed my surprise at her sudden change of heart and made it clear that if we were to start again, it would require rebuilding trust and taking things slowly. This agreement might have lasted a week or two, but soon we found ourselves fully immersed in our relationship once more as if nothing had occurred before.

As her birthday approached, Ally mentioned that birthdays were a big deal in her family. Aware of her love for oysters, I decided to take her on a special outing along scenic Highway 1 near the Hog Island Oyster Company. We made a stop at a nearby restaurant, where we indulged in fresh raw oysters and savored a bottle of wine while gazing out over the picturesque Tomales Bay. Afterward, I went to my car and surprised her with a birthday cake, complete with a lit candle, and encouraged her to make a wish. It wasn't a lavish or extravagant celebration, but the thoughtfulness and effort put into creating those little moments meant the world to her and brought a smile to her heart on that day.

I introduced Ally to Devon, and they immediately hit it off. They bonded over their shared love of witty sarcasm, dry humor, and classic movies like *"Breakfast at Tiffany's," "Casablanca,"* and *"Auntie Mame."* They often danced together, singing along to Frank Sinatra's "Fly Me to the Moon," or convinced Devon to serenade us with old Billie Holiday tunes after enjoying dinner and a few bottles of wine. Their camaraderie added an extra layer of joy and laughter to our evenings together.

During gay pride week, Devon threw a lively party at our place. The sun was shining brightly in San Francisco, setting the perfect backdrop for the celebration. Devon extended invitations to a diverse group of friends, all eager to gather, drink, dance, and share laughter while reflecting on their experiences and discussing current events within the

LGBTQ+ community, both locally and globally. This vibrant atmosphere was where Ally truly thrived. She reveled in the excitement of a good party, especially one filled with opportunities to meet new and fascinating individuals. Ally effortlessly glided from person to person, attentively listening to their stories and offering her support or relevant insights into the struggles faced by the gay rights movement. It seemed as if she had a deep-rooted connection to standing up against injustice and advocating for those who had endured hardships, much like the burdens she had experienced in her own upbringing.

As someone who also enjoyed socializing, I fully immersed myself in the festivities, catching up with old friends and forging new connections. At one point, I caught sight of Ally on the balcony, sitting on another man's lap. Instantly, a pang of jealousy coursed through me as memories of past betrayals resurfaced. Seeking a private moment to address my concerns, I asked Ally if we could speak alone. She agreed, and we retreated to my bedroom, where I expressed my distress over her seemingly inappropriate and disrespectful behavior. Without missing a beat, she retorted, "He is GAY! You have nothing to worry about. I am a sure thing." Her response instantly put things into perspective, and I felt foolish for overreacting as if I still needed to win her over as I did in the early stages of our relationship. With a newfound understanding, we rejoined the celebration and continued to revel late into the evening. From that point forward, Ally became a familiar presence in our townhouse, joining Devon and me for shared meals, engaging conversations, and cherished moments.

CHAPTER 9

A Promise

After completing my first full year at Nordstrom, I found myself tantalizingly close to achieving the prestigious million-dollar seller status, with just $100,000 left to reach the milestone. Several department managers took notice of my success and approached me with offers to become their assistants in their respective departments. It was an enticing prospect, but deep down, I knew I couldn't accept their offers. My heart yearned to leave behind the demanding life of retail and return to my original profession once my practice had gained enough momentum.

Coincidentally, during this time, a friend of mine from Seattle reached out to me. Aware of my modest accomplishments in energy work, particularly with cancer patients, he asked if I would fly out to Virginia Beach to see if there was anything I could do for his uncle. His uncle, a retired man of 75 years, had been diagnosed with tongue cancer and was undergoing chemotherapy treatments. In his generous gesture, he offered to cover all my expenses, as well as the cost of any treatments. If there was a chance, it could enhance his uncle's chances of survival. Energy work remained relatively unknown to many, with only a select few having firsthand experience of its potential benefits in their lives.

Upon our arrival, we were met with palpable resistance and a lack of enthusiasm regarding my presence. His uncle had just completed a grueling round of chemotherapy, leaving him weakened and plagued by severe nausea. The cancer had spread throughout his body, and his ability to have a regular meal was nearly nonexistent, relying instead on a PEG tube for necessary nourishment. Furthermore, he suffered from excruciating lower back pain, likely exacerbated by immobility and prolonged bed rest. The pain hindered his movements, making it challenging to perform essential stretches and exercises prescribed by his private trainer.

During our initial days together, our conversations remained brief and inconsequential, often cut short by his fatigue. His perception of me was reduced to that of a mere massage therapist, a service he already had at his disposal. However, by the third day, his back pain had intensified to the point of debilitation, rendering him incapable of getting out of his Easy Chair or bed without full assistance. Sensing an opportunity, I revealed my identity as both a chiropractor and an energy worker and proposed examining his condition. Familiar with chiropractic care and desperate for relief, he reluctantly acquiesced, granting me permission to begin by reading his energy. To my discovery, his hip flexor muscles were in severe spasm, causing pain and inflammation in his lower back. Lacking the means to maneuver him onto a chiropractic table, I resorted to applying energy work to his lower body, aiming to release the muscle tension. For 30 minutes, I diligently performed the treatment, channeling my focus and intention toward his healing. With the session concluded, I cautiously requested that he attempt to stand. Supported by our assistance, he mustered the courage to take his first step, then another, and another until he was walking with ease, free from pain, and reinvigorated by a renewed sense of energy and enthusiasm. Overwhelmed by the transformation, he proclaimed it to be nothing short of a miracle. Filled with gratitude and awe, he made his way to the backyard, gazing up at the sky with closed eyes, basking in the warmth of the afternoon sun.

In that transformative moment, he became an instant believer in the power of my work, expressing a desire for me to relocate and become his private physician. However, the practical considerations weighed heavily on my mind. It was not only my own life that I had to take into account but also the responsibilities, commitments, and relationships I had cultivated in San Francisco, including Ally, my work, and my patients. "I will pay you $10,000 a month!" he exclaimed as his answer to all of my problems. Reluctantly, I informed him that we would be departing the following day, as planned, to return to our lives in San Francisco. However, I proposed an alternative arrangement to maintain his care and further our concentrated energy work. We agreed that I would fly out for a week every month, ensuring regular treatment sessions to enhance his chances of survival. It was a compromise that allowed me to fulfill my professional responsibilities while continuing to support his journey toward healing.

Upon my return home, I shared the entire experience with Ally, including the agreed-upon treatment schedule. She greeted the news with excitement and happiness for me, intrigued by the energy work that I had undertaken. She expressed a desire to receive an energy session herself, curious to explore this aspect of my practice. While I agreed to perform a single session on her, I emphasized the importance of seeking long-term treatment from a practitioner who could provide an unbiased perspective. The intimate nature of our relationship had the potential to cloud judgment and hinder clear and objective treatment, unencumbered by emotional entanglements. With open hearts and a shared understanding, we embarked on this new chapter, where the worlds of energy work, healing, and our relationship converged.

Having been in a relationship with Ally for six months, I had gained some insight into her life and experiences. Early on, we had agreed not to delve into each other's pasts, aiming to avoid preconceived judgments and biases that could hinder our connection. However, as an energy worker, I realized that conducting a session would grant me access to information about her past, potentially shedding light on unresolved issues. We scheduled a private session at my clinic on a day when we had the space to ourselves. I guided Ally to lie on the table. Her eyes closed as I prepared for the session. Placing my hand gently on her abdomen, I tuned into her energy field, immediately sensing the presence of profound pain and sadness. It became evident that she carried deep-rooted emotions of abandonment and anger stemming from her parent's divorce, alongside various other incidents that had compounded her sense of sorrow. The weight of this emotional baggage was palpable, casting a dark and heavy cloud over her energy. As I began to articulate what I perceived within her energy field, a profound shift occurred. Her body trembled, tears welled up in her eyes and streamed down her face. It was a cathartic release, a testament to the authenticity of what I was sensing. At that moment, she opened her eyes, taking in a deep breath. In a gentle voice, I shared with her the importance of finding a way to forgive and release the negative energy that she had been holding onto. I emphasized that if left unresolved, such emotional burdens could have far-reaching consequences, potentially even impacting her physical health and manifesting in serious conditions like cancer.

She turned to look at me and said softly, "I know, but I don't know how to."

I tried comforting by telling her, "We will figure out a way to help you get through this and let it go."

With Ally's consent, she closed her eyes once again, and I began the energy work to facilitate the release of negative energy that resided within her, aiming to bring about a sense of grounding and balance. As I worked on her energy field, she gradually drifted off to sleep, her body relaxing in response to the healing energy. Meanwhile, in order to accommodate my new treatment schedule for my friend's uncle, a significant shift was required in my own professional life. I made the decision to finally resign from my position at Nordstrom, freeing up precious time and energy to dedicate to building my practice and shaping my life according to my true calling. It was a pivotal moment as I transitioned away from forty-hour workweeks, allowing me to invest more deeply in my energy practice.

Interestingly enough, it was this shift that led to a surge in the growth of my energy practice, surpassing even the progress I had made in chiropractic care. This newfound momentum and availability allowed me to spend more quality time with Ally, who, in contrast to my unconventional schedule, held a regular corporate job with a Monday through Friday routine. Our schedules began to align more harmoniously, offering us the opportunity to nurture our relationship and create meaningful experiences together.

After the energy session, a shift occurred in Ally's demeanor. She began to exhibit greater vulnerability and trust in our connection, opening up about her family dynamics and the traumatic experiences she endured during her upbringing. She shared the challenges her father faced in raising two teenage girls, feeling ill-equipped to provide the guidance and support they needed. As her older sister moved away, Ally found herself longing for guidance, and a sense of abandonment settled within her. She disclosed that she had been estranged from her mother for nearly five years and sought my perspective on the matter.

Pausing to reflect, I carefully chose my words before responding, "Your mother is your mother by birth and blood, which means that she will always hold that role in your life. We all carry regrets and mistakes from our past. Perhaps your mother made decisions that, at the time, she believed were best for her, even if they caused you pain and feelings of abandonment. It's possible that she carries her own burden of guilt and regret. Ultimately, the decision of whether to have your mother in your life rests with you. If you choose to welcome her back, it will require forgiveness and a commitment to rebuilding trust from this moment forward. It doesn't have to happen all at once; you can take small steps or approach it one day at a time. On the other hand, if you feel that forgiveness is beyond your reach, you must come to terms with the idea that she may no longer be part of your life. Only you can determine what is best for your well-being."

Later that week, Ally mustered the courage to make the long-awaited call to her mother, and she asked me to sit by her side for emotional support. We settled on the couch in her living room as she dialed her mother's number, and as soon as her mother answered, Ally tightly held onto my hand, seeking comfort in our connection. They engaged in a conversation, catching up on the events of their lives, bridging the gap that had persisted for so long. When the call ended, Ally let out a deep sigh of relief, accompanied by a genuine smile gracing her face. It was a moment of triumph, representing a significant first step on her journey toward forgiveness and liberation from the burdens of her past. Ally recognized that she couldn't have undertaken this transformative path alone, but with me by her side, she felt the strength and support she needed to embark on the healing journey that awaited her.

To lift her spirits and create new memories together, we decided to embark on our first road trip during the 4th of July weekend, heading to Los Angeles. The purpose was twofold: introducing Ally to my friend JR and some other acquaintances and enjoying a change of scenery. We extended an invitation to Devon, asking him to join us for the five-hour drive to the City of Angels. As we made our way down the I-5 corridor, approaching our final destination, we began to hear an intermittent pinging sound every few minutes, piquing our curiosity about its source. After a few more pings, we collectively realized that it was Devon's Grinder app, indicating that men in the area were expressing interest in connecting with him. As we neared Los Angeles, the pings became more frequent, and we couldn't help but chuckle at Devon's newfound popularity, as he received far more attention in LA than in San Francisco. For a brief moment, Devon basked in the role of the new Queen of LA, delighting in the weekend of attention and seizing the opportunity to fully enjoy his momentary fame.

During our first night in Los Angeles, we collectively decided to forgo the idea of going to a club to meet JR and his friends, as it didn't align with Ally and Devon's interests. Instead, Ally found joy in the simple pleasures of ordering room service and watching movies, a favorite pastime of hers while traveling. Devon, on the other hand, had plans to meet with a "John" later that evening, so he ventured out on his own.

The following day, JR invited us to a 4th of July weekend barbecue at his community pool, nestled in his high-rise condo near downtown LA. The combination of sunshine, poolside relaxation, and refreshing drinks proved enticing enough to convince Ally to join in the festivities. As we mingled, indulged in delicious food, swam, and enjoyed the company of others, Ally and I discovered a cozy corner on the veranda, offering a captivating view of the silhouetted backdrop of Los Angeles. We settled into a lounge chair, embracing each other's presence. In that intimate moment, I turned to Ally, my heart brimming with affection, and uttered, "I will give you the world if you give me enough time." She met my gaze, a radiant smile gracing her lips, before planting a tender kiss on mine. With those words, I aimed to convey my commitment to providing her with everything she desired and dreamed of, even if I currently lacked the means to do so. We sat there, cherishing the warmth of our embrace in blissful silence. In our hearts, the unspoken understanding blossomed: We yearned to spend the rest of our lives together, bound by a love that knew no limits.

THE MIDDLE

CHAPTER 10

THE BIG QUESTION

    In the midst of autumn's embrace, I sensed a shift in the air, signaling that change was imminent. Reflecting on the whirlwind of events since my previous ayahuasca journey, which had sparked the transformative decision to relocate our lives from San Francisco to Seattle, I couldn't ignore the call from JR inviting me to join him on his annual pilgrimage to the sacred ceremony. Intrigued by the opportunity to reconnect with me and seek guidance for the path ahead, I readily agreed.
    As the evening unfolded and we gathered within the sacred ceremonial circle, I settled into a state of meditation, focusing on my intentions with unwavering resolve. What did I need to discover that remained concealed from my awareness? Where did healing and growth beckon in my life? What were the next steps awaiting me? Enveloped by the sacred medicine, I traversed the depths of my subconscious, yet only one vision stood out

from the ephemeral tapestry. It depicted Ally, adorned in a resplendent white dress, while I stood beside her in a classic black tuxedo. Together, we turned to face a gathering I could only assume comprised of our cherished family and friends, raising our entwined hands in triumphant unity. The vision unmistakably revealed that we were destined to be wed. This profound revelation ignited a fervent determination within me and solidified my unwavering commitment to ask Ally for her hand in marriage. I resolved that we would exchange vows within a year, for the medicine had never steered me astray, and I entrusted its message to be undeniably true. Upon returning home, Ally inquired about the visions I had witnessed during the ceremony. Hesitant to reveal the depth of my revelation, I dismissed it with casual nonchalance, offering vague references to work-related matters and areas in need of release. I chose this approach to ensure she didn't perceive anything extraordinary or suspect my true intentions.

After receiving a resolute answer during my last meditation, I felt a strong sense of clarity. Acting upon this newfound certainty, I reached out to Jules via text to arrange a time for an important conversation. I understood he might find this unusual, as serious discussions were not our typical realm of interaction. Our conversations had always remained light and casual, limited to inquiries about each other's well-being and recent activities. The deeper conversations, the ones that held significance, were reserved exclusively for Jules and Ally. I was determined to proceed with our planned discussion, one that needed to occur discreetly without Ally's knowledge. Surprisingly, Jules agreed, and we coordinated a suitable time that aligned with both of our schedules.

I started our conversation with, "Hey, Jules. How's it going?"

He replied with a slightly skeptical demeanor in his voice, "Good. How are you, Minh?"

I blurted, "Good. Thanks for taking my call. I have decided to propose to Ally and wanted your advice on what type of engagement ring I should buy for her.

There was a long pause of silence before Jules replied, "Are you sure this is something that you really want to do, considering your history of ups and downs the two of you have had over the years?"

Indeed, it was undeniable that Ally and I had experienced many incidents that could lead one to question the eventual outcome of our relationship. Throughout our five years together, Ally consistently raised the inquiry of why we hadn't taken a step toward marriage. My responses were often comprised of excuses, citing that the timing wasn't ideal or that we lacked sufficient financial stability. However, deep down, I recognized that there would never truly be a perfect time, and at some point, I needed to confront the reality that we had to make a decision. As they say, one must ultimately "shit or get off the pot." In light of this realization, I promptly replied to Jules, expressing my certainty by stating, "Yes, I am aware of the challenges Ally and I have faced, but I am genuinely sure about this."

His voice perked up, and then, without missing a beat, he replied, "Well, if that is truly the case, then it is simple. She would want a vintage-style engagement ring, specifically, an emerald cut diamond. Something simple like a plain platinum band or maybe a setting in a half-eternity band. Something of that nature."

"Thanks, Jules. I really appreciate it," I replied.

"No problem, Minh. Keep me posted. I am very happy for both of you and look forward to seeing how this all unfolds."

"Yes, for sure! And I am sure you will be one of the first people to know," with that information, I hung up the phone and began my search for the perfect engagement ring for Ally.

After an extensive search spanning over a month, meticulously scouring through a vast inventory of emerald-shaped diamonds from reputable online merchants, I finally discovered the perfect gem. While jewelers often emphasize the importance of color, cut, and clarity, we all know that size is the most significant factor. Thus, I selected the largest diamond that fit within my budget, ensuring it met the criteria of the other three C's as well. With the gem in hand, I reached out to a trusted jeweler friend, someone I had known for a long time, to assist me in crafting the ideal ring for Ally, following the specifications provided by Jules. Once the diamond arrived at my office, I wasted no time in delivering it to the jewelers, trusting them with the task of having it birthed into creation. The jeweler estimated the ring would be ready by the beginning of December, just in time for a potential Christmas surprise. The only remaining step was to call up Ally's father and request his blessing for his daughter's hand in marriage.

Considering the time difference of three hours between JB on the east coast and ourselves, it was crucial to reach him before his bedtime, which was typically before 7:00 pm our time. After careful consideration, I settled on calling him on a Sunday evening, knowing that Ally would be occupied, enjoying some time with one of her friends. This would allow me to have a private conversation with JB raising no suspicions or jeopardizing the surprise I had in store for Ally.

"Hey, JB... How are you doing?" I spoke.

"Hey, buddy. I am doing pretty good. How are you and Ally doing over there in Seattle? I hear it is all rainy and cold," he replied. "I need to get out there for a visit real soon."

"Yeah, it's pretty cold and wet here. It is Seattle, you know."

He just chuckled, "Yeah... I bet."

I had to cut him off before he got to talking. The one thing about JB was that he would talk your ear off if you let him. So, I immediately said to him, "Hey, JB. I am actually calling for an important reason."

For a moment, things suddenly got really quiet on his end. He was probably thinking something bad had just happened, and he was preparing himself for the news I was going to tell him. "Go ahead... what's going on?"

I started with, "Well... You know Ally and I have been together for a while now."

"Yup, go on," he replied.

"Well, I just wanted to do what is right and ask you for Ally's hand in marriage.

You could sense that JB had a great big smile on his face and said to me in a calm, sincere demeanor, "Well... you have my blessings. That is some of the best news I have heard in a long time."

"I haven't quite figured out the details of when I will ask, but it will be either Christmas or New Year's Eve," I told him.

"I am sure either one will be just fine. I am so happy for the two of you and can't wait for you to be part of the family," he said.

"Thanks, JB. You have a good night," I told him.

Christmas or New Year's? I finally came to the conclusion that Christmas Day would be best because it'd be more personal without so many people around. One of Ally's friends gave me the idea to wrap the tiny ring box within a bigger box so that Ally could open a special gift. I thought to myself that was a great idea.

Aware of Ally's disappointment in not receiving teaching assignments for the fall term due to low student enrollment, she expressed her concerns about not being able to afford Christmas presents that year. It was disheartening for her, as she took great joy in giving gifts, particularly during special occasions like birthdays and Christmas. The upcoming holiday season seemed less merry for her, and I understood the weight of her financial situation. Despite secretly spending a significant portion of my savings on her engagement ring, I was not in a much better financial position than Ally. However, this was not a new experience for us, as we faced various challenges together throughout our years. We had always managed to make do with what we had, finding solace in each other's presence. Even though this Christmas would be modest in terms of material possessions, I was determined to make it a memorable one, regardless of Ally's current mood.

Despite the uncertainty surrounding gift exchanges that year, I wanted to make sure that Ally felt special during Christmas. I handpicked a few extra presents, including our traditional wool socks, which held sentimental value in our relationship. I purchased a long dark dress that I knew Ally had been eyeing, as it would perfectly complement her already-fashionable wardrobe. To add an extra touch of excitement to the holiday season, I also secured tickets to a New Year's Eve party at the Columbia Tower Club (CTC). We had attended the same event the previous year and had a fantastic time, so I hoped it might become a cherished tradition for us. I was thrilled at the thought of celebrating with an even larger group of friends as our close-knit circle had expanded.

Knowing that Ally wasn't sure if she would receive any gifts that year and feeling unable to reciprocate the gesture, she had come to terms with the possibility. In order to maintain the surprise and create an even playing field, I wrapped all her gifts at work on Christmas Eve and hid them in the trunk of my car. My intention was to make Christmas feel like just another day so that Ally wouldn't feel any pressure or guilt about not being able to give me a gift.

Christmas morning had finally arrived. I got up early to grab Ally's gifts from my car before she would wake up and set them on the coffee table. After letting her sleep in for a bit, I finally couldn't wait any longer and woke her up at around 10:30 am. I entered the bedroom and quietly sat next to her on the bed. I then began to gently shake her body and said in a soft voice, "It's time to wake up. It's Christmas, Babe."

She slowly opened her eyes, met my gaze, and greeted me with a warm smile. Stretching her arms, she let out a tired groan before asking, "Merry Christmas. What time is it?"

With a smile of my own, I yelled, "It's time to get up and open presents, babe!" I could see a mix of curiosity and anticipation in her eyes as she rolled onto her side to face me. The festive spirit was in the air, and we were ready to make this day special. "You want to get up and get ready. We have a big day ahead of us. Maybe wear something nice since it is Christmas," I mentioned.

In a slightly reluctant mood, Ally kicked off the sheets and got out of bed. With a hint of dissatisfaction in her voice, she murmured, "Fine, I'll get up and get ready, but why do I have to get all dressed up?" as she headed towards the bathroom and closed the door behind her. When she disappeared into the bathroom, I couldn't help but smile to myself. Little did she know, I wanted her to look nice because I had planned to capture the moment on video, something for us to cherish in the future. Plus, I knew she would playfully strangle me if I let her appear anything less than her best on such an important occasion.

After what seemed like an eternity, she finally emerged from the bathroom, wearing a stunning black, long-sleeved, form-fitting dress complemented by her cozy, long wool grey cardigan to keep her warm. "Sit over here on the couch," I suggested, motioning towards the comfortable spot. With a quick nod, she settled herself on the couch as I hurried to our guest room, retrieving the carefully hidden Christmas gifts. Placing the three wrapped presents on the floor, I approached her with anticipation.

"Here's the first one," I said, handing her a small, wrapped gift. The excitement in the air was palpable as she eagerly accepted the package.

"Thanks, babe, but you really shouldn't have gotten me anything. It's not really fair that I can't reciprocate this year," she said, sounding a little downtrodden.

With a touch of disappointment in her voice, she murmured, "Thanks, babe, but you really shouldn't have gone through the trouble of getting me anything. It's just not fair that I can't reciprocate this year."

A warm smile illuminated my face as I replied, "But it's Christmas, babe. It's not about what you can give in return. I simply wanted to bring a touch of magic to your day, to make it extraordinary for you."

Eagerly, she seized the first gift, eagerly tearing through the wrapping paper and a burst of delightful laughter from her lips. "Yayyy... A pair of cozy wool socks. Thanks, babe!" Her genuine joy resonated in the air.

As her hands embraced the weight of the larger box I presented to her, a shimmer of curiosity danced in her eyes. Delicately, she unveiled the layers of anticipation, each motion filled with careful intention. Finally, she unveiled a stunning long, dark dress, and an astonished gasp escaped her lips. "How did you know I wanted this, babe?"

I smiled, "Your friend told me that you wanted this dress to wear for New Year's Eve this year. So, I went ahead and got it, as well as two tickets for us to go to the CTC New Year's Eve party again this year."

"I love it!" She then stood up and held it up against her body to make sure the length of the dress was ok and then carefully put it aside neatly in its box.

With anticipation bubbling within me, I swiftly rushed to my laptop, its vibrant screen reflecting my excitement, connected to the enchanting sound bar. As my fingertips danced over the keys, I selected "The Blower's Daughter" by Damian Rice, carefully choosing the perfect soundtrack to weave an enchanting ambiance. Grasping the final gift, both colossal in its physical presence and grand in its heartfelt intention, I approached her with a glimmer of anticipation. "Here you go," I murmured, my iPhone poised to capture the magical moment.

Her brows furrowed with curiosity, her eyes locking onto mine as she questioned, "You're acting strange, babe. Why are you recording me?"

A tender smile danced upon my lips as I reassured her, "Don't worry about it."

She shifted her focus to the box nestled in her hands, her voice barely a whisper as she pondered, "What is it?" Carefully, she jiggled the package, attempting to untangle the layers with meticulous grace. Yet, her patience waned, and the temptation of diagnosis attracted her to surrender control. Swiftly, she tore away the colorful wrapping paper, only to discover a steadfast fortress of tape guarding the treasure within. Searching for a tool to dismantle the barrier, she explored her surroundings until she surrendered to the perseverance of her own fingertips. "Geez, babe," she exclaimed, finally freeing the box from its adhesive restraints, revealing a sea of transparent Amazon air pillows and a diminutive silver-wrapped package adorned with a graceful bow. Ally's gaze lingered upon the petite box, her curiosity mounting before venturing into the realm of its contents. Sensing the perfect moment, I deliberately switched the song, allowing the dulcet tones of "What Are You Doing for the Rest of Your Life" sung by Na Leo Pilimehana to weave its romantic spell. She peeled away the layers of the box, retrieving a small grey velvet jewelry case. For a fleeting moment, she cradled it, uncertainty flickering in her eyes, before summoning the courage to unveil its secrets.

A symphony of emotions painted across her face as a delighted chuckle escaped her lips, resonating with pure, unbridled joy. "Yayyy..." she exclaimed, her laughter becoming an intimate conversation with herself, an echo of happiness unfurling in the room. The opened box became the object of her unwavering gaze, and amidst the blissful chaos, she murmured, "Oh my gosh, I'm trembling," extending her right hand to confirm the incredible reality she held within her grasp.

"What is it?" I asked. She then turned the box around and proudly held up the engagement ring. I then took the box from her hand and got down on one knee. I held up the ring and said, "Will you marry me?"

She quickly answered, "Yes!" as she held out her left hand. I slid the ring onto her engagement finger. She then extended both of her hands, trembling, "Oh babe..."

"Do you like it?" I asked.

"Yes, I love it," she quickly replied.

I then said, "Merry Christmas!"

She then jumped up and down and, with utter joy, screamed, "Merry Christmas!" She then immediately gave me a big hug and a kiss. "Oh my God," she said as she took a couple of deep breaths to try to calm her down. "Oh my God, I can't stop shaking," as she stared at the one gift she had always dreamed about.

CHAPTER 11

WISHES DO COME TRUE

Seattle, WA – 2016

I reached my sister's house at 6 a.m., greeted by a scene of cold, darkness, and somber shades of gray. The rain persisted in a gentle drizzle that threatened to escalate into a torrential downpour, echoing the tempestuous night before. In the realm of Seattle, October showers were an ordinary occurrence, but yesterday had brought forth the wrath of two fierce windstorms, one even rumored to be a tornado. These violent tempests unleashed their fury, promising not only drenching rains but also gusts of 30-50 mph that uprooted trees and plunged the city into widespread power outages. It was undoubtedly an ill-fated weekend to celebrate a wedding. Fleetingly, a question lingered in my mind: was this a sign, an omen of troublesome times ahead?

Yet, amidst this gloomy backdrop, a glimmer of solace emerged. The incessant rain shielded Seattle from the biting grip of colder temperatures that were to be expected. Grateful for this small respite, I wrapped myself in the warmth of my dependable old gray hoodie, a faithful companion that offered refuge from the misty showers threatening to get through to my skin.

The neighborhood slowly stirred awake, with flickering lights illuminating each house as families began their routines, marking the end of the workweek and rallying their sleepy children for school. At that moment, my sister, Minh, was likely doing the same. To avoid any confusion between us, I adopted our family name, Vo, while my sister, being the eldest, went by Minh. However, as fate would have it, when I moved to Los Angeles, I reclaimed my given name, for it was how people addressed me. Curiosity nudged me to question why they called me Minh instead of Vo, to which they simply replied, "Because it is your first name."

Pausing for a moment, I tried to gather my thoughts, my senses still groggy and disoriented from a mere four hours of sleep, remnants of the previous night's festivities. However, such weariness did not matter. I knew, without a shadow of a doubt, that I had to be here this morning, no matter how heavy the fatigue I battled. A deep sense of duty compelled me to pay my respects to my mother, who had traveled all the way from Texas a few days prior to gracing my wedding with her presence. Scarcely a minute had passed when the door suddenly swung open, and my sister, positioned at the threshold, exclaimed with urgency, "She has been waiting for you."

"I know. I know. Traffic was so bad driving up from Seattle. There was literally nothing I could do about it," I replied, my voice tinged with weariness. Navigating past her, I squeezed my way through and embarked on the ascent up the stairs, each step bringing me closer to the room where my mother resided. As I neared the door, faint murmurs of voices reached my ears, hinting at the conversations taking place within. With a soft touch, I knocked gently, signaling my arrival in the most unobtrusive manner.

Without delay, the door swung open, revealing my mother's eager countenance. "Wow, you've finally come to visit me. Where is Ally?" she inquired, her words striking me with an unexpected wave of guilt. I stood there, silent and transfixed, absorbing her presence. Clad in her formal Buddhist attire, she emanated an air of significance, donning a flowing Zen Buddhist gown in a soft shade of gray, complemented by a radiant saffron-colored robe gracefully draped over her left shoulder, symbolizing the importance of the occasion. These past few days had been a whirlwind, a frenetic juggling act, as I endeavored to finalize wedding details, tend to the needs of out-of-town relatives and friends, and navigate the festivities of last night's rehearsal dinner.

Struggling to conjure a suitable explanation, all that escaped my lips was a feeble excuse. "Ally is getting ready for the pictures at the hotel, and she couldn't make it with everything going on," I murmured, aware of the flicker of disappointment crossing my mother's face. A heavy sigh escaped her lips, a momentary proof of her implied wish. Yet, she swiftly brushed aside any trace of discontent. With a graceful gesture, she beckoned to Daisy, her steadfast Buddhist companion who had been by her side for countless journeys. In response to my mother's call, Daisy approached her, holding out a small bag and two vibrant red envelopes, offerings of affection and significance.

She looked over to me and said, "Hello, Vo Minh. How are you?" as she smiled and put her hands together in prayer and bowed.

"Hello, Daisy. I am well. Thank you for coming to Seattle with my mom," as I also bowed with a prayer to give her the same respect that she deserved.

My mother retrieved four Buddhist bead bracelets from her possession, each one unique in its material—wood, stone, black onyx, and white onyx. Fondly cradling them in her hands, she started a muted prayer, her words a gentle caress upon the sacred beads. Then she entrusted them to me, her voice filled with a sense of reverence and caution. "These bracelets are very expensive and were blessed by one of our venerable monks. These three are for you, and this white one is for Ally. It is white onyx. Very rare. Be careful with them, and don't lose them, okay?" Instantly, I adorned my right wrist with the three bracelets she gave me, wearing them proudly on this momentous day as a testament to my deep connection with my mother. The white bracelet, intended for Ally, found a temporary home within the confines of my pocket, awaiting the perfect moment to be given to her. Alongside the bracelets, my mother handed me two red envelopes, one representing her own offering and the other from Daisy.

Suddenly, my Aunt Dì Tám emerged from the background, having journeyed all the way from Vietnam to attend my wedding. Lost in my mother's presence, I had overlooked her presence until that very moment. Speaking in Vietnamese, she approached me, extending a red envelope as she imparted her words. Burdened by my limited awareness and linguistic abilities, having departed the motherland at such a tender age, I could only respond with a smile and a nod, expressing gratitude in Vietnamese.

I then looked at my mother and said, "I am so sorry, Mom, but I can't stay that long. I have to head home to meet up with Leo by 9 o'clock to get ready and head to the hotel to take wedding pictures with Ally and the wedding party."

She simply shook her head, a gentle smile gracing her lips. "It's okay. I know you don't have much time, Vo." Waves of guilt surged through me, realizing how poorly this significant moment had unfolded. My mother, a devoted Buddhist nun, could not attend the wedding. In her spiritual path, she had been guided to release attachment to worldly thoughts, emotions, and pleasures, including taking part in joyous public occasions unrelated to her religious commitments. For her, being present in the same city was the utmost expression of her love, mirroring the support she had shown my brother Billy during his wedding three years ago.

I leaned in to give her a hug, "I love you, Mom. I am so sorry that Ally couldn't make it."

She just smiled as she patted me on my back, "It's okay, Vo. I love you too. Thank you for coming to see me."

Weeks leading up to my mother's arrival, I would tell Ally, "Babe, I know we will have a lot going on, but it is very important that we make time to see my mother when she gets here before the wedding so we can pay our respects to her." In Asian culture, this was customary and essential, especially for a wedding. Things like lucky money, jewelry, and blessings bestowed upon a couple by their elders are extremely crucial to the longevity, good health, and prosperity of the newlyweds.

At first, she would smile and say, "Yes, of course."

Then suddenly, when it was only two days before the big event, we had a house full of family in our small two-bedroom condo, helping us prepare party favors and table decorations for the wedding. Not to mention a whole slew of family and friends still arriving in town. I pulled Ally aside to try to remind her one last time, "Babe, we still need to figure out a way to go visit my mom at my sister's house before the wedding."

Ally's piercing gaze bore into me, her head shaking in frustration. Stress had become an unwelcome companion, pushing her to her limits. Throwing her hands up in exasperation, she unleashed her words, a blend of desperation and defiance. "How would that even be possible with everything going on here and all the things that we still have to do?! Just tell me how!" I found myself drawn to the ground, examining the weight of her statement. There was little room for argument, given the packed schedule that lay ahead. A family dinner awaited us that very night, followed by a rehearsal dinner the following evening. A host of friends and relatives would soon arrive in town, relying on me to pick them up and transport them to their accommodations.

This was Ally's special day, and her vision of perfection embraced the core of her dreams. She longed for us to occupy the central roles throughout the weekend, with her positioned as the center of attention. It was the manner in which she had been raised and the norm she had grown accustomed to—a more Americanized approach, straying from the weighty obligations implanted in Asian culture. I had to set aside my responsibilities and prioritize her needs and desires, ensuring her happiness. Compromise became necessary as we merged our two distinct cultures, placing her aspirations at the forefront and safeguarding the sanctity of our long-awaited six-year celebration.

The limited moments I shared with my mother stood as the greatest compromise I had made. It weighed heavily upon me, casting a shadow of concern. Seeking solace, my sister would console me, acknowledging the challenges posed by my mother's rules and conditions. In their own unique ways, both my sister and mother wished for my happiness and sought to ease the wedding-induced stress. Thus, I dedicated as much time as possible to be with my mom and aunt, cherishing those precious interactions before hastening back home, battling the morning rush-hour traffic to meet Leo by 9 a.m. to begin our preparations.

With a mere ten minutes remaining, I secured a parking spot along the street in front of my building. Hastening inside, I made a beeline for the kitchen, desperate to savor a cup of coffee I had brewed earlier to restore my strength and my senses. As I took a few sips, the front door swung open, and Leo crossed the threshold, his presence filling the room. "Hey..."

"Hey, you made it on time," I smiled.

"Where are the tuxes," he asked.

"They are hanging in the closet," I pointed to my room. You would think that it would be messy, considering how early I had to be at my sister's house. But coming home so late the night prior, I fell asleep with my clothes on my face planted on my bed due to one too many drinks after the rehearsal dinner with a few friends who arrived late last night from out of town.

As we both began dressing, Leo looked over at me and asked, "Are you ready?"

A gentle smile adorned my face as I replied, "As ready as I'll ever be." With our attire carefully donned and our preparations complete, Leo and I embarked on our journey to the hotel, where Ally and the rest of the wedding party were eagerly getting ready for the grand day.

The boutique hotel we had chosen exuded an eclectic charm, with its lofty ceilings, expansive windows, and a fusion of contemporary aesthetics and inviting European warmth and charm. Ally had spent the previous night in our wedding suite, accompanied by her two closest friends, Jules and AT. It was a peaceful respite, a final night of solitude before the whirlwind of festivities began. In the early hours of the morning, they would rise before dawn, adorning their hair and makeup alongside Ally's mother and sister, preparing for our much anticipated "first look" and the subsequent wedding party photos.

Stepping into the hotel, I was promptly directed to stand at the top of a staircase overlooking the bustling street below. With my back turned, I patiently awaited the moment. My gaze wandered through the expansive windows, observing the glistening streets of downtown Seattle, still wet from recent rainfall. A few fleeting minutes passed before I felt a soft touch brush against my shoulder. I turned to behold Ally, radiating grace. She was adorned in a sleek, elegant white gown, its short sleeves embellished with delicate, sequined embroidery reminiscent of the vintage charm of the 1940s and '50s. Her hair was elegantly styled into a bun, accentuating her face and her mesmerizing azure eyes—the very eyes that had captivated me during our serendipitous encounter in a San Francisco gay bar. Words failed me, and for a moment, I gasped before breaking into a wide, joyous grin. A surge of love engulfed me, sending tingles coursing through my entire being as if I were a young boy witnessing the most wondrous spectacle imaginable. She was a vision of radiant beauty in her exquisite white wedding dress.

Her smile was equally immense as we both leaned in to embrace each other. I whispered into her ear, "You look so beautiful, Babe."

"You look so handsome, my Asian Tom Cruise," she said. It was a funny moniker she had made up for me, considering that I looked nothing like him, but it was her way of letting me know how much she adored me. I then leaned in and stole my first kiss of the day from my future bride. After all these years of dreaming and waiting for this moment, our dream had finally come true.

Despite the significance of our first look, we swiftly transitioned into a whirlwind of activities dictated by our tightly packed schedule leading up to the main event. We promptly shifted gears, embarking on a photography extravaganza within the confines of the hotel. Countless pictures and portraits were captured, immortalizing the essence of our union, before venturing forth with the wedding party to the charming Olympic Sculpture Park. There, amidst the captivating sculptures, we continued to pose for more portraits, group shots, and cherished family photographs.

To ensure a lighthearted and carefree atmosphere, Ally and her close-knit crew opted for separate Uber rides, reveling in their jovial camaraderie. Meanwhile, Leo and I maintained our focused demeanor, attentively progressing through the planned itinerary. After capturing a series of images featuring us and the wedding party, a steady stream of family members eagerly joined the fray, seeking their moments to pose with the radiant bride and groom, commemorating this significant scene.

Ally finally paused for a moment and exclaimed, "Wooo… I need a drink!"

I chuckled in agreement, saying, "Absolutely! They weren't kidding when they warned us that this day would fly by." Wise words from our married friends echoed in our minds, urging us to pause and cherish every moment as time slipped away in the blink of an eye. Amidst the bustling photo session, we realized we hadn't taken it all in, and we were only halfway through the picture-taking extravaganza. Several hours had swiftly passed, resulting in the capture of hundreds more snapshots. By the end of it all, nearly a thousand photos had been taken, commemorating and preserving the culmination of our long-awaited wedding.

Now, it was time for us to make our way to the wedding venue, where a few of the last photos with the wedding party awaited before we could steal a momentary break. Nestled in Seattle's industrial district, affectionately known as SODO (South of Downtown), the chosen venue was a beautifully transformed warehouse, marrying artistic elements with industrial-chic aesthetics. Its brick walls, wood paneling, and cement floors exuded charm and character. The space was divided into four distinct areas, each adorned with gigantic sliding barn doors showcasing its unique ambiance. A covered rooftop deck provided a breathtaking view of the distant downtown skyline. When we finally arrived at the venue ninety minutes early, the festivities were already in full swing. The diligent caterer and their team were busy arranging chairs and tables while selected family members and close friends attended to the final touches, adorning the reception area with exquisite table centerpieces and other embellishments.

We were immediately greeted by the event manager with a great big smile and a hug. She then asked, "Do you all need a drink?!"

We looked at her and said, "YES! Of course."

She grinned at Ally and asked, "Something light or something a little stronger to take the edge off?" She promptly noted our preferences and scurried off, swiftly returning with our chosen drinks in hand. Two double whiskies on the rocks were our personal go-to when we desired a little boost of energy. With our spirits lifted, the photographer guided us upstairs to the enchanting rooftop deck, where the last set of pictures awaited us. Our beloved wedding party, along with our dear friend Jomoses, who had graciously agreed to officiate our ceremony, joined us in capturing these last moments.

The final shot was of the two of us cheering each other on with our whiskeys. We finally had a moment to ourselves. I looked at her and said, "Are you ready?"

She responded with a beaming smile and softly exclaimed, "Yes!" while embracing me tightly and planting a gentle kiss on my cheek. We finally retreated to our separate but adjacent bridal and groom suites, bidding each other farewell for the time being to spend precious moments with our respective wedding parties.

Upon entering my suite, I wasted no time in unveiling a hidden treasure—a bottle of exquisite Japanese whiskey that I had discreetly stashed away in my backpack, along with some disposable cups. It was time for a pre-wedding toast with Leo, my soon-to-be brother-in-law, and my closest friends, who were standing by my side on this special day. A few strong drinks were exactly what I needed before the whirlwind began. As we engaged in light-hearted banter, they teasingly threw remarks like, "It's not too late to escape" and "Are you sure about this?" However, in between laughter, each of them expressed their genuine support and heartfelt congratulations, assuring me I had made the right choice and that they were proud to be part of this momentous occasion.

Afterward, seeking a moment of silence for myself amidst the bustling atmosphere, I slipped away from the clamor and stepped outside, yearning for a breath of fresh air and a quiet moment of introspection. Gazing up at the somber grey sky, I found myself lost in contemplation of my life and the imminent transformation it was about to undergo. Memories flooded my mind, harking back to my earliest recollection of departing Vietnam—a vivid image of standing hand-in-hand with my mother, peering through a vast airport window, and embarking on the journey that led me to this very moment. I realized just how far I had come. Now, it was our turn to embark on a new chapter, building a life and a family together. Lost in my profound musings, I was abruptly interrupted when a voice bellowed from the entrance, informing me, "We are about to begin." Collecting myself, I took a couple of deep breaths and readied myself for what lay ahead. With a last gulp, I finished the remaining sips of whiskey, fortifying my resolve, before returning inside to prepare for the grand spectacle that awaited.

Aware that the momentous ceremony was on the cusp of commencing, the pews filling up with eager guests and the last-minute touches in place, I sought Ally's father, who stood at the entrance, ready for the significant task of walking her down the aisle. Hastening towards him, I gently draped my arm around his shoulder, drawing him close, and whispered, "Hey JB, I have a little surprise for Ally before we begin the ceremony. So, I need you to hold off for a moment before you walk her down the aisle."

He smiled at me and gave me a great big hug, and said, "No problem, buddy." He was so excited that this day had finally arrived, and I would soon be a part of the family.

Although Ally and I had decided against writing our own wedding vows, I yearned to do something extraordinary to honor my love for her and make our day even more remarkable. Embracing the hopeless romantic within me, I concocted a plan straight out of a rom-com movie—I would serenade her as she walked down the aisle. I enlisted the help of one of my patients, a seasoned musician and professional singer, to perform live music at our wedding. I shared my idea with her, expressing my desire to serenade Ally with Train's song "Marry Me" during her procession. She enthusiastically embraced the concept, and we agreed to perform a duet rendition, considering my less-than-stellar singing voice. For months leading up to the wedding, we secretly rehearsed the song, tweaking it slightly to fit our unique story. Yet, no amount of practice could quell the knot of anticipation that formed in my stomach. Ready or not, the moment had arrived.

Positioned at the front to the right of the aisle, accompanied by Leo by my side, I took my place. My patient took the microphone, announcing to the audience that a special opening song awaited. A hushed silence filled the space as Ally emerged through the large barn doors, her face beaming with a radiant smile as she took her father's arm. The music began, and we both started singing "Marry Me" to Ally. In an ideal world, it would have been just me and my less-than-stellar voice serenading her. The gazes of the audience members intensified my nerves, but all my anxieties melted away when I glimpsed the sheer joy and tears in Ally's eyes. Striving to stay focused on the lyrics and maintain the rhythm, I knew it certainly didn't sound like Train or Frank Sinatra crooning "Fly Me to the Moon." Yet, in the grand scheme of things, it didn't matter how imperfect my singing was. What mattered most to me was the sentiment behind it. As Ally walked toward me, tears glistening in her eyes, I knew my friends would likely poke fun at my less-than-stellar performance later on. However, at that moment, all I could see was her. The look of love and the swirl of emotions on her face reassured me I had achieved what I had set out to do. I simply wanted this day to be exceptionally special for Ally, an unforgettable memory etched in her heart for a lifetime.

The song slowly ended as Ally walked down the aisle with her father, and he gave his baby girl away. Jules started the ceremony with a reading. Jomoses, our officiant and close friend, shared a story about the two of us uniting our two cultures as we began our journey together as one. We then exchanged rings.

Jomoses announced *la pièce de la résistance*: "By the power of love vested in me, I now pronounce you husband and wife. Vo, you may now kiss your bride."

With huge smiles on our faces, we both leaned in for our first kiss as husband and wife and then turned to face the audience with our hands interlocked and raised in triumph.

"For the first time ever, making their married debut," Jomoses declared, "I give you Mr. and Mrs. Minh Vo!" The crowd roared in excitement as we walked down the aisle hand in hand. We were finally married.

CHAPTER 12

WHAT'S GOING ON?

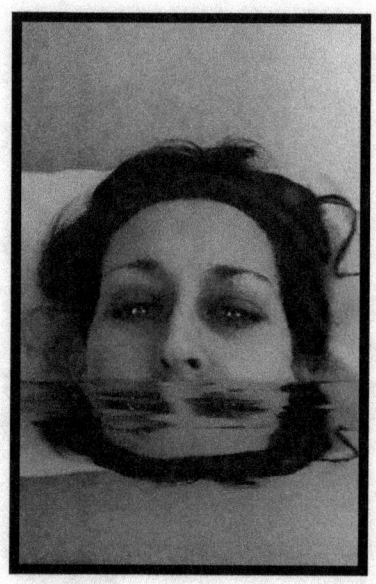

A few days after our families and friends had left town, Ally caught a severe flu bug. It had been going around the day of the wedding. Members of the wedding party and several of our wedding guests had caught the same bug as well. Ally became bedridden. She had a severe headache, body aches, and chills that lasted for a little over a week. She could barely move or get out of bed. It was a good thing that we had decided not to take our honeymoon immediately after the wedding; Ally would've been lying sick in bed the entire time somewhere in a foreign country. Instead, we opted for a honeymoon in the spring around her birthday to visit Paris and see my cousins. We then planned to head over to Italy and visit Tuscany, the place where she dreamt of having her wedding. Deferring to the spring would also allow me time to rebuild my depleted vacation hours at work while she focused on finding another job.

We had also decided to enjoy our first year of marriage before trying for a baby: the final wish she had always longed for, especially now that we were married. She stopped taking birth control shortly after the wedding to prepare her body for the possibility of conceiving a child in the near future. If pregnancy accidentally happened within the first year, we wouldn't complain. Ally and I just wanted to enjoy finally being married and all the happiness that came with it.

When Ally finally felt somewhat well enough to function again, she began noticing that she was experiencing more frequent stomach aches than usual. I thought it to be normal, given the severity and duration of her illness. She hadn't really eaten or drunk anything during her recovery, so the introduction of solid foods could possibly irritate her digestion for a little while till her body was able to adapt. Short-term side effects from such a nasty virus were considered normal as her body began to regain its strength and constitution.

In the past, Ally would occasionally have stomach sensitivities from time to time and would need to rest for a moment to let it subside. This might occur once a month or even longer. Unlike her stomachaches in the past, these new stomach issues were causing her short bouts of sharp stabbing pain in her abdomen. These symptoms seemed to appear shortly after eating but then would subside. At first, we both didn't think much of it, but as the weeks went on, the pain grew increasingly more intense and would last a little longer each time. Eventually, Ally would have to take a moment to rest for a bit on the couch or in our bed before it would fully subside. After seeing her deal with this half a dozen times, I had finally had enough.

We had just eaten burgers and fries that we picked up from a nearby restaurant when sure enough, not more than thirty minutes had passed, and Ally grabbed her stomach and bellowed out, "Owww... I think something is wrong, Minh." She normally wouldn't address me by my first name unless it was something serious.

"Yeah. I think you are right. Your stomach issues seem to be getting worse. Maybe you should call your doctor in the morning and try to get an appointment as soon as possible," I told her.

She nodded her head and said, "Yeah," in agreement and whispered, "I will call and make an appointment tomorrow." Luckily Ally still had medical insurance from her employer till the end of the year. "I think I need to lie down for a moment," as she headed to the couch and curled herself up with a throw blanket and a cushion on the couch. As usual, The Food Network would be playing in the background for her mind to focus on with her eyes closed and her arms wrapped around her stomach. Ally would continue to make little grunts and moans as she waited for the pain to subside. After cleaning up the table, I came and sat next to her and began to rub her back to give her some sort of comfort until she finally fell asleep.

In the morning, she called her doctor, who worked at the main campus building on Capitol Hill. She was able to get in to see her later that week. During the visit, after taking her history and prodding around her abdomen, the doctor felt that they needed to run a few more tests. They scheduled her for x-rays and did a barium test to check for ulcers. She was able to schedule the tests for the following Saturday morning so that I could drop her off and pick her up afterward.

During her follow-up visit, the doctor diagnosed her with irritable bowel syndrome (IBS) and assumed her discomfort was stress-related from losing her job in late August and then being severely ill after the wedding. Ally's treatment plan was to take over-the-counter meds, such as Tums and Pepto Bismol, to help alleviate her pain and add yogurt, digestive enzymes, and other natural remedies to help with her digestion. Ally was also placed on the BRAT diet, which consisted of bananas, rice, applesauce, and toast, along with the addition of probiotics in hopes of helping ease her pain.

Things seemed normal at first with the doctor's recommendations. Ally wasn't feeling any intense stomach pains on her restrictive diet, and things seemed to be getting back on track. JB was back in town for his annual Thanksgiving visit. We would take him around Seattle, doing mostly local activities, trying out a few local restaurants, and ending the week by having Thanksgiving dinner at my sister's house. By the end of the night, Ally's intense pain reared its ugly head once again after indulging in savory turkey, mashed potatoes, stuffing, and gravy. Once we got home, Ally spent the rest of the night curled up on the couch again, waiting for the pain to subside. Ally, knowing she had made the mistake of overindulging her diet during Thanksgiving and resumed her regimen to help stabilize her condition before her trip to visit her sister's family in Oklahoma for the holidays. This year would be a little different due to the fact that I was extended an invitation to come as well, mostly due to the fact that we were now married.

This was a big step in my relationship with Ally's sister and her family since their approval of me and our relationship was far from welcoming until we had finally tied the knot. Ally was extremely happy and excited about us spending time with her sisters as a married couple. She hoped that this would be the first of many more visits to come and eventually evolve into joint family vacations together. Ally went to Oklahoma a few days before me to spend quality time with their family, especially with her two nieces, as they were getting bigger and were able to talk and play. I arrived during the weekend for the tail end of her trip.

When I landed in Oklahoma on a Friday, Ally, her sister, and the girls picked me up at the airport, and we headed to a local restaurant that had outdoor seating so that we could grab some food and enjoy the beautiful 70-degree weather they were having. I thought this was highly unusual since Christmas was a week away. Oklahoma was known for having what they called bipolar weather, considering it would be snowing the next day with temperatures reaching negative degrees during the night. Whatever the case was, we would enjoy the short period of time we had to spend with each other. When we reached the house, the festivities would continue with a few drinks followed by a nice family dinner together before retiring a little early in preparation for going to the niece's Christmas recital the next morning.

As we woke, you could feel the temperature had dropped considerably with the coolness in the air. Armed with sweaters and winter coats, we headed to the church to see the girls perform on stage their Christmas play. Walking towards the auditorium, little flakes of snow began to fall from the sky as the wind picked up and the winter cold quickly set in. Once inside, we were happy to be in the warmth of the small theater as we watched a children's version of the old manger and its celebration of the birth of Christ.

Back at home, we opened Christmas gifts by the fire. Ally had hand-picked both of the gifts for the girls. They tore them open and screamed with excitement at what they had received, which made Ally very happy to witness the joy that they had received in their hearts. Ally was given a matching Christmas beanie that lit up and had "Sup Gnomie" printed across the front, along with a few other stocking stuffer items. We ended the night going out to eat while hitting a few golf balls at the new Top Golf establishment that was located just a few miles away. We ate your typical affair of things such as chicken wings, burgers, and fries and washed them down with a few cold beers before calling it a night to get up early the next day to catch our midday flight back to Seattle.

That night the weather had dropped to negative degrees as predicted, and we were snuggled under a heavy down comforter for the night. Early in the morning, I was awakened by the sound of Ally moaning and groaning as she grasped tightly to her stomach, withering in pain. I rolled over and asked her, "What's wrong? Is everything ok?"

Small droplets of tears were streaming down her face as she tried to catch her breath in between the waves of pain she was feeling. "Something is really wrong with me. My stomach hurts really bad," she grimaced.

"Is there anything I can do to help?" I asked.

"No," she said, "It is starting to lessen a little."

I snuggled my body up next to her and held her close as if anything I was doing was even remotely helping her. "Sorry, babe. I wish I could do something for you."

"I am fine… Everything was going so well, and now it is happening again. I need to call my doctor when I get home, so she can figure out what is wrong with me. This isn't normal," she said.

"Yeah. I agree. Let's just get home, so we can figure this out, babe," I told her.

When we returned home from Oklahoma, Ally made another appointment with her doctor and was, once again, turned away from any further recommendations or treatment. They refused to give her any further tests. As the frequency continued to increase, Ally would make weekly doctor appointments, even a few ER visits when the pain was bad enough, to see if there was anything else they could do or prescribe to help with the pain she was experiencing. Various doctors would look at her chart and test results but remained confident in their diagnosis of IBS and told them she'd just have to deal with it.

Christmas was upon us, and the sharp stabbing pain became more intense, more frequent, and lasted much longer in duration. A friend of ours had a few Vicodin leftover from some previous condition and offered them to Ally. She took them when the sharp stabbing pain came on, and the pills pacified her pain for a few hours. Knowing that her health insurance would soon end in December, On New Year's Eve, Ally made one last attempt since her pain became almost unbearable. She called and pleaded with the on-call doctor over the phone for a prescription of painkillers to help with her pain since her Vicodin stash was now gone. The doctor stood their ground and refused to extend medical help or pain prescriptions her way, saying that her condition did not warrant any narcotics for pain relief and that she would just have to deal with the pain.

My frustration continued to grow. I hated seeing Ally, my wife, the love of my life, in so much pain. I felt helpless since this was outside of my scope of practice being a chiropractor. All I could do was watch and give her emotional support. I knew we needed to get her a second opinion, but since her health insurance was an HMO, it didn't allow her to see any doctors outside of her provider network. We would've had to pay out-of-pocket for visits and further testing, which could be financially crippling since we were, once again, living on a single income. I even tried to put her on my insurance in December after being mistakenly informed that I could add her as my spouse within the first three months of marriage. My insurance broker at work corrected me, saying that it had to be done within the first 30 days of a major event, such as marriage.

Instead of going out to celebrate our first New Year's as a married couple, Ally and I, along with a few close friends that came over that night, knowing her current condition, in support and in friendship, stayed with us in our little two-bedroom condo to celebrate. We would sit around chatting, sharing conversations. Ally never wanted to be the cause of any reason not to celebrate, and she wanted people around her, even though Ally laid on the couch in a fetal position writhing for hours as we counted down to the new year.

Several of our close friends were well aware of Ally's escalating stomach pain and found people willing to sell their leftover Vicodin, 5, for $50. We were desperate and took whatever we could find. These pills came in the nick of time since Ally and I booked a joint getaway with our close friends Kahan and Mimi to attend the Consumer Electronics Show (CES) in Las Vegas the first week of the new year. It would be our first vacation together as a married couple. They went the year before and told us how much fun it was and wanted us to join them this year along with a few others. Ally would cut her Vicodin loot in half and use it sparingly whenever she felt the pain was becoming intolerable. Leading up to the event, Ally felt relatively good. She was back on the BRAT diet to calm down her supposed IBS. It had been a long time since we were able to travel anywhere for pleasure, and she was determined not to let her stomach pain stop her.

When we arrived in Las Vegas, we were definitely not disappointed. Sin City is always alive with action. Instead of the usual party dudes, bachelor and bachelorette parties, it was swarmed with lots of professional tech people from all over the world. Kahan, being well-known in the technology field, had a number of colleagues hosting some of the private events. We arrived just in time for Happy Hour at one of them, and, thanks to Kahan, we got into a free all-you-can-eat-and-drink event hosted at a well-known Southern soul food restaurant at the hotel where we stayed. For Ally and me, this was our jam since she was originally from the south, and who doesn't like fried chicken and all things fried with a side of bourbon? Ally was feeling good after a few glasses of bourbons on the rocks and decided to be bold by eating some mashed potatoes, a little mac and cheese, and a small piece of fried chicken. I hadn't seen Ally so happy in laughter and smiles in quite a while. Afterward, there was a free concert, but Ally didn't want to push her luck since she was starting to feel the onset of discomfort again. She opted to take a Vicodin and stayed in, going to sleep content.

The next day, we broke into groups: the guys went to see guy things and the girls to see girl things among the thousands of vendors showing off the latest technology gadgets in their field. Of course, Ally and Mimi focused on beauty and baby stuff since these were items that would be useful in the not-too-distant future. At night, we got all dressed up and attended another free nightclub event for attendees featuring some famous DJs. After the crowds poured in and packed us in like sardines, it became so unbearable that we opted to finish the night at one of Kahan and Mimi's favorite Asian restaurants before calling it a night.

The next day, we scoured the event one last time before it closed shop at noon. Afterward, we indulged in lobster rolls nearby since Ally loved anything lobster before packing up in time for our late checkout and flight home. As we were finishing up, a series of unbearably sharp stabbing pains ensued that brought Ally to her knees and into tears. By now, Ally was out of painkillers. Her only alternative was to lie on the bed and ride out the pain. As it began to escalate, we considered taking her to the ER, but she couldn't move because she was in so much agony. Ally didn't think she could even make the flight home. All we could do was wait to see what Ally wanted us to do as we tried to think up other ways to help. Then suddenly, after what seemed to be over an hour of feeling helpless, Ally finally sat up and took a few deep breaths. She said she thought everything was going to be alright and could make the journey home. Who would have known that this would be our first and last vacation as a married couple?

The next morning after we arrived home, I called my insurance broker and asked if there was any way I could get Ally on my insurance since she had just lost hers at the end of December. By luck, my broker said that losing prior insurance coverage due to loss of employment was considered a major life event, and they could add her to my policy. The only drawback was that it would probably take a week for everything to go through. At this point, I was elated and asked them to start the paperwork immediately. I told Ally right away, which made her thankful that a solution was in sight. I booked an appointment for her to see Dr. Tony, my primary care provider, with whom I had full trust. The earliest appointment we could get on such short notice was a week out, which was perfect since it would take a week to get Ally activated with my insurance carrier. I assured Ally that everything was set and that all she needed to do was hold on for one more week to be seen by my doctor. I was certain that he'd find a solution to her health concerns. Ally was just thankful that she'd have insurance again. There was a possible end to this nightmare.

Days leading up to her doctor's appointment, Ally became increasingly curious as to what was the cause of her pain. At night she would try to poke and prod her abdomen, searching for her own answers. The night before her appointment, we were lying in bed, and Ally was feeling around her abdomen. She then turned and said to me, "Babe, what do you think it could be? I think I feel something. I think I feel a lump." She dug into her abdomen and pointed to where she felt all of her pain originate. "Can you feel it?" she asked as she grabbed my hand and asked me to push deep into this one spot in her stomach to validate what she was feeling.

I reached over to try to locate whatever she thought she had found. I couldn't necessarily feel a mass or a lump and told her, "I don't feel anything, babe."

Ally continued to press down at the spot. "Do you think it's cancer? Can you read my energy again to see if you can see anything?" she asked.

Being a chiropractor and an energy medicine practitioner, I could read people's energy and had some insight into medical intuition. But it is very hard to treat someone you are emotionally attached to, especially with Ally being my wife and my future. I could tell she was worried, so I indulged her wishes and placed my right hand on her abdomen and began reading her energy.

After I was done, I told her, "I can't see anything, babe. I only see black. I am sure Dr. Tony will figure it out tomorrow at the appointment. He is a really good doctor. Don't worry. I am sure it is not cancer, babe. Everything is going to be okay. You will see tomorrow."

In the past, when she asked me to look early on, I often saw black, which usually meant one of two things: either her energy was blocked, and I wasn't allowed to see, or in extreme cases, it meant there was something I didn't want to think about. During the last month of Ally's escalating pain, I thought back to my chiropractic schooling and remembered one of my teachers who taught clinical diagnosis saying, "Whenever you had a patient who'd wake up in the middle of the night with uncontrollable sharp stabbing pain, it was usually a sign of cancer." When Ally began having pain, the truth of this became a possibility in my head, but I chose to keep that to myself instead of sharing it with Ally. I didn't want to scare her. I also didn't want to consider that notion. I just prayed that the medical doctors would find a solution to fix the problem so we could get on with our life together.

"You should get some rest. Tomorrow is a big day, and we will finally get the answers to your pain," I told her as I reached over and gave her a big hug and a kiss. "I love you, babe. Everything will be good again real soon."

She looked at me and said, "Promise?"

I smiled and said to her, "Yes."

CHAPTER 13

So, It Begins

On Monday, January 16, 2017, Ally took an Uber to the clinic on First Hill, where my doctor practiced near downtown Seattle. As much as I wanted to be there, I had to work to ensure we had some income coming in. I also needed to work full-time to maintain eligibility for the insurance coverage that we desperately needed for Ally. Dr. Tony ran the standard physical tests, did a workup on Ally, and collected blood samples to produce a baseline. After recording her medical history and palpating her abdomen, he asked her to schedule another appointment for a computed tomography (CT) scan. This would allow him to see what was going on with the soft tissue and organs inside Ally's abdomen. He then prescribed Vicodin since he knew that it helped her pain and sent her home. Ally immediately called me afterward and was extremely happy with her appointment with Dr. Tony. She was happy to finally get some painkillers legally. She was in a very good mood and totally trusted his plan of action. I reassured Ally that he was one of the best and that he would figure out a solution. That night, we had a mini-celebration and hoped for good news on the next visit.

Two days later, Ally once again took an Uber back to the clinic for her scheduled CT scan and a follow-up with Dr. Tony afterward. While she sat waiting for the results, Ally texted me a play-by-play of what was happening to fight off the nervousness of what we might find from her scan.

Ally: Just finished.

Minh: How are you doing?

Ally: I am nervous, babe. What if it shows something bad?

Minh: You will be fine. Everything is going to be great.

Think positive, babe.

Ally: Yeah, you are right.

Minh: The CT will tell us what the problem is. Nothing to worry about.

Ally: You promise?

Minh: Yes. You will see.

Ally: Ok. They just called my name.

Minh: Ok, babe. Good luck. Everything will be great!

After an hour of solemn silence, I took a moment away from the world to grab some lunch. Just as I parked my car, my phone rang, jolting me from my thoughts. It was Ally. But instead of her usual cheerful voice, all I could hear were wrenching sobs interrupted by coughs and choking. I knew something bad was coming in, and nothing in this world could've prepared me for that exact moment when Ally finally uttered, "I have cancer. Please come pick me up. I need you here with me right now!"

Her voice was filled with emotions that one could only feel in extreme agony. I could already envision her face and what she would be feeling right now simply by hearing her voice. All I knew was that I had to be by her side that instant and nothing else.

"I'm on my way. Just hold tight, and I will be there as fast as I can," I reassured her, my voice trembling with a mixture of fear and determination.

She handed the phone to Dr. Tony, who spoke in a somber tone, "I am so sorry, Minh. Ally has terminal cancer. I think you need to be here with her right now." In the background, Ally's cries echo, "Hurry, Minh! Hurry!"

"I'm on my way. I'll be there as soon as I can," I screamed into the phone before hanging up.

Tears streamed down my face as I sped toward the freeway, consumed by a tumultuous storm of emotions. My mind raced, and I felt the weight of the world crashing down upon me. In a desperate attempt to inform my office, I called and practically shouted into the phone, "Ally has cancer. I need to be with her right now. I am so sorry, but I can't come back to work."

Sydney, my coworker, responded with a calming voice, "You just go be with her and don't worry about the clinic."

"FUCK! FUCK! FUCK! ARGHHH!!!" I unleashed my anguished cries on the car, my grip tightening on the steering wheel. Thoughts swirled within me, searching for comprehension in the face of this devastating news. "What the FUCK just happened?" Feeling the weight of uncertainty pressing down on my soul.

I immediately phoned my sister and blurted out, "Ally has cancer!"

"WHAT?!" she replied.

"She just got her test results back and told me she had cancer! I am heading there right now!" I screamed.

In a calm voice, she said, "I know some people at Seattle Cancer Center (SCC). I will try to pull some strings and see what I can do. Don't worry. Just go be with Ally, and I will work on the rest Vo."

"Thanks, Minh."

I hung up the phone and then immediately called Leo. He was speechless and didn't know what to say except that he was so sorry to hear the news and to let him know if there was anything he could do for us. I am sure that during the time I was driving, Ally called Jules and her family, and I remembered seeing missed calls and texts coming in asking me to call them as soon as I could. But I had to focus and get to Ally as soon as I could.

Arriving at the clinic, I rushed to Ally's patient room, where Dr. Tony stood, trying to offer her solace. As Ally caught sight of me, she leaped up, embracing me tightly, her tears soaking my shoulder. "I just want to go home. Can we please go home?" Her plea pierced my heart, her vulnerability palpable in every word.

Dr. Tony turned to me, his eyes filled with sorrow, saying, "I am so sorry, Minh." He explained that a biopsy was necessary to confirm the type of cancer, but based on the CT scan, it appeared to have metastasized to multiple areas, leaving little hope. He promised to forward the report once he received it, an ominous reminder of the grim reality we now faced.

During the ride back home, Ally clutched her phone and engaged in a heart-wrenching conversation with her sister. Overwhelmed by grief, she struggled to find the right words, eventually conceding her inability to speak at the moment. It was then that I held her hand tightly, locking eyes with her tear-streaked face.

"Everything is going to be okay," I whispered, my voice filled with unwavering determination. "We will find a cure, and we will beat this cancer. You just have to believe and have faith."

Her eyes searched mine, seeking reassurance amidst the darkness that threatened to engulf us. "You promise?" she choked out, her voice trembling with fragile hope.

I tightened my grip on her hand, channeling all the love and strength within me. "Yes. I promise. We will find a cure, and everything will be okay." At that moment, I held onto that promise, believing it with every fiber of my being. For now, I knew that I had to be Ally's emotional rock, her steadfast support in the face of unimaginable hardship.

Back at home, Ally curled up in bed, her thoughts a tempest of fears and uncertainties. I nestled beside her, enveloping her in my arms, offering silent support as we grappled with the weight of our newfound reality. Together, we sought solace and strength, knowing that the path ahead would be fraught with challenges but united in our unwavering love.

A few days later, I received the CT report and began reading. Being a chiropractor, I had to learn and understand medical terminology, so it was easy for me to comprehend what the report said.

IMPRESSION: CT SCAN 01/18/2017

1. Mesenteric soft tissue mass 9.1 x 7.1 x 7.4 cm likely arising from the adjacent jejunum suspicious of gastrointestinal stromal tumor.

2. Peritoneal disease in several areas as above, seen with small volume ascites.

This explained Ally's severe sharp, stabbing pain. Basically, she had a mass the size of a tangerine sitting on the left side of her small intestines. Something that big would cause blockage and make it difficult or prevent anything from moving through whatever canal the tumor obstructed. It was most likely that whenever Ally ate something dense, the food had a hard time moving through her digestive tract, which sent sharp shooting pain to the surrounding area. The fact that smaller masses in other areas in her abdomen were forming meant that the cancer was spreading, hence why Dr. Tony had stated that her condition was terminal. Unfortunately, there was nothing we could do until we learned the type of cancer she had. We had to wait another week for the biopsy results. We began sharing the news with all our closest friends to create a support group for whatever happened next. In the meantime, Dr. Tony referred us to one of the clinic's gastrointestinal (GI) oncologists.

A week later, I took the day off work and took Ally to her biopsy appointment. I wanted to be there this time to give her the strength she needed now that we knew it was cancer. They took a small sample of her tumor from her abdomen and sent it to the pathologist for cancer identification to see what we were dealing with so we could treat it accordingly. We were also given a referral to see one of the cancer specialists the following week.

My sister and I accompanied Ally to her first visit with the oncologist. When we arrived for the appointment, the oncologist was running around, stepping in and out of the room frantically, looking for something. So, we sat there waiting for her patiently. After 10-15 minutes had elapsed, she finally stepped into the room and sat down before us. She had some papers in her hands. "So, sorry to keep you waiting. I was waiting for the pathology report so I could go over it with you. Unfortunately, they were inconclusive, and we had to send the slides to a specialist in the field to get a more accurate diagnosis." Feeling a little confused about what we had just heard, we sat there quietly and continued to listen. Her face became very solemn. "I am so sorry, but Ally has terminal cancer," she said. "I think it would be best for you to start to prepare yourself for this."

Ally let out a great moan and then cupped her face with both hands as tears began to stream from her eyes.

The doctor continued, "Both of my parents had terminal cancer. So, I know what you are going through. I will do my best to make you as comfortable as possible with what time you have left."

"When do you think the cancer started?" I asked.

"Most likely around August."

"How much time do you think she has left?"

"About a year is my guess, based upon what we have seen," she responded.

Ally let out another loud moan and then screamed hysterically, "I don't want to hear this anymore! I want to go home!"

Even though I couldn't believe what I was hearing, I had to know the answers to all of my questions. "Are you sure there are no other solutions?"

"No... I am sorry."

Ally grabbed my arm and shrieked, "I want to go home, Minh! I just want to go home..."

My sister suddenly stood up and said in a stern voice, "We want a second opinion. Let's go!" She then motioned for us to leave the appointment. As we left the facility, my sister said, "Call SCC as soon as you get home and let me know what they say."

Ally sat quietly in the car as she stared out the window. I grabbed her hand and said, "Everything is going to be ok. I will call SCC when we get home, and they will find a cure."

She turned and looked at me as she tried to manage a smile, "Ok."

When we got home, I immediately asked if we could schedule an appointment for Ally to be seen right away. The appointment specialist asked me what her diagnosis was. I told her that she had terminal GI cancer, but we could not confirm what type of cancer it was yet since the biopsy report was inconclusive, and they needed to send it to another pathologist for confirmation. The scheduler responded that Ally, unfortunately, couldn't make an appointment until she had a confirmed diagnosis.

I could not believe what I was hearing. She had terminal cancer. Wasn't that a good enough diagnosis to warrant an immediate appointment? This news was even more disheartening since our only two choices at the moment were to wait for the report or to wait for Ally to die. It seemed that all we could do was hold off for the pathology report to come back before taking steps forward. Naturally, we canceled our follow-up visit with the oncologist and waited day by day with bated breath for the pathology report to arrive.

Once the news of Ally's cancer spread among our circle of friends, an outpouring of love and support washed over us like a comforting wave. Texts and phone calls flooded in, each one a lifeline offering help in any way they could. Our friends offered to buy groceries, prepare meals for us, and provide transportation for appointments. Gifts poured in, a tangible manifestation of their care and concern—books, blankets, crystals, anything and everything that held the promise of healing or solace for Ally. It was an overwhelming display of kindness that left me in awe and disbelief. Yet, amid this sea of generosity, I grappled with a deep-rooted struggle. Perhaps it was my upbringing, ingrained with a sense of self-reliance, or the echoes of cultural influences, but accepting help proved to be a challenge for me. Gratitude filled my heart with every offer extended, but I hesitated to impose upon others. It was only within the embrace of my family and closest friends, those who Ally held dear as well, that I felt comfortable enough to seek their aid. These were the individuals on whom I knew I could lean, especially during the darkest moments that lay ahead. In this vulnerable time, I marveled at the strength of our connections, the unspoken bond that tied us together. The love and support we received were not just gestures; they were lifelines, threads that wove a safety net beneath us as we navigated this treacherous journey. And in the face of adversity, it was the unwavering support of our chosen family that provided us with the courage to face each day, knowing that we were never alone.

My sister, who worked for the University which was directly associated with SCC, helped to create and establish connections and necessary appointments that Ally would need for any future appointments. My brother suggested that we start a private group on Facebook to keep everyone informed of Ally's progress and successes instead of having to text everyone individually. Di, my brother-in-law's sister, who was familiar with cancer given the fact that her mother was going through her own battles with breast cancer, committed to bringing us meals every week and volunteered to take Ally to all of her treatments and appointments that I couldn't make. This was extremely helpful since I had to continue to work full-time. Leo was mainly there for me, as was Ally. He is always the one that I turn to if I need someone to talk about something or just to listen to me ramble and vent and give good advice when I feel lost. There were several others who were close to both of us and would drop everything to help out if we were to ask as well. The people that showed us actions versus words were the ones that we could count on the most.

My actions counted the most because I was the one that Ally needed the most. I had to dig in deep and remain strong for her so that she would not quiver or give into her own fears of the unknown ahead of us. I had to face the reality that I needed help preparing for the difficult journey ahead. I began scouring the internet for books on how to best prepare for what was to come. How to be the best caregiver I could be for Ally. My research found books on how to fight cancer, how to beat cancer, diets for cancer, and, of course, how to deal with cancer after someone passes away. Something that I really didn't want to have to read someday. After hours and days of searching, I found nothing that could prepare me for what was to come. I felt frustrated and a little hopeless, not being able to find anything that was suitable to help me. I came to the realization that I would just have to wing it and muster every bit of strength I could for Ally's sake, doing whatever she needed or wanted from me. People often asked how I was doing through it all. I would reply, "I am living the dream." They'd smile or chuckle at my response. It was my own sense of irony when in reality, a dream could also be your worst nightmare, which was what we were both facing together during our first year of marriage and the possibility of losing a life when we were just beginning.

Many opinions were thrown at us about how we could fight cancer, even though we still didn't know what kind of cancer we were dealing with yet. As they say, opinions are like assholes: everyone has one. Some of them were good, and some of them were not the best. These included using essential oils, incorporating daily juice cleanses, trying hyperbaric chambers, buying a Rife machine, getting acupuncture and herbs, and eating honey every day. The list went on for days. I did what I thought would be helpful and within our means and tossed the more ridiculous suggestions aside. The reality was that I could only do what Ally was willing to do since it was her body. She was the one who had to either eat it or go through it, and Ally had always been a selective eater.

A few of our friends suggested going to Mexico to do alternative treatments that had high success rates for survival. Upon researching these programs, I found that most of them started at $30,000. Unfortunately, we didn't have that kind of money lying around. It took this long for Ally and me to begin to feel somewhat financially stable until this "terminal cancer" thing happened. When I mentioned to them that we couldn't afford it right now, one of my replies was, "Wouldn't you do anything to save Ally's life?" I couldn't help but feel overcome by guilt. I felt inadequate as a husband for not having endless resources to help my wife fight this deadly disease. To feel condemned by anyone with their opinions and judgments, thinking that I wasn't doing everything I possibly could to save Ally, was something that I really didn't want to deal with either. I had to bookmark the Mexico idea and hoped if the time came that, our financial situation would have changed, and the treatment might become possible.

To make things easier to relay the progress of Ally's cancer to all of our friends and family, we decided to form a private Facebook group called "Ally's Healing Circle." This allowed us to relay current information about Ally's progress efficiently to our family and friends all at once versus through separate texts and emails. So, we dipped in with our first post.

February 4, 2017 (Ally's Healing Circle)

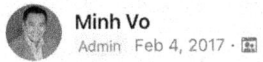

Minh Vo
Admin Feb 4, 2017 ·

Hello Everyone! This is a private group to keep you posted on the latest developments of the road to Ally's journey of health, healing, and recovery. Thanks for all your love, prayers and support. We wouldn't be able to do this without all of your help. We feel very blessed.

👍❤️ 20   1 comment

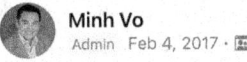

Minh Vo
Admin Feb 4, 2017 ·

Update: The pathologist at the ▆▆▆ clinic wasn't able to determine for sure what type of cancer it was. They sent the slides to Boston for a specialist to review the slides and hopefully give us an exact diagnosis by next Friday. So unfortunately another week of waiting before we are given a plan of action and treatment steps.

👍❤️ 5

As each day passed, I could see Ally just wanted to feel a little peace, comfort, familiarity, and normalcy. To Ally's relief, Jules decided to fly up from San Francisco for the weekend for a visit to help ease her mind. They had been through a lot together and had faced many hard times. Jules was the only other man in her life that she felt safe to lean on besides me and her dad.

Jules flew into Seattle late that Friday night. As we pulled up to arrivals at SeaTac Airport, where Jules was waiting, Ally immediately jumped out of the car, squealed, and then gave him the biggest Ally hug she could, her dear friend. They both got into the back seat and immediately went into their banter. I could only smile to myself, seeing how much joy this had brought to Ally. When we arrived home and got Jules settled into his room, the two of them stayed up a little longer and continued to catch up with their friendship where they had left it when they had last seen each other back in San Francisco.

The next morning, they already had their day planned out; lunch in Seattle, followed by a little shopping and good quality time spent in each other's presence. I had to show my face to a few commitments that we had made a while back, but I knew Ally needed her time alone with Jules. When I came home from the first event, I found Ally and Jules sitting next to each other on our bed, looking at fashion magazines and discussing which luxurious scarf Ally should wear if she were to lose her beautiful long brown hair while undergoing chemo. In his way, he prepared her for the possibility of what may come in the most elegant, fashionable way possible. That was their love language, and that was Ally's comfort. They talked and laughed, delving into their witty banter. Time stood still for a moment that weekend. Birthdays, weddings, even the Superbowl didn't matter to the both of them. All that mattered was that Jules was there for her as they had promised each other when they had first met till the moment Jules had to leave his dearest friend once again.

Almost a month had passed since Ally got her first CT scan. I was at work when I got a text from Ally that she had finally received news from Dr. Tony's office that the report from the oncopathologist had finally arrived with a confirmed diagnosis. I called up the office and asked them to email me the report so I could read the results and forward them to the rest of the family. The report concurred with the findings of the original pathologist regarding the diagnosis of biphasic peritoneal mesothelioma (PM), but nothing much more was explained. I knew that mesothelioma was asbestos-related and that it was usually associated with the lungs. Peritoneal means that the mesothelioma was located somewhere in the abdomen.

As I began to research the diagnosis, specifically for peritoneal mesothelioma, my heart sank. PM was a rare form of mesothelioma that affected 20% of known cases. This form of cancer was very rare and was often misdiagnosed it. It was even rare for it to be found in patients under the age of 40 since mesothelioma had a latency period of 20+ years before symptoms could manifest. I began reading about survival rates, with lung patients having a median life expectancy of 15 months for lung patients and abdominal patients having better survival rates within the 3–5-year range. Tears began to slowly drip from my eyes as I could taste the bile rising in my throat and my heartbeat drumming in my ears. How could this be happening? It hadn't been more than four months when

Ally was a beautiful bride with her entire life ahead of her – kids, soccer games, Christmases, vacations, growing old together. How could this beautiful future disappear so quickly?

I forced myself to keep reading and quickly turned to researching all possible treatment plans and cures for PM, which led me to the inventor and pioneer of hyperthermic intraperitoneal chemotherapy (HIPEC) surgery for peritoneal mesothelioma patients. If caught early enough, they could essentially surgically remove the tumors in the abdomen and let the organs soak in a warm chemo bath. The timing of diagnosis ideally was within the first three months, but this method could lead to a 100% success rate in full life expectancy. We were now in the fifth month if our first oncologist was right in suggesting that the cancer began to grow in August. I sat there thinking to myself that we still had a chance, but I also knew that time was quickly running out.

Knowing that Ally had already read the report but probably didn't know what it meant. I immediately called her, "Babe. Whatever you do, promise me you won't do any research on the diagnosis."

"Why? What's wrong? Is it bad?" she replied frantically.

"Just promise me you won't do any research until I get home. I don't want you to freak out, especially when you are home alone," I told her. "I will call SCC and make an appointment immediately. There is hope."

"Ok. I promise," she said as she hung up the phone. I knew she was already completely scared and petrified at this point. All she knew was that it was bad.

I immediately called SCC with the diagnosis and tried to schedule an appointment. Their first availability was still a few weeks out. My heart sank hearing that the appointment was so far away. Ally needed help now if we were ever going to have a chance to beat this cancer and find a cure. The reality was that we were not the only ones who had cancer, and we were not the only ones who had terminal cancer. We were just the current ones dealing with cancer, and everyone who had cancer was just as important as Ally. Realizing this put things into perspective of how vast cancer had affected so many lives. My focus was on Ally and how I could help her find a cure so that she could live and grow old together.

After reading more horrific facts about PM cancer, I hit a breaking point. I remember my drive home from work that evening, I called my sister and began crying, wailing to her about all I had read. I couldn't believe this was happening to us, to Ally. My sister listened attentively as I vented all my fears and frustrations about what I had read throughout the day. When I finally stopped to take a breath, she said, "We will get through this. I know the head of the cancer center. I will try to pull some strings to get Ally in as soon as possible."

When I got home, Ally was on the phone with her sister, who had also researched cancer and wanted her to book an appointment to see a specialist at a cancer center in Houston for immediate treatment since it was also one of the best cancer centers in the U.S. Ally told them that she had to talk it over with me and would get back to them. That night, we had a serious talk about what I read, but Ally already knew a lot about it after talking with her sister. I told her that I was going to reach out to the doctor who invented Peritoneal metastasis - Hyperthermic Intraperitoneal Chemotherapy (PM HIPEC) surgery to see if she was a good candidate. I also told her that my sister was working to get her in for an appointment at the SCC. The reality was that we didn't know how things were going to play out, and there were still a lot of unknowns. If Ally chose to go to Houston, then she'd have to go alone since I'd have to stay back and work to maintain our insurance. If she chose to stay in Seattle, then at least she'd have support from me, my family, and our friends. These were the things she had to seriously consider when choosing the next steps. I told her I'd support her decision 100% whichever way she chose, but we had to make a decision soon.

I lay in bed that night, and my heart began pounding heavily as my mind began to recollect everything that had occurred. I became increasingly angry at the doctor who originally diagnosed her with IBS. We had lost so much time because of it. I was fixated on the fact that her oncologist stated that the cancer probably started in August. If her original doctor had done a CT scan back in November when the sharp pain occurred, then maybe we could have done something sooner. We were coming up four months past the original date of symptoms and seven months from the suggested date of August when the cancer would have first appeared. Mesothelioma is a deadly disease, and the odds of survival with PM HIPEC are significantly higher if it is discovered in the first phase of cancer. Now that the cancer cells were biphasic, the odds of survival seemed slim to none. Unfortunately, it's unlikely that a provider would suspect something as deadly as mesothelioma or even a more common form of cancer in a 38-year-old healthy woman who presents symptoms often associated with abdominal pain. In essence, we couldn't expect all doctors to be superheroes, so I had to squelch my anger and sweep it under the rug for another time.

The next day, Ally placed a call to schedule a tentative appointment to see the mesothelioma specialist in Houston, a few weeks out while my sister was hard at work trying to get Ally an appointment at SCC. That evening we asked our close friends, Richard and Lisa, to come over for support and help us figure out the best course of action.

Lisa and I went to chiropractic school together. When I returned to Seattle to begin practicing, I was surprised to find that Lisa was practicing in the same building as me downtown. Richard, who also practiced there, was our senior and was the most experienced out of the three of us. We all developed a friendship and grew close throughout my first ten years of practice. Lisa and Richard, now married, were two of the very first people who welcomed Ally and me with open arms in Seattle. We shared many adventures of hiking, exploring new places together, and, most of all, enjoying many nights over dinner and wine at their peaceful place on the water. Ally loved to snuggle up by the fire during the cold fall and winter months. Ally felt safe and loved being around them as we engaged in deep conversations about life, relationships, and spirituality. These times enriched Ally's heart and soul with happiness, understanding, and a newfound purpose whenever she felt lost in her own life.

Now it was a serious decision time to determine Ally's fate; to receive treatment here in Seattle with her sister or with me in Houston. I know that we both had Ally's best interest at heart, even though we didn't see eye-to-eye on which place was best and where she should seek treatment. As the four of us settled into the living room, it was hard not to feel the unwanted big elephant that sat in the middle of the room staring at us in the face. Ally sat on one side of the couch, silently staring at the floor, with arms wrapped around her knees drawn close to her. I sat next to her for support as I decided to jump straight into it. "Thanks for coming over and helping Ally with her decision on where she should seek treatment."

"Of course. We are so honored that you have asked us to be here," Richard replied as Lisa nodded in agreement.

"We can all agree that we want what is best for Ally. The real question is where the best place for Ally is to receive the best treatment for her cancer. Here at SCC or over in Houston with her sister?"

Richard immediately butted in, "I really don't think there is a question here to be had. Any sort of cancer treatment will be extremely hard on Ally, both physically, mentally, and emotionally."

"Yeah, Vo. Ally needs your support the most. And you not only have us, but you also have all of your friends and family here in Seattle to help her, and you get through this together," Lisa emphasized.

"Of course, that is what I prefer," I said, "but…"

"No. No… They are right," Ally whispered with tears running down her face, "I want to be here with you. I can't imagine being in a hospital bed by myself and not having you next to me. I can't do this without you babe," she cried as she reached over to wrap her arm around me.

I turned to look into her eyes, "I am glad. I don't want you to be away from me, either. We will get through this together, and we will find a cure," I said as I leaned in to kiss her.

"Hey, hey!" then we are all in agreement," Richard yelled as we all gathered in for a group hug to rejoice in Ally's decision to remain here with me in Seattle.

Now it was time for Ally to call her sister and inform her of her decision. There was a lot of yelling and screaming back and forth as to what was best for her. The phone call ended with Ally screaming into the phone, "IT IS MY LIFE AND MY DECISION!" before she hung up the phone in tears. "Argh!!!" she screamed as she threw up her fists in frustration.

I knew it was hard for Ally to stand up to her sister since all her life, she longed for her approval. I reached over to hold her, "Everything is going to be okay. You made the right decision."

Ultimately, all Ally wanted was to be with me, the other half of her heart. We then called my sister and told her about our decision. "Good! I was able to get Ally an appointment tomorrow at SCC to see one of the nurse practitioners, and I'm working on getting an appointment with a specialist early next week. I will pick Ally up around 10:30 am and take her to her appointment tomorrow." This was a real blessing, considering all the obstacles we had faced earlier. We couldn't help but smile, knowing that we had made the right decision and things were finally quickly moving in the right direction.

Chapter 14

Commitments

February 10, 2017, was Ally's first visit to Seattle Cancer Center in Seattle. Ally and my sister met with the physician's assistant (PA) assigned to the oncologist she would see the following Tuesday. The PA prescribed Dilaudid, a faster-acting derivative of morphine that offered Ally significant pain relief. The only drawback was that she'd have to give up her love of wine, but that was a small price to pay to be virtually pain-free. Before Ally was seen by her chosen oncologist, we were informed that her case was escalated to the cancer board. This meant that several of the top oncologists from around the U.S. would meet to discuss the best course of treatment for particularly rare cancers. She was too young to have such a rare form of mesothelioma. One of the members of the board was a world-renowned mesothelioma expert. She was doing clinical trials using an immunotherapy drug called Keytruda that showed promising results in reducing and even stopping the cancer's growth. A patient had to undergo a few rounds of failed chemotherapy treatment to be considered for the trial. Those who carried the genetic marker of the PD-L1 protein yielded a higher success rate with the immunotherapy treatment.

Earlier that morning, knowing that the PM HIPEC doctor was located on the east coast. I called his office as soon as it had opened, hoping to speak to someone right away to talk about Ally's case, but I was met by a few rings and was prompted to leave a voicemail. There was only so much I could say in a 5-10 second recording besides, "Hello, my wife has terminal cancer, and you are our only hope. PLEASE CALL ME BACK ASAP!" So, I left a brief message with my phone number and decided to email a more detailed description of our circumstances before giving Ally a deep hug and a kiss, wishing her luck at her appointment before heading to work.

(Email to the HIPEC Doctor)
To: Hello Dr. ███████████ - Allyson Vo
From: Minh Vo

Hope you are well. My wife has just been confirmed after months of discovery and waiting to have peritoneal mesothelioma. The pain began in late October/November. Her doctor thought it to be IBS and refused to do any further testing other than blood labs. I put her on my insurance, which didn't kick in till mid-January, to see my internal medicine doctor, which did tests and a CT scan right away. It showed a 3.5-inch stromal-type tumor in the mesentery, along with several nodules with ascites in the peritoneal cavity. The following week they performed a biopsy, and the pathologist at the ███ clinic in Seattle wasn't confident to determine the diagnosis after a week. They sent it to the head pathologist at ██████ and confirmed this Wednesday that it was indeed mesothelioma. Her chest scan is clear.

Her pain is escalating by the day, and her pain meds are barely working. I just left a message at your clinic. We would love to have her seen by you as soon as possible since time is

of the essence. We have an appointment with ▮▮▮ Cancer Center ▮▮▮ associated with ▮▮▮ Cancer Institute, but the earliest they can get her in is Tuesday.

   Ally is a 38-year-old Caucasian female. We were married on the 14th of October 2016. Please contact us as soon as possible. Thank you so much. I can be reached at 206-▮▮▮▮▮▮▮

   Blessings,
   Minh Vo

A few hours passed before my cell phone rang. It was the receptionist at the HIPEC office. "Hello, Mr. Vo. The doctor has read your email. He would like you to email him a copy of the confirmed diagnosis and CT scan so that he could review it."

"Yes! Of course. I will email it right away. Thank you so much!" I immediately went to my MacBook and replied.

   (Email from HIPEC)
   To: Minh Vo
   From: Dr. ▮▮▮▮
   Dr. ▮▮▮ has looked at the information that you provided.
   His recommendation is to begin systemic chemo with cisplatin and Alimpta, the standard mesothelioma regimen.
   Have you had a consult with a med onc?
   The biphasic pathology is not a diagnosis with which we have done well. Unless the systemic chemo works, these tumors seem to defy any treatment, including cytoreductive surgery combined with HIPEC.
   The issue with the somewhat uncontrolled pain is not something usually seen.
   Please send the actual disc of the CT for the doctor to review. He has looked at the report, which indicates limited involvement of the peritoneal cavity.
   ~OM

Given all the information that happened at Ally's appointment, I immediately forwarded the email to Ally's cancer team at SCC, hoping that this information would be useful, and replied to Dr. HIPEC with the information I was given.

>(Email to HIPEC Doctor)
>From: Minh Vo
>To: Dr. ███,
>Thank you so much for your response. We are seeing the director of GI at ███ Cancer Center ███ associated with ███ Cancer Research Center and ███ Medicine. I showed him your email, and he said that was exactly what he was thinking. They put Ally's case in front of the cancer board so that several eyes could look at it, as well as consult with experts in Chicago as well. They are going to do additional staining slides to confirm things that they were questioning. We have them as a backup, based upon your confirmation, since you are the expert in this field. I will mail out the CD tomorrow for Dr. ███ to review.
>
>Thanks again for looking at Ally's case. We are very grateful. If you have any other recommendations or suggestions, please let us know.
>
>Blessings,
>Minh Vo

February 12, 2017 (Ally's Healing Circle)

Minh Vo
Admin · Feb 12, 2017 ·

Update: Ally is diagnosed with peritoneal mesothelioma. She was admitted to SCC yesterday for pain management. She will be seeing Dr. ███, Director of GI cancer on Tuesday to map out treatment and begin chemo next week. Her case, being so rare, was placed in front of the tumor board yesterday for specialists to review her case here, and other parts of the country. Thanks for all your support and prayers.

👍 30   11 comments

I couldn't be with Ally to attend the first meeting with her new oncologist, but my sister went with Ally to support her while he reviewed her diagnosis information, treatment plan, and expectations moving forward. Afterward, my sister called me with a recap of the discussion. "Vo! We just finished the appointment with Ally's oncologist.

It wasn't pretty, and honestly, Ally is still upset with what happened at the appointment."

"Why, what happened?" I inquired.

"The doctor's bedside manner was absolutely horrible. First of all, he was so casual about the whole thing when reviewing information about her diagnosis and treatment plan. He was on his laptop the whole time and was very distracted when talking to Ally," she said. "What really set Ally off was when he discussed with Ally about her life expectancy with mesothelioma and stated that, on average, she had about 6-18 months to live. Ally totally freaked out and screamed at him that she was told it was 3-5 years. I had to calm Ally down. He then apologized and corrected himself, telling her he had made a mistake and quoted lung survival versus abdominal survival."

"Yeah. That is not good," I replied.

"He then told her she most likely got cancer from the use of talcum powder as a baby and that there were current studies showing high levels of asbestos in talcum powder in the '70s and early '80s. He then went into the treatment plan and what drugs would be administered, the side effects, and what to expect during chemo and afterward. He didn't really even acknowledge or show much concern about Ally's emotional well-being, especially considering it was their first meeting! You need to talk to her Vo!" She then handed the phone over to Ally.

"Hello," Ally said as she gasped for air seeking composure.

"Hey, babe. I am so sorry that your first appointment didn't go too well," I calmly said. "Not every doctor has good bedside manners. What matters most to me is that you are getting the best treatment possible that was recommended by the Cancer Board, and they are the best doctors in the world. All I really care about is that they find a way to help cure you."

"Okay," she murmured.

"I also have some great news to tell you, babe. The HIPEC doctor emailed me back this morning. After reviewing the CT scans that I sent him, he said that you have a good chance of being a surgical candidate. He said the tumor was most likely coming from your mesentery. After two or three months of chemotherapy, he thinks that he could possibly see you at his clinic in Washington, D.C., for surgery!" I exclaimed. "Everything is going to be great real soon, and you will be cured!"

"That is great news, babe!" she replied. Her voice was more cheerful now.

"We will get through this. You just have to trust the process," I said with conviction. "I will be home soon. I love you."

"Love you too, babe," she said before she hung up the phone.

To me, this was the most exciting news since he had considered her a possible PM HIPEC surgical candidate after two successful rounds of chemotherapy. We shared the good news with both of our families, and everyone felt really happy and excited. Ally was extremely pleased for the first time since her diagnosis. She had felt hope and a small sense of relief. Our next step was beginning her chemo treatment.

February 16, 2017 (From Ally) (Ally's Healing Circle)

Allyson
Admin Feb 16, 2017

Hi Friends and Fam from Ally,

Update: We have chemo lift off this Friday beginning @ 7:30 am. As I embark on this crazy journey, feel free to ply me with cancer humor. I need something other than yet another study that offers grim survival rates, scary-sounding side effects or another medicine that has more vowels than consonants. It can span the spectrum from silly to biting. Game on

Love and Luck,
Ally

👍❤️ 54   37 comments

Love, prayers, and humor flooded the private healing circle:

"Ally/Minh. I know the water is deep, keep the faith and never ever give up hope, the fight is ahead let's kick ass and take names!!!" ~

"Ally, sending you lots of love from SF. Good luck with your treatments and we're rooting for your recovery. You are strong. After seeing your marathon pics, I got inspired to run...a half...

barely finished it. So you're my inspiration. I love you and sending lots of hugs. You got this!!!!! Let's kick cancer in the ass!! ~

"Love you Fartface. I'm here for you when you need me." ~

As Ally began to mentally and emotionally prepare herself for her first round of chemo, we asked around about the side effects. Ally was told by her doctor, nurses, and a few others that symptoms usually don't occur until a day later. Some may experience nausea and vomiting that could last up to 3-4 days. They also ensured us that they had all the necessary medications we'd need to combat these side effects. The fact was chemo is like administering napalm to the body. As it enters, it kills everything, hopefully targeting more bad cancer cells than healthy cells.

Just days leading up to her first chemo treatment, Ally got a call from one of the nurses at SCC asking her if she wanted to have her eggs frozen before she received her first chemo treatment. The procedure would be costly, and we'd have to wait for a full menstruation cycle in order to harvest healthy eggs.

This question hit Ally like a ton of bricks from out of nowhere. "Wait! What?!" she screamed into the phone hysterically. "What do you mean?"

"Once you have chemo, you won't be able to have viable eggs if you and your husband ever plan to have kids in the future," the nurse replied.

"I... I can't talk about this right now! I have to talk to my husband," she yelled as she hung up the phone.

Ally began to wail in tears, "Babe... babe, I can't have kids?! I can't believe this is happening to me!" Ally threw her hands into the air as she slumped onto the couch, grabbing her hair. "Argh!! This is not fair. This is so not fair!" Having a child was the only thing left that Ally really wanted in her life.

This news caused her severe emotional distress. I sat down next to her on the couch and took her hands into mine. "I know this is hard for you to hear. It is hard for me as well," I told her. "But we can't delay your treatment, babe."

"But what about our baby?" she softly cried.

"Maybe we can adopt one day," I said.

"That's not the same, babe," she replied in frustration, "it won't be from you and me."

"Ally," I said, trying to calm her down, "I would rather have you live and adopt than delay your treatment and risk losing you. That is what is most important to me. I can't lose you."

"Arghhhh," Ally screamed as she shook her head. "Okay… okay. I hate this fucking cancer!"

"I know you don't want to hear this, but everything is going to be ok. We will figure it out later," I whispered. "We just need to get you better as fast as possible."

She nodded, her face still streaming with tears. Time was something we didn't have on our side, and finding a way for Ally to survive the cancer was at the top of our priority list.

In the beginning, it was mostly just the two of us left alone to try and figure out what to do next. We were both walking through foreign territory. Often times I would find Ally sitting alone on our bed, deep in her thoughts. I couldn't imagine what was going through her mind. All I could do was sit next to her to put my arm around her for comfort, and we would sit in silence together. She would then burst into tears and scream, "I can't fucking believe this is happening to me!" I would just hold her tighter and try to calm her down. She then screamed, "You don't deserve this life, Minh. You should leave me. I can't even have babies!"

I looked straight into her eyes and told her, "Babe. I wouldn't change a thing. There is nowhere else I would rather be than here with you."

"But I can't even have a baby. All of our dreams, our plans, our future! They are all gone now." She was devasted and cried, "Where are we going to get the money to pay for all of this?!"

"Don't worry about the money Ally. Let me worry about it. I will figure out a way. You just need to focus on yourself and stay positive," I told her. "We will get through this. We will find a cure, but you are the one that has to fight the fight. I will be with you every single step of the way." I just needed her to focus on herself and remain positive since I truly believed that a person's mental outlook played a big role in determining the outcome of surviving cancer along with the body's ability to heal. Ally had to put herself first now.

We asked Ally's mom to fly in for Ally's first chemo treatment and to help out the following week when I would be at work. With the appointment being so early, I had hoped to be present long enough for her first infusion to begin before having to leave for work. Ally was finally ready to begin her fight against cancer with her first chemo treatment. Ally, Marie, Di, and I arrived at the cancer center that morning to begin her day with a blood draw, which I assume was to establish a baseline prior to starting the treatment. We then headed upstairs to the infusion clinic to check-in. When we got there, they reviewed her vitals, gave her a medication list for pre- and post-chemo side effects, and we discussed the chemo treatment plan for the day. She would be given Pemetrexed for 60 minutes, followed by Cisplatin + Hydration for another 60 minutes. The chemo drugs chosen by the tumor board were congruent with the recommendations by the PM HIPEC doctor to treat her mesothelioma. Ally's first day of infusions would take a total of six hours to complete.

Two hours had almost elapsed as we were waiting for the infusion to begin. I figured that maybe this was normal since people are usually waiting for hours in the emergency room before they are able to be seen. Not having much time left before I had to leave, I was able to get ahold of the nurse in charge. "Sorry to bother you, but we have been sitting here for quite a while now and were wondering when Ally would be starting her chemo treatment," I said.

"I am so sorry, Mr. Vo, there was some miscommunication. The orders for Ally's drugs were not placed the day before as directed by her doctor to get preapproval for her treatment today," she said.

"What? What did you say?" Ally said, listening nearby. "What does that mean? Am I not getting treatment today?" she yelled out. "I have been mentally preparing myself for this all week!" she screamed as she began shaking her head in tears and frustration.

"We are working on this as fast as we can," the nurse said apologetically. "Ally's doctor is on the phone as we speak, trying to get rush approval. The worst-case scenario is that Ally would have to begin her treatment tomorrow, but we are trying our best to get Ally's drugs approved for today. Please bear with us a little longer to see if we can resolve the situation, Mr. Vo."

I looked at the time on my phone. I, unfortunately, couldn't stay any longer as I was already late for work because of the confusion. I walked over to Ally, who was being consoled by her mom. "Babe, I am so sorry, but I have to leave for work. They are doing their best to try to get you approved for today," I told her as I held her hands.

"But I am ready today, babe. It took all the courage I had to prepare myself for today," she replied, feeling downtrodden.

"Everything is going to be okay. They are still working on getting you approved today. Have faith, babe," I told her before I gave her a big hug and kissed goodbye.

"Okay...," she said as she wiped away her tears. All she could do was wait and leave it in the hands of her doctor and our insurance carrier.

I asked Di to keep me posted and let me know what the final outcome of the insurance issue was and if it would be resolved. I also asked her to keep me posted on how Ally was doing throughout the treatment if we were lucky enough to get approval.

On the same day as Ally's first chemo treatment, when all hell broke loose that morning, I was hiding in my office that morning when my phone rang. It was my friend Lee from San Francisco. Ally and I spent a lot of time with him and his girlfriend once they moved in together in the neighboring Fillmore District perpendicular to Lower Haight and the Panhandle where Ally and I lived, respectively. We cooked several dinners at their place and watched movies together. He had returned to Seattle for his annual family visit and to catch up with Ally and me. I told him I wasn't available to hang out while he was in town this time since it was the day of Ally's chemo treatment. I don't know if it was from the stress of Ally potentially having to delay chemo that day, but he managed to convince me that I needed a break. He wanted to be a good friend to me and give me some emotional support by at least taking me out to dinner for a few hours and trying to take my mind off all the stress I was going through with Ally's cancer. "I will confirm a little later once I know what is going on with Ally. The hospital messed up and didn't get her drug orders in for today. They are working on getting them approved."

"Alright, I will be at the restaurant around 8 pm. If you show up, then you show up. I have to eat either way. Just let me know," he said before we hung up.

Ally knew he was in town, and because she couldn't partake in the normal things we used to do together, we had a conversation a few days prior, and she told me, "You should go and meet up with Lee for a few hours."

"No... no, I should stay with you your first night of chemo," I told her.

"Minh, you should go and have a few drinks, at the very least. Hell, I would go if I could," she chuckled. "At least one of us should have some fun. Besides, I will have my mom here with me, and it will only be for a few hours."

It made a little sense, but I had to ask again, "Are you sure you are okay with it?"

"Yes. Just go. What is the worst that can happen? It's just a few hours, babe," she smiled. Thinking back to what we were told about chemo symptoms not manifesting until the second day and because we had Ally's mom here to help, I finally agreed to meet Lee for a few hours.

Three hours had passed at work when I finally got a text from Di.

Di: Ally's doctor got the approval for her to begin treatment.

Vo: That is great news! How is she doing?

Di: She is calm now and is doing well with the infusion. Her mom is sitting with her. We should be done by the time you get off work, and then I will bring them back to your place.

Vo: Thank you so much, Di... for everything.

Di: Of course. I will let you know if anything else happens.

Vo: Sounds good.

This was a great relief for me. I hated leaving Ally when she was so distraught. It broke my heart to see her so upset and hopeless. She had her mom and Di with her during the infusion, and my sister checked in on her later that day. We were so thankful for Di and her flexible schedule that allowed her to accompany Ally to most of her appointments.

When I got home, Ally was sitting in our room. I immediately asked Ally, "How are you feeling, babe? Are you tired? Any nausea?"

"I am feeling a little tired, but I am doing good," she said.

"Yeah, you have been through a lot today," I told her. She nodded in agreement. "So… Lee called me earlier at work and asked if we were still on for dinner and a few drinks tonight."

She reiterated her thoughts, "Oh yeah? You should go, babe."

I still felt a little torn, "Are you sure? I don't have to go, you know,"

"Yes! We will be fine. You go have fun with Lee," she said.

"Ok, I will let him know." Before I left, I made sure that Ally was feeling alright and had no signs or symptoms of any side effects from the chemo. I also made sure they had all the meds and the instructions that they would need if anything was to happen to Ally. As I opened the door and was about to leave, Ally suddenly grabbed my arm. I turned around and looked at her. A sudden veil of fear eclipsed her face, "I am scared, babe."

I smiled at her and said, "You have nothing to be scared about. I will only be gone for a few hours. Dinner and a couple of drinks," I reiterated to her. "And if anything goes wrong, you can call me, and I will be home right away."

Her face calmed, and with a little smile, she said, "You are right. I don't know why all of a sudden, I freaked out for a moment."

"If you really want me to cancel, I can if you want me to," I told her.

"No. Go have fun," she then reached over to hug me and give me a kiss goodbye.

I then yelled out to Ally's mom, "Call me if you need anything."

"Have fun," she replied. "We will be fine."

In hindsight, I was never going to find peace or get any sense of sanity by having dinner with Lee. Instead of feeling emotional relief, all I did was stare off into the distance while silent tears streamed from my eyes. There was nothing my friend could say or do to cheer me up or to change what I felt: helpless fear. After a little while, I had an overwhelming feeling that I needed to be home with Ally. Having dinner with Lee was certainly not worth being away from Ally, so I cut the visit short and headed home early. As I walked through the door, I saw Ally violently throwing up in the bathroom, as Ally's mom was trying to help her by holding up her hair. I felt instantly enraged; various scenarios started running through my head as to what might have happened during the short period of time I was gone. Ally was completely fine when I left, and now she was throwing up uncontrollably. I began screaming at Marie, "What the fuck just happened!" Thinking that Ally wasn't given her post-chemo medication on time, I began blaming Marie for Ally's current condition. "Why is Ally throwing up? Did you not give Ally her meds?!"

Marie looked at me, horrified and speechless. She was getting very upset with me as I was directing all of my anger and blame toward her, which didn't help Ally's situation at all. Ally couldn't help but immediately notice what was going on, and when she finally stopped vomiting momentarily, she pushed me back and yelled, "Go to the bedroom Minh. Me and my mom got this. Just go to bed." Frustrated, I turned and just walked away instead of trying to make something bad worse. I headed straight for the bedroom and closed the door behind me. I could still hear Ally vomiting and dry heavying most of the night as she couldn't control the side effects from the chemo coursing through her body. By morning, I woke up to find Ally resting on the couch with her head on her mom's lap as she slowly stroked her long brown hair, finally able to rest from the exhaustion of staying up all night.

It was Saturday morning the following day, and unfortunately, I had to get ready for work. I checked in on Ally as she was fading in and out of sleep. In a sheepish voice, I said to her, "Sorry that I lost my temper last night. I shouldn't have left you last night."

She opened her eyes and looked at me, "It's okay. My mom and I did everything we were told to do. I took the meds exactly when I was supposed to. Then all of a sudden, I couldn't stop throwing up, and there was nothing we could do to make it stop."

I then looked at Marie and said, "Sorry that I yelled at you. I just lost it when I saw Ally was throwing up."

She just smiled at me and said, "It's okay. We did do everything right."

I then kissed Ally on the forehead and told her I would be back from work as soon as I could. She just smiled and then drifted back to sleep.

After an hour or so at the office, I received a phone call from my father-in-law. "Hey Minh, what the hell happened last night over there? I have been getting a few phone calls and some angry texts from different family members saying some bad things about you."

"What are you talking about?" I said confusedly.

"They were calling you every single colorful name in the book, saying how you were such a horrible person for leaving Ally last night," he confessed.

"Hey JB, all I did was have dinner and a few drinks with my friend Lee from SF," I replied. "I was gone for less than a few hours. Ally and I had agreed that I needed some time away to help deal with my stress."

"Well yeah, of course, buddy. That is what I figured. I told them that you and Ally are dealing with a lot out there on your own and that they shouldn't blame or throw you under the bus for trying to take a breather, especially when Marie was there to help out. I just wanted to call and let you know what is going around the family and that I defended you, buddy," he said. "Don't worry about them. You did nothing wrong."

"Thanks, JB, for letting me know."

"Of course. I will be out there soon to see you guys in a week or so to help out," he said. "Keep your head up, and don't worry about their nonsense. Love you, Minh," he said before hanging up.

I immediately began freaking out and called Leo. "Fuck Leo. People are talking shit about me behind my back, saying that I am such a horrible person for meeting up with Lee last night during Ally's first night of chemo."

"You know Vo, studies have shown that it is just as important that the caregiver also takes the time to take care of himself and that it is alright to breaks at times so that he can be at his best when looking after those they are caring for, especially when it is a loved one or a spouse," he said.

"You sure I didn't fuck up?" I replied.

"Don't worry about it. You did nothing wrong," he said before hanging up the phone.

I then called up Lee, "Shit, Lee. Family members heard about me going out with you last night and are talking shit about me. What the fuck?!" I yelled.

"Shit…. They don't know you. They don't know how stressed you are," he said. "I could see and feel the pain in your eyes last night. Fuck them. You needed a break," It was his way of trying to give me encouraging words to ease the negativity being heaved in my direction, but the damage was done. I couldn't stop thinking about it.

I know I haven't always made the best decisions in life, but hearing everything being said behind my back put me in further distress. Now I regret trying to find a moment of peace or believing that symptoms didn't occur until the following day after chemo. Looking back, leaving that night was one of my biggest regrets. Then suddenly a few texts flashed across my phone screen, 'What is wrong with you?', 'What kind of a husband would leave his wife on the night of her chemo treatment?' This sent me over the edge, and I began to crumble emotionally. I felt worthless. I called my sister, gasping in tears, "Minh! All of these people are saying all of these bad things about me, all because I went out for dinner with a friend last night during Ally's first night of chemo. I am under so much stress, and I just can't take it anymore!"

In a calm, stern voice, she said, "Vo, listen to me. You did nothing wrong. Stop listening to people who are not walking in your shoes. I will take care of the whole situation. I am going to shield you from all of this. From now on, everything will go through me. You don't have to talk to anyone anymore. They will all have to go through me. You just need to focus on you and Ally." My sister had always been my protector when I was growing up. It wasn't any different now. She shielded me then, and she would once again shield me now.

When I arrived home later that night, I was even more furious at Marie and all that had transpired from Ally's family. There were only three people who knew what went on the night before, and Ally was preoccupied with throwing up the entire time. I was enraged at Marie for spreading gossip. As I walked through the front door, my intent was to rip Ally's mom a new one. The anger and redness on my face were quite noticeable. Ally saw that I was livid and uncontrollably upset to the point where I was literally shaking. She immediately took my hands and led me into our bedroom, and closed the door. "What's wrong, Minh? What is happening?"

"I am so furious with your mom Ally!" I yelled in a whisper. "I want to throw her out of the house right now!"

"Why? What happened?" she said frantically, "What did she do?"

"She called everyone in your family and told them how bad of a person I was for leaving you last night when you got sick from your chemo," I shared. "Now everyone is blaming me and talking shit about me about how bad of a person I am. I can't deal with any of this anymore!"

"Look at me, Minh," she said in a calm voice as she grabbed both of my hands and looked me straight in the eyes. "From here on out, Babe, it's just you and me no matter what. We don't need any of them. We just need each other. I just need you by my side to get me through this."

I took a few deep breaths and started to calm down. 'You and me, no matter what.' From that day forward, this became our mantra in fighting cancer together as one. People were allowed to have their own opinions and would be so quick to judge you for not being perfect in their own eyes, but we were no longer going to listen to those who were not going to help us in the ways we needed. No more gossip, no more opinions, no more unnecessary noise. Nothing else mattered except the love we had between us.

All the noise in my head came to a halt after that conversation. Even in her weakened state, Ally knew exactly what to say to me to give me back my strength. I came to my senses, and once again, I became that calm, strong rock that Ally needed me to be. The following day, I apologized again to Marie for lashing out at her when my emotions got the best of me. We agreed that we were both there for Ally's best interests and that we would work together as a family, a team, to do everything we could to help her get through her battle against cancer. My sister squelched all the negative gossip going around about me, reminding everyone that this was about Ally and Minh getting through an extremely difficult time. All of the negativity and nonsense had to stop and was detrimental to the progress of the uphill battle we were facing. If anyone had a problem with anything or needed any information, she would be our point of contact. After hearing about all the unnecessary drama, my brother Billy told me that he would be taking over all public communication in the Healing Circle regarding Ally's treatment, health, and well-being. I provided him with all the information he needed so he could best relay our message to everyone in the group.

February 22, 2017 (Ally's Healing Circle)

Admin Feb 22, 2017

Hi everyone -- I'm Ally's brother-in-law, and myself and Minh Vo Sum, are going to do our best to keep all of updated on how Ally's doing. Here's a recap of the last few days:

1) Ally started chemotherapy last Friday, Feb. 17. The first 3-4 days after receiving chemo is generally very difficult, and this was also the case for Ally -- she was experiencing lots of nausea and pain.

2) On Monday, Feb. 20, we took Ally to the Seattle Cancer Center (SCC) to consult with her medical team. She received an IV that day for hydration, and additional nausea and pain relief. And, she a lot better afterward.

3) On Tuesday, Feb. 21, Ally did great and had her best day yet! She wasn't feeling much nausea or pain, and was also able to each much more than usual. She had a couple bowls of spaghetti, and since Ally has no dietary restrictions -- Minh was able to take Ally out for some sushi! Ally told me last night that she was able to eat five pieces of sushi, and she even had a piece of uni!

We are really thankful for the medical and care team we have at SCC for Ally. They have been awesome, and have been an answered prayer for us.

Just a note to this FB community: given Ally's energy level, she likely won't be able to respond to your emails, messages, and texts at this time. Rest assured, she is feeling your love and prayers for her -- and will be drawing strength from your continued love and prayers in the days ahead.

Please use this FB group to share your continued love, thoughts, and prayers for Ally and let's continue to lift her up in every way we know how as we continue to walk this journey together.

Much love, everyone!

👍❤️ 70   25 comments

It took almost a week with several calls and a trip to the cancer center to consult with her medical team during a follow-up when they decided to implement IV hydration and anti-nausea medication. They needed to rehydrate and stabilize Ally's condition after her first round of chemo. Ally was put on a strict medication regimen to combat her pain and nausea, which she would need to take to alleviate symptoms for one or the other, with a multitude of medications every 3-4 hours, 24 hours a day, until her symptoms stabilized. Considering everything that Ally was going through, I tried to make life seem as normal as possible when she was feeling well enough to do things.

The past few months were extremely stressful not only for Ally but also for me. To hear that your new bride, the one you've chosen to build your life with, had terminal cancer and would not survive the next few years throws your whole life into a downward spiral. Who would have known that on the day I made a commitment to spend the rest of my life with Ally, I would soon be making another commitment to do whatever it took to save her life.

I am not a person who knows or has ever learned to show emotions, especially sorrow, but I often found myself sitting in my office in between patients with silent tears streaming down my face. I felt so helpless not being able to do more for Ally. If I could, I would have traded my life fo hers and taken her place, taking on cancer myself so that she could live. There was no magic wand to wave to make this nightmare go away.

I told Leo early on when we were sitting alone together, "Man, Leo, I must have done something extremely horrible in a previous life to deserve such a fucked-up life as this one. I finally got married to Ally, only to find out that she has terminal cancer and might die. WHAT THE FUCK!"

He would just nod and say, "Yeah, man. I am sorry." What could he really say to me? Him being one of my closest friends, even though he didn't have the magical words that would make me feel remotely better about Ally's cancer. At the same time, I tried to be Ally's immovable rock so that she could lean on me no matter what she was going through.

When I arrived home from work every night, we would try to do something together, such as make dinner or go out and grab a bite to eat or do what we always did on a work night: watch a movie or food shows together. At night, we crawled into bed together and talked about things that happened during the day until it was time to sleep. I was sleep deprived during this time since I'd have to wake up whenever Ally needed to take meds to stay on her strict regimen. She'd often wake up in the middle of the night when she was in pain, and I would have to call the on-call doctor to see if she could take more pain medication or to help her when she needed to throw up or go to the bathroom. In essence, Ally and I were both exhausted.

On our follow-up visit with her oncologist, we were given a review of Ally's progress and how he felt things were going. After reviewing the information, he looked at Ally and said, "How are you doing after your first treatment? Do you feel like you are getting good support at home?"

Ally was staring at the floor, pondering everything she had just heard from her oncologist. Then in a soft scared voice, she murmured, "I don't feel safe at night and am usually awake. I tend to get scared of the dark when Minh turns off the lights for bed."

I immediately looked at her. "Wait, what?!" "How come you have never told me this, Ally?" I pleaded.

She looked at me and began feeling a little upset, "I know you have to get up for work in the morning, and it is important for you to get sleep."

"Oh Ally... you should never ever be afraid to tell me anything, especially if it is anything that you need from me," I told her. "It is way more important for you to feel safe than you to worry about me or my sleep."

"But we need the money," she cried.

"Don't worry about the money Ally. I have it taken care of. Your health and safety are my number one priority," I told her. Ally reluctantly agreed that we would sleep with the lights on from that day forward. We also finally agreed that whatever it took, her health, comfort, safety, and well-being always came first.

Ally always puts other people's feelings or needs before her own. It was hard for Ally to put herself first; she cared so much about others. My dad had always been tough as nails and sometimes a mean son-of-a-bitch when we were growing up as kids. Now as adults, his temper and his ways had mellowed throughout the years. I remember the first time my dad met Ally. We were having a glass of wine after dinner at our home. We got on the topic of Vietnam, my childhood, and then the war. Ally asked him, "So, what was it like for you during the Vietnam War?"

His mood suddenly changed, and his face went blank. He stared past us, and tears began to stream down his face as he tried to muster the words, "It is almost indescribable what happened there." Then he stopped speaking as though the words were too painful to say aloud.

There were times growing up when I heard him yelling and screaming in the middle of the night, but he'd wake up and brush it off or laugh about it. That night was the first time I saw true pain in his eyes as he thought about the war. Ally felt his pain and began to weep. She reached over and embraced him deeply, as if she would never let go, letting him know he didn't need to finish answering the question. Afterward, he smiled while wiping away the tears from his eyes. He then took a deep breath along with a few sips of his wine and then just sat there smiling for a moment. And just like that, all was normal again, but a bond between him and Ally was forged. I'd hope Ally will be able to live through this terrible ordeal without the thoughts and nightmares of the possibility that she may not survive.

PART 3

THE ENDING

CHAPTER 15

ALLY'S BIG RACE

Seeing Ally go through her first round of chemo and its aftermath, I did everything possible to try to ensure the best outcome in beating her cancer. I added alternative medicine options to supplement her treatments. She began seeing an acupuncturist who prescribed herbs. My mom sent Ally a case of Fucoidan, a brown seaweed known to help cure people with stage 4 cancer. We used aromatherapy essential oil diffusers to help with her general well-being, anxiety, and other side effects of cancer. Finally, I purchased a Rife machine to help detox and strengthen her body while sending specific frequencies to theoretically destroy the cancer virus in her body. Most of these things required little effort on Ally's part besides taking the herbs, which was good since she began to lose energy, whether it was due to the pain, the chemo, or the tumor that prevented her from eating and exercising to keep her body strong. I could only push Ally to do so much in her condition, and oftentimes, I had to acquiesce to what she wanted and was willing to do. Ally often asked me to stop pushing her, but all I wanted was for her to get well. If no one pushed her, then she probably wouldn't do as much, I thought. It took me a while to figure out that there was a fine line between pushing and helping versus pushing and not helping. I often didn't know how much she could really handle at any given time. All I could do was have her try anything and everything that could possibly help save her life.

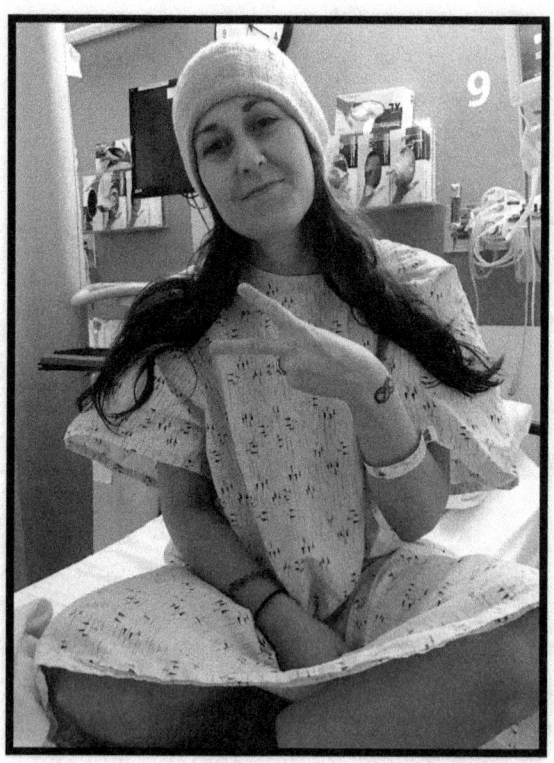

March 2, 2017 (Ally's Healing Circle)

 is with **Allyson**
Admin · Mar 2, 2017

Hi everyone -- I just wanted to give you an update on how Ally's doing and some things you can thinking and praying about this next week.

Ally has been doing good, and is adjusting well to her medication for pain and nausea. She has been experiencing some of the common (and uncomfortable) symptoms from chemotherapy, including tiredness, and dryness, inflammation, and sores in her mouth and tongue. These symptoms, along with the nausea, can make eating particularly difficult. So, we appreciate your continued thoughts and prayers for her to maintain a good appetite, and for these challenges with eating.

We're also continually thankful for the great care and support we're receiving from Seattle Cancer Center. This past week, we've met and been in communication with a social worker who has been assigned to Ally. She has been providing a lot of helpful as we begin this journey (e.g. finances and support, etc.), and one thing we are hoping to work with her on is seeing if we can connect Ally with a peer support group of those who are also fighting cancer.

We appreciate your continued love, thoughts, and prayers for Ally as she deals with these symptoms and we try and connect her with a support group.

As for what's ahead: next Tuesday (3/7), Ally will go to SCC to get her chemo port which will greatly assist with receiving chemotherapy. Then, next Friday (3/10), Ally will receive her second round of chemotherapy.

(Ally's mom) will be leaving Seattle tomorrow morning. We're thankful that she has been here to help with providing care and support for Ally during these last couple weeks. This next week, (Ally's sister) will be in Seattle to be with Ally for her second round of chemo, and we look forward to having her with us to assist with providing Ally (and Minh) with the support care that they need.

(Attached are a couple of photos of Ally for you all. The first is of Ally during her biopsy appointment, and the second is during (near the beginning) of her first round of chemo)

Much love to you all. Let's send Ally into this next week with all of our love, strength, encouragement, and prayers!

My Ally Sunshine. Love you! Thinking about you. Prayers for you from my lips to God's ear, he is your healer! Hugs & Kisses! ~

Sending some love and support today hon. Big hugz. ~

Ally, I've known you a long time and we have all had a lot of fun times together, I know you are going thru a tough time right now but you are as tough as they come and you will get thru this. Just remember "ITS GAME DAY BABY AND TIME TO WIN." I'm in your corner. Love you with all my hear. ~

We were in the thick of it now, and Ally's fears began to amplify. She often told me, "I am scared, babe. I can't help but think, what if these treatments aren't working? What if I am going to die?! I don't want to leave you, but I just don't know how to cope with what is going on inside my head."

"I know you are going through a lot, Ally. I can't even imagine how much stress you are dealing with inside your head. I wish I could help you deal with this, but I think you need to talk to a trained counselor or maybe other survivors who are going through the same things that you're going through to get the right advice." Being a chiropractor and energy medicine practitioner for many years, I listened to and counseled thousands of patients on confronting and dealing with their emotions. But this was so different, and Ally was my wife. I knew her mind was racing with fear, but I felt like I couldn't really give her the right advice because I was emotionally too close to her. I'd never experienced anything like this in my life, having someone so intimate to you fighting for their life.

There were group cancer patient talks at the cancer center, but Ally wasn't ready to share openly with a bunch of strangers. She had never been one who wanted the spotlight to share her story, let alone her feelings. Luckily, Di had a friend who was in remission from cancer, and he shared his thoughts on life, fear, and will live while he was in the thick of his own fight.

Ally knew she was in this fight for the long haul. Since she was afraid of needles and the sight of blood, it was recommended that she have a chemo port installed to make it easier and virtually painless to perform blood draws or infusions. At first, the thought of getting a port terrified her. It solidified in her mind that all of this was too real. But when she was told that it could easily be removed if or when she went into remission, she felt more at ease about having the procedure.

Life kept moving all around her. Holidays, birthdays, and weddings came and went. Things that Ally and I would normally celebrate together with our family and friends were no longer the same. She didn't feel well most of the time, whether it was intermittent sharp bouts of pain or moments of nausea. She was often curled up on the couch in front of the television or trying to get some rest in our bed. With her current condition, she felt trapped in a bad dream that she couldn't wake from. Long lost were the days of constant laughter, the fluid bombardment of activities and exploration, and all the celebrations that went with it. Ally often felt alone and solely responsible for what was happening to her. She didn't want to burden anyone. She wanted me to have a normal life, to break away from this nightmare, to take a breather and step away every once in a while. Of course, she knew I was there by her side, along with both of our families and friends, near and far. Ally knew that she would ultimately have to walk this path on her own since it was her body and her own private race to beat this cancer. Although I could walk beside her like I had when she ran her marathon in Greece, she knew she would have to be the one to cross that finish line alone in order to receive the ultimate goal: life.

To me, you either enjoy running or you don't. People tend to spout off their clichéd bucket list items. "You've got to run a marathon at least once in your life." My reply? "I'm good." For Ally, it was a little trickier. She'd had asthma since she was a child and needed an inhaler from time to time. Her immune system wasn't strong, which often caused her to become sick or catch a cold or flu all too easily. So, running in this marathon was a big feat for her since she had only run half-marathons in the past. It also gave her something else to focus on, and it helped build up her mind, body, and spirit to accomplish this goal of running a marathon. I am all for people bettering themselves, and I supported her in every way I could so that she wouldn't stress during that time.

Ally trained diligently leading up to the event, putting in long weekends to build up her lungs and endurance. Greece would be our first real vacation together in another country. After a long 20-hour flight with two layovers, we finally arrived in Athens. We were both ecstatic to be in such a famed city as Greece. It was odd to see ancient ruins and pieces of history centuries old strewn about everywhere amongst the city's current architecture. We enjoyed our first meal in Greece, followed by a sampling of the local anise spirit, ouzo. We didn't last long before jetlag took over and put us in bed before 8 p.m. We'd be wide awake by 4 a.m., trying to adjust to the local time, or at least until we heard the first sign of a coffee shop opening nearby. We later met with team members and moseyed over to the convention center to register for the marathon and pick up her bib number and tags for the big race the following day.

People from all around the world flew in to participate in and attend the race, especially since it was the original course of the very first marathon ever held in Greece. The city was alive and flourished with runners and tourists. We met with Ally's friends from her team and made new ones from other parts of the U.S. who were also there for the marathon. We were given the option to rest for the afternoon or to sightsee in Athens. Of course, Ally and I decided on the latter since we were scheduled to leave for Santorini the day after the race. We headed toward the Parthenon and the Acropolis before taking a tour of the Acropolis Museum. We took pictures from the hilltops and with other runners from other countries before grabbing a bite and falling asleep again before 8 p.m., which was a good thing since we had to meet with the team early in the morning for a group motivational rally.

I awoke to Ally already dressed and ready to meet with her team downstairs. I suspected she hadn't slept much. Ally and her teammates huddled together, motivating one another with their purpose for being there and who they were running for, getting pumped for the grueling race. I decided to meet up with the husband of another runner, and we would head to the halfway point to wait for Ally and his wife to cheer them on around noon. The race didn't begin until 9 a.m., and Ally's group began at around 10 a.m. with an estimated run time of around 5 hours, give or take, based on her training. This allowed the serious runners to run ahead of the pack without the slower masses of runners inhibiting their run times. I wished Ally good luck and gave her a great big hug and kiss. Then off she went with her team to begin the marathon.

We arrived at the halfway point of the marathon, theoretically two hours from the estimated start of the race since the husband's wife was a lot faster than Ally, and he didn't want to miss seeing her run by. We waited with other supporters and cheered the first runner as he whizzed by. More runners started coming around the bend, some dressed in Roman costumes, some barefoot or wearing flimsy leather sandals as if to experience how it might have felt to be in the very first race. To me, that was crazy because they were running on paved streets and not dirt roads. *To each their own*, I thought as I cheered them on while we both waited patiently for our significant others. An hour passed, and we still didn't see either of them. The husband was a little concerned, knowing that three hours was far below his wife's run time, and there was the possibility that he might have actually missed her. He decided to take leave and look for her at the finish line. This made me worry for Ally, but I knew that two hours wasn't past her run time, so three was acceptable. It must have been another 45 minutes before I saw her walking with another runner, literally in tears. I jogged over to her and asked, "What's wrong? Is everything ok?"

Ally was elated to see me as she forced a smile on her face. "I don't know what happened, but my shins hurt so bad. I thought I was already this morning, but something must be wrong. I must be dehydrated or something. It hurts too much to run," she said with tears streaming down her eyes as if she felt a little defeated.

Unfortunately, I showed up in flip-flops and couldn't run along with her for very long to provide some encouragement. "I am going to go back to the hotel and change into some shoes. I will meet you at the quarter mark and help you run the rest of the way." She nodded as she kept her waking pace before I rushed off to catch the subway back to the hotel.

I must have waited on the side of the road for about an hour before I saw her rounding the corner. At least this time, she was jogging at a slow pace versus walking and crying in pain, which was a good sign. I was relieved that she was feeling better. I began jogging toward her to see if I could be of any assistance. Not that there was anything that I could really offer her except for my company and encouragement along the way. I learned something about marathons that day. They were more than just a physical feat of conditioning and endurance. It was also a mental, emotional feat of the endurance of the mind. Running and being with yourself for that long with whatever aches and pains the body produces tests your ability and belief in yourself, challenging you to achieve the goals that you set out to accomplish. I knew that finishing this race was very important for Ally's mental state and confidence, not only in herself but also in her life. I chose to walk and run the rest of the quarter marathon with her so that she would be sure to finish the race. When Ally finally crossed the finish line, she was overcome with immense joy and relief, and I was so proud that she finished the race like a true champion and didn't give up. To Ally, the marathon was a symbol that she could achieve anything that she set her mind to. For me, it was a way to let her know that I would always be with her every step of the way, no matter how tough our road together became. We were a team in life; team AVO. Now, Ally was running a different kind of race. A race against cancer. The finish line was either life or death. All I could do again was to walk beside her and support her as best as I could.

Ally finally felt back to normal heading into the week before her second chemotherapy treatment. Ally always had some degree of abdominal pain, but it slowly grew worse even as her dose of painkillers increased and she was prescribed more medication. Now Ally had to, once again, mentally and emotionally prepare herself for the next round of chemo. At least she knew what to expect this time. We asked her oncologist if a CT scan could be performed after the first treatment, but since they were three weeks apart, he thought it would be best to wait, especially since most insurance plans wouldn't approve CTs so close together. We had to wait until after the second round of chemo before we could see what was happening with the cancer inside Ally's body.

March 10, 2017 (Ally's Healing Circle)

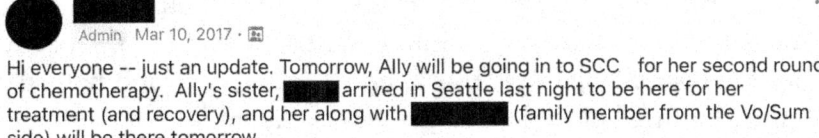

On Friday, March 10, 2017, Ally went in for her 2nd round of chemotherapy. Her oncologist prescribed the same two drugs, Pemetrexed for 60 minutes, Cisplatin Sub Dose + Hydration for 60, and he added Bevacizumab Sub Dose for 60 minutes, which was a biomarker that helped target cancer cells. The total treatment time was just over 10 hours. Since Ally's session was scheduled for a little later in the morning, I wasn't able to attend the beginning of her treatment but was able to get there before she finished.

It wasn't more than a few minutes after we arrived home when Ally rushed to the bathroom and began heaving and vomiting as expected. Ally's sister and I took turns supporting her as best as we could, Whether it was helping her up from the couch or the bed to the bathroom, making sure the toilet area was clean before the next round, or giving her a sip of water or some sort of nourishment to give her strength to endure the exorcism of the demon insider her body. I took the first night's watch over Ally so that her sister could settle in as best as she could since she just flew in from a different time zone. Ally's vomiting lasted throughout the night. With little to no sleep, now I finally knew what Ally and her mom went through on her first night of chemo. Nothing, and I mean nothing, that was prescribed to Ally to help her control nausea or vomiting was working.

Knowing what I knew from the previous chemo treatment, I called first thing in the morning to see if we could get Ally an appointment at the cancer center for IV hydration and medication to help her get some relief. We were in luck as the scheduler on the other line said that there was an opening late that morning. We packed a little travel bag for Ally, her meds, a change of clothes, and a toothbrush and helped Ally endure the morning before heading to her IV hydration appointment for much-needed relief.

I pulled up to the entrance and searched for a wheelchair for Ally to be carted around so that she could conserve her energy before leaving her with her sister as I found parking nearby. Once checked in, Ally was hooked up to her IV, and her body was given the much-needed fluids that had violently left her body during the first night's battle with the poisonous chemo that ravaged her being. Ally's symptoms somewhat subsided after receiving the first round of IV hydration, but several other patients were also waiting for relief. So, we headed home to see what the next night had in store for Ally and her sister.

It wasn't more than an hour or so that the vomiting continued as violently as the first night. Ally's sister, somewhat exposed from the day prior, tended to Ally's needs as her body continued to battle with the chemo. I stayed to help as long as I could before exhaustion from not really sleeping for over the past 24 hours crept in and crashed, leaving Ally and her sister to man the rest of the evening till the break of dawn.

Luckily the day prior, I had made another appointment for the following day for another round of IV hydration and medication. That way, it ensured us an earlier appointment for Ally to receive her much-needed relief. Unfortunately, this time it was even worse. After several hours of nurses trying to control Ally's symptoms, nothing seemed to work. Ally would continue to uncontrollably vomit and dry heave whatever remains she had to empty her stomach. That was when the Certified Physician's Assistant (PA-C) at SCC pulled me aside and said, "I am going to make a judgment call. I think we need to admit Ally to the University Medical Center (UMC). SCC has a special cancer wing there for our patients. There is only so much we can do here, and Ally's body isn't responding to anything I give her."

"Okay. When do we leave?!" I said worriedly.

"Just wait a few minutes. I will have the nurse call ahead to see if there is a room available for her," the C-PA said. "They have a whole team of resident doctors and nurses there who can attend to Ally around the clock in their special cancer wing." The phone rang in the room. "We are in luck. They have a room ready for Ally. Just head to the ER at UMC and check-in."

"Thank you so much for all your help," I said as I rushed off to inform Ally and her sister that we were leaving immediately for UMC to check Ally in for more intensive treatment.

I drove Ally and her sister as quickly as I could, considering we were right in the middle of rush hour traffic. Luckily the medical center wasn't too far away. I parked the car and grabbed a wheelchair to head straight to check-in. Since both SCC and UMC were in direct partnership, they already had all of Ally's medical records and insurance information on file. With a few quick signatures, they wheeled her up to the cancer wing of the hospital. She was promptly admitted, and a team of doctors and nurses began to attend to her worsening condition. A new IV was administered along with several orders of various IV drugs en route. All we could do was watch and pray as Ally's medical team did its work. An hour or two had passed before the doctors let us know that it could take up to a week before Ally was stable enough to be released. With only one visitor's lounge bed in Ally's room, her sister insisted that she wanted to stay with her sister during her last few days here before she had to fly home. I was sent home to gather all of her things to prepare her for her overnight stay at the hospital.

Unprepared for all of this, I made a call to (AT) to see if she could fly in on Tuesday to stay with Ally at the hospital for the remainder of the week since I had to work after Ally's sister's departure. I did not want Ally to be alone by herself without someone she knew by her side. AT immediately said yes, whatever we needed since she had the flexibility to work remotely.

I went home to grab Ally's sister's suitcase so she could stay at the hospital with Ally. I stayed as long as I could with Ally the first night until I had to go home to get some rest for work the following day. Every morning, I'd wake up early to swing by the hospital and visit her for an hour, hopefully long enough to hear her team of doctors report on the progress of her condition. If I couldn't be there, my sister, who worked nearby in the Health Science Department at the university, which was connected to the medical center, also checked on Ally throughout the day and sat in on meetings with her doctors. After work, I would head back to the hospital and stay with Ally for as long as I could and also give Ally's sister or AT a break for dinner or take a breather. This daily schedule continued until Ally was finally released and came back home.

March 13, 2017 (Ally's Healing Circle)

 is with **Allyson** ▉ and **Minh Vo**.
Admin Mar 13, 2017

Hi everyone -- just a quick update. Ally received her second round of chemotherapy last Friday. As I mentioned, the first few days afterward are very difficult, and this was definitely the case this time around as well.

Ally has been experiencing lots of nausea, and came back into SCC on Saturday and Sunday morning for hydration and treatment. Yesterday evening, Ally was transferred to ▉ Medical Center ▉ and stayed over night -- ▉ spent the night with Ally, which allowed Minh to get some much needed rest.

Ally will likely remain at ▉ for a couple more days to allow her medical team to perform more testing, and to determine how best to treat her nausea (so she can regain her appetite).

One very positive highlight from this weekend is that we received the results from her blood work, and the results confirmed that after one round of treatment, the chemo appears to be working. (Ally's cancer markers CA 125 V2 went from 173 down to 108.) Needless to say, we were very encouraged by this news!!!

As for what's ahead, ▉ who has been huge help this weekend, will be leaving this Tuesday. And, Ally's close friend, ▉, will be arriving tonight to be with Ally this week.

Let's continue to keep Ally in our thoughts and prayers -- for her nausea, for her appetite, and for the healing!

Below is a picture taken of Ally after chemo on Friday night.

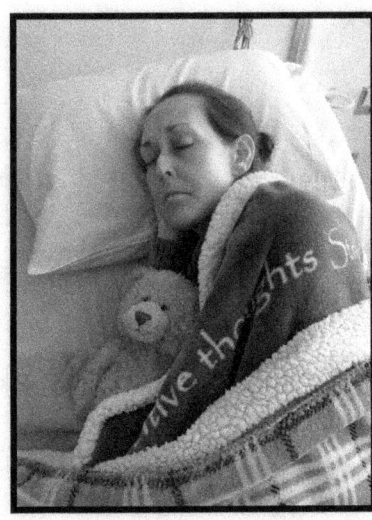

One good thing that came out of Ally's stay at the medical center was that they decided to perform a CT scan to see a deeper picture of the cause of Ally's increased pain levels. I asked her doctor to email me a copy of the CT report so that I could read it for myself. As I sat in Ally's hospital room, I began reading the report. I really didn't know if this sounded like it was good news or bad news. Sure, the markers were going down, but the main tumor was still growing along with new smaller lesions in the liver which weren't there before. Ally was staring at me intently from her hospital bed. I could feel that Ally was scared as she barked at me, "Minh. What does it say? Is it good news?"

I didn't want to alarm her with my own personal fears. I just wanted this nightmare to be over with. I just wanted her to get better so that we could get on with our lives. I walked over to her bed and mustered the courage to put on my happy face, and said, "Yes, babe, it is good news! The report says that the cancer markers are going down, and we are on the right track. This is a big win for us!"

A smile lit across her face, "Thank God! This makes me so happy!" The reality for me was that unless the tumor growth had stopped or other lesions were beginning to disappear, I wasn't really all that confident that we were winning. I had to hide my doubts and fears and just trust that our oncologist was telling us the truth and that we were actually winning the race against Ally's cancer.

IMPRESSION: CT SCAN 03/15/2017

Increase in the size of a large necrotic mass seen in the left mid abdomen with multiple other smaller nodular metastasis seen in the abdomen diffusely spread throughout the peritoneum. Multiple necrotic nodular masses were seen along the serosal surface of the bowel. There is no evidence of bowel obstruction. Multiple enhancing nodular opacities are also seen along the serosal surface of the uterus and bilateral ovaries. Overall worsening of the disease in the abdomen Bilateral small pleural effusions.

We did a follow-up visit with Ally's oncologist after she was released from the hospital. He went over the report and showed the growth and lesions on his monitor. Compared to Ally's original CT scan on 1/18/17, her abdominal tumor had grown from 9.1 x 7.1 cm to 14.3 x 8.2 cm, which was alarming to us now that it was the size of a small grapefruit. New smaller lesions were forming in the liver as well. Although it was startling, these results were considered normal with untreated cancer. Our oncologist assured us that even though the tumor had grown significantly, the cancer marker was going down, which meant that the chemotherapy treatment was doing its job. So, his recommendation was to continue with the same treatment since it seemed to be working in Ally's favor. He also agreed to perform our next scheduled CT a few weeks later at the end of the month as planned for a closer comparison of the two scans once the second round of chemo had enough time to do its job.

CHAPTER 16

CHANGES

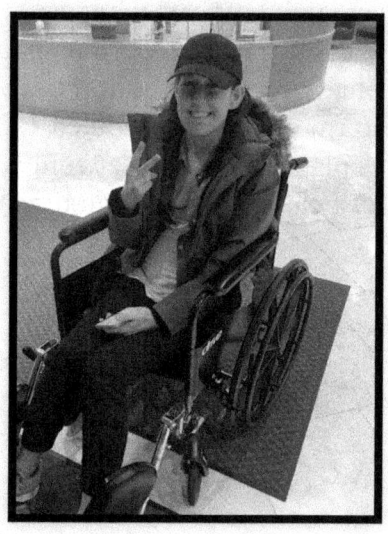

Knowing that we didn't have a lot of disposable income to pay for Ally's cancer treatments, a close friend of ours suggested that I start a donation site to help pay for medical bills, supplies, and possibly raise enough money to go to Mexico for experimental alternative care as a last option if everything else failed. I was hesitant and uncomfortable with the idea when it was first presented. I had too much pride in asking people for financial help and wanted to somehow figure out how to take care of it on my own. After a few days of debating and resistance on my end, my friend finally said that if I didn't do it, then she would start one for me. I thought to myself, *we could definitely use the money, and it would help ease the financial burden of high deductibles and enormous medical bills that were beginning to roll in*. I eventually surrendered to the idea and began researching which site would be the best to start the process. We chose a free crowdfunding site, and with the help of our healing circle and social media, I swallowed my pride, took a deep breath, and launched it.

March 23, 2017 (Ally's Healing Circle)

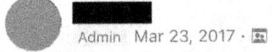
Admin Mar 23, 2017

Hi everyone -- just an update. Ally received her second round of chemotherapy on Friday, March 10 and wound up staying in the hospital for a whole week until last Friday, March 17. This was unexpected, but her medical team felt they needed to monitor Ally further because her nausea was lasting much longer than expected. (Thankfully, Ally's sister ▇▇ and one of Ally's best friends ▇▇▇ were right there to support Ally around the clock.)

After running further tests, they discovered some mixed results for Ally's cancer. As we mentioned, Ally's blood work tested very positive at the time of our last update - the cancer in her blood stream went down from 178 to 108.

However, a CT scan was performed last week and her tumor (and smaller lesions) has grown from 9cm to 14 cm since January. Her doctors believe this aggressive growth took place before Ally began chemo, but it is unclear at this time.

Ally's scheduled to have her blood tested again this tomorrow, March 24. If the blood tests are positive again, then Ally will remain on chemo. However, if the results are negative, then her medical team will consider an alternative treatment path -- including the possibility of treatments that are in clinical trial.

On behalf of Ally and Minh, thanks so much for your continued encouragement and prayers. We have also set-up a special fundraising page for those who wish to share their support for Ally and Minh in a more tangible way:

They will certainly need this support and our continued thoughts and prayers in the weeks and months ahead.

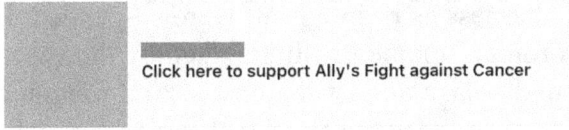
Click here to support Ally's Fight against Cancer

18   10 comments

Donations began to flood in from everywhere as family and friends immediately started contributing. Ally and I were completely shocked and tremendously grateful to all those who were donating and sharing our page with others, even people who we didn't know joined the cause. Ally was feeling good after her release from the hospital and after receiving news that the chemotherapy treatments were working and her cancer markers were decreasing. This gave her tremendous hope, and she was able to spend the day with AT, eating and shopping downtown like they used to do back in San Francisco and Florida. Ally returned home with a gleaming smile on her face that made my heart melt. It had been a while since I had seen Ally that happy.

Later that evening, when we were alone in our room, Ally's tears cascaded down her cheeks, catching me off guard. Concern etched across my face, I gently inquired about the cause of her distress. Her voice trembled as she poured out her emotions, sharing the depth of her vulnerability with me. She spoke of the cherished moments spent with AT, reminiscing about the laughter they shared over plates of sushi and the precious girl time they had together. It was a glimpse of the past, a fleeting taste of normalcy that had become so elusive. But amidst the joy and connection they experienced, a bittersweet shadow cast its presence upon Ally's heart. It felt as if fate were playing a cruel trick, allowing her to relish in the simple pleasures of friendship and happiness, only to shatter the illusion with a haunting whisper of doubt. The fear of losing this newfound sense of normalcy consumed her, creating a dissonance between the beauty of the present moment and the uncertainty that loomed ahead. As Ally's words hung in the air, the weight of her vulnerability settled upon me. I wrapped my arms around her, offering a safe harbor within my embrace. In that tender moment, I whispered words of reassurance, reminding her it was okay to revel in the happiness she had found. Together, we vowed to cherish each fleeting moment, to savor the laughter and togetherness as if time itself were suspended. For it was in these seemingly ordinary moments, illuminated by the warmth of friendship, that Ally found solace amidst the chaos. And though the fear of what lay ahead lingered, I pledged to stand by her side, a steadfast presence in the face of uncertainty. Together, we would navigate the intricacies of life, celebrating every glimmer of joy and finding strength in the love that bound us together.

"Maybe it was all just a façade," she said since she still had cancer and feared that she might possibly die soon. "I don't want to die. I don't want to leave you."

I looked her straight in the eyes and told her to believe that miracles do come true and that we would find a cure. It was all true. She was getting better, and the blood labs and CT scans proved it.

"Everything is going to be okay, and we are going to beat this thing." She deserved to be happy and pain-free. We would have many more days like this to come.

As she wiped the tears from her eyes, she said, "Do you promise?"

"Believe in the miracle because it's happening. We are going to beat this and find a cure. I promise."

She smiled and embraced me for a moment before giving me a kiss goodnight.

Time seemed to accelerate as AT left, and her father, JB, was about to fly in for a week to help take care of Ally. Jules would arrive thereafter to help with Ally's 3rd round of chemo. With all the nausea, vomiting, and increasing pain, she didn't have much of an appetite. Eating less meant she was obviously losing weight. JB focused on getting her to eat as much as she was willing while taking her on little walks during the day to keep up her strength and endurance in preparation for the next round of chemo. With such good news after the last CT scan, JB wanted to be there to see the results of the next CT scan. Ally started to get nervous about what it would show while trying to prepare for the next chemotherapy treatment.

>(Email to GI RN)
>
>**From: Ally**
>**To:** ▇
>**March 27, 2017: Chemotherapy and Pain Questions (Email)**
>**Hi** ▇**,**
>
>**Before chemo on Friday, are there any other meds or med adjustments that I need to be aware of besides the prescriptions I am currently taking? I've run out of Dronabinol and Dexamethasone and wanted to know if these two drugs are crucial to my chemo recovery. Also, I've been experiencing a dull soreness on the right side of my abdomen close to my belly button, that has now moved to my left side. Currently, I am taking 4 mg every 3 hours of the Dilaudid coupled with 25 of**

the Ativan, but I feel like I may be getting diminishing returns. Perhaps a higher dosage? Can we cover this after my CT scan today? I want to make sure I'm well equipped this time so I can avoid any hospital overnighters.
Best,
Ally

(Email from GI RN)
From: ▮
To: Ally
SUBJECT: (RE) Chemotherapy and Pain Questions
Hi Ally,
Your oncologist would like to see the CT scan results first and then come up with a plan and the need for additional prescriptions.

When you say that you may be getting diminishing returns, does that mean your pain level is not going down as much as it was before, or does it mean that you are needing more pain meds earlier than every 3 hours? What would you say your pain level is at now as opposed to before?
Thanks,
▮

(Email to GI RN)
From: Ally
To: ▮
SUBJECT: (RE) Chemotherapy and Pain Questions
Hi
I think the pain level is not distilling as much as before. Currently, because my current dullish pain, my level is about a 2-3 and I find myself more weary than I have in the past. I would assume the tiredness would have to do with treatment, but don't want to assume or overthink this right now. Will I be getting results from the CT scan today?
Best,
Ally

(Email from GI RN)
From: ▓
To: Ally
SUBJECT: (RE) Chemotherapy and Pain Questions
Your CT scan results will not be out today. Possibly tomorrow depending on the radiologists. Once reviewed, we will give you an update on the plan. definitely before Friday, hopefully by tomorrow or Wednesday.

Would you say that your pain level is tolerable? I will have to defer to ▓ **or** ▓ **to see if it's best to increase your Dilaudid dose.**

The next day we received Ally's CT scan.

IMPRESSION: CT SCAN 03/27/2017

1. 38 yo female with metastatic peritoneal disease, decreasing CA-125. Stable to slightly decreased metastatic peritoneal disease within the abdomen and pelvis.

2. Small volume ascites has significantly decreased.

3. Interval decreased size of segment 7 lesion in the liver. There are few (3 in number) lesions in segment 8 and 2 of the liver are new since March 15, 2017. Attention on follow-up imaging is recommended.

4. Stable right upper lobe pulmonary nodule, indeterminate.

Continued attention on follow-up imaging recommended.

Once again, the latest CT scan showed even more positive results in comparison to the previous one. Some tumors and lesions were beginning to shrink. The blood markers continued to decrease. If we moved on at this rate, it was possible that Ally would be a candidate for PM HIPEC surgery. Her oncologist considered her cancer to be stable and continued with her current chemotherapy protocol. Based on Ally's history post-chemo, the cancer center scheduled her for multiple days of IV hydration and meds following her chemotherapy treatment.

> (Email from GI RN)
> **March 28, 2017**
> **From:**
> To: Ally
> **SUBJECT: (RE) Chemotherapy and Pain Questions**
> Hi Ally,
> So, this is the plan we have come up with:
> **Pain:** Increase Dilaudid 4mg 1-2 tabs with a max of 8 tabs per day. We will refill the Dilaudid and Ativan at the cancer center's pharmacy by tomorrow.
> **Nausea:** continue the Ativan, Granisetron, and Compazine as you are now. We called in Dronabinol to the pharmacy. Please take this 2 times per day as needed. I asked the pharmacy to call you when it is ready for pick up today.
> **Constipation:** Since your bowel movements are irregular and constipation may be contributing to both the pain and nausea, continue the Docusate and Senna twice a day. Increase Lactulose to 2 times per day, holding for loose stools. Make sure you're drinking fluids and getting up and walking as much as possible/tolerated.
>
> You will not need Dexamethasone prior to chemo but your oncologist will decide if this is recommended for after chemo when he sees you on Friday. He can write a new prescription at that time.
> **Best,**
>

As much as Ally was going through, she continued to stay aware and concerned about my own mental and emotional well-being. When all of this started, we had to cancel our honeymoon, trips planned to visit friends and family, and a wedding in Arizona for one of my closest friends. Ally was almost healthy enough to attend, but their wedding date landed on the day of her 3rd chemo treatment. For a brief moment, Ally thought about rescheduling, but her cancer team emphatically recommended that she stay on her every 3-week treatment plan, as if it was the magical number that couldn't be moved. She pleaded with me to go without her since we knew that Jules would be in town to take care of her that weekend. Even if it were just to fly in for the day of the wedding and then fly back out. But I made a commitment to Ally after what happened during her first chemo treatment: "You and me, no matter what." As important as it was for me to attend my friend's wedding, I was not going to leave Ally's side again; saving her life was what mattered most to me. So, in lieu of our circumstances and with the aid of Jules, we decided to send a video recording as a surprise per the secret request of his beautiful bride-to-be. It was played at their wedding so we could personally congratulate the two of them on their special day.

On the day of my friend's wedding, I drove Ally and Jules to SCC so that Ally could begin her 3rd round of chemo. I escorted them in for check-in and got them both settled before having to leave for work. I pulled Julies aside and said, "Are you all good? Is there anything you need?"

"We are fine Minh. I will text you if anything comes up," he said nonchalantly. Nothing ever really rattled Jules. There was a way about him that kept everyone around him calm, cool, and collected. If anyone could keep Ally from going off the deep end, it would be Jules.

"I know she is in good hands. Thanks for everything Jules," I said as I gave Ally a kiss and wished her the best with her treatment.

Pemetrexed 60 minutes, Cisplatin Sub Dose + Hydration 60 minutes, and Bevacizumab 60 minutes were prescribed again since the combination had worked in our favor. Ally would be visited by a chaplain and psychiatrist assigned to check in on her overall well-being over the course of the 6-hour treatment. Jules would Uber the both of them home prior to me getting off work.

As I entered the door, Ally was once again violently thrown up nonstop as Jules and I took turns to comfort and tend to her with what little we could do. We stayed up all night making sure she was never without help, giving each other breaks so that we could both catch up on some much-needed rest before the morning came. Time couldn't move fast enough as we eagerly waited for Ally's appointment at SCC to arrive. During the day, we spent long hours at the cancer center making sure Ally received the proper IV hydration and medication needed to help calm her symptoms since IV was a faster-acting form versus the pill form. It was always a blessing to come to the cancer center for her hydration. On-staff physicians and nurses knew us on a first-name basis. We became a regular fixture in the ward. Ally always felt nurtured and well taken care of by the entire staff, as if we were special to them. Their motto was to put the patient first before their own needs, and they'd have to try harder if patients didn't get the help they needed. We were thankful every time we came to visit because we always felt we were getting the very best care while in their hands.

April 4, 2017 (Ally's Healing Circle)

Admin Apr 4, 2017

Hi everyone - just another update. Ally received her third round of chemotherapy this past Friday, and has been in and out of SCC   hydration, nausea and pain relief. She's back at home resting tonight.

We also got the results of her blood tests and CT scan last week and the results are positive. The cancer markers in her blood has gone down from again from 108 to 50 and her CT scan showed that there was no growth in Ally's tumors. This is all great news, and demonstrates that the chemotherapy is working. That said, ultimately, we want to see the Ally's tumor and lesions shrink so that they can be removed by surgery.

Ally's next round of chemo will be on April 21. We continue to covet your thoughts and prayers as April and May will be critical months to determine Ally's treatment plan going forward. Her doctors will also perform another CT scan on May 12 to see if there is any further progress in her condition.

Minh and Ally are extremely thankful that ▮▮▮ (Ally's dad) and ▮▮▮ (Ally's close friend) were here to support these last couple of weeks. They are also thankful that ▮▮▮ (Julian's mom) is here to pick up the torch and take great care of Ally during this first week of recovery.

A huge thanks to everyone for your love and support. Through your generosity we've been able to raise almost $16K to assist with Ally's medical expenses in just 1.5 weeks! Please consider sharing their ▮▮▮▮▮ story on Facebook, especially with friends and family of Ally and Minh.

Much love to you all.

Although Ally's cancer was considered stable and even improving, her health, strength, and weight were rapidly declining. Side effects of the chemo and cancer were taking a toll on her body and appetite. With constant nausea and vomiting after chemo and an increasing level of pain, Ally rarely had an appetite to eat. She was rapidly losing weight after the third round. She went from being 5'5" at a healthy 125 lbs. to now weighing just slightly over 100 lbs. in less than two months. All of her clothes hung as if she was a child trying on adult clothing; it was heartbreaking. I knew that if her weight dipped below 100 lbs. at her height, it could prove fatal. The body begins to lose its normal physiological functions, such as the ability to digest and absorb nutrition and begins to eat away at itself. I was beside myself with worry, and now she was no longer able to be on her own without some level of supervision. Julian stayed for one weekend to witness the severe side effects that Ally and I went through after a round of chemo. With each new round that Ally endured, the effects became worse, and much to my dismay, her frame continued to shrink. Although the largest tumor in her abdomen had theoretically stopped growing in size, with the reduction of her body weight and frame, the same tumor took up more space in a smaller body, which began to wreak havoc on Ally's ability to eat in order to stay strong enough for any further treatment.

Luckily, Julian's mom was able to fly in and help Ally and me for a week while Ally tried to stabilize from her 3rd round of chemo. She was like a mom to Ally. Being a former teacher, she had the patience and experience to help encourage people to do the things they needed in order to accomplish a daunting task ahead. Ally's diet now consisted mainly of protein drinks and meals the size of one or two strawberries before she felt full. Baby steps would be the key to getting Ally to eat a small amount multiple times a day. Sometimes it would be a few blueberries or chopped strawberries supplemented with protein drinks and other fluids that Ally was willing to drink. With a lack of nutrition, Ally's strength and endurance began to fade as walking to the end of the block outside of our place became a difficult task for her to achieve.

Spring had arrived, which meant that the famous Cherry Blossoms were in full bloom at the University of Washington. Being usually cooped up at home most of the time, I decide to take Ally for a walk to see the cherry blossoms in The Quad at the University. We would park nearby so that it would be a short walk for her. Ally was able to walk a few minutes at a time with my support before needing to pause a moment to take a longer break so that she could build up her energy to walk a few more minutes down the beautiful rows of trees that were in full bloom. Maybe 15-20 minutes had passed before we opted to sit on the steps and marvel at the view before Ally requested that I take her home so that she could get some rest. That was the last time Ally, and I were able to walk hand-in-hand together as her strength and mobility finally faded. She was now limited to walking from one room to another in our small two-bedroom apartment. We'd have to rent a wheelchair for transport if we ever wanted to go on an outing other than to the doctor's office.

After our previous follow-up with her oncologist to me, it was evident that Ally's health was quickly declining, and now everything was beginning to move in the wrong direction. Her oncologist disagreed and considered Ally's health as being stable, which was considered a success. So, we were kept in a lull period as we waited for Ally's 4th round of chemo to start.

Seeing Ally's condition deteriorating on a weekly basis, my sister asked, "What's the doctor's plan for Ally? She is not doing well at all. Have you talked to her oncologist?"

"Yes, I talked to him at our last follow-up visit. We are just waiting for her next round of chemo to begin," I told her.

"That's not good enough, Vo! What about immunotherapy or HIPEC surgery? Ally's health is rapidly declining. He needs to do better," she said. "I am going to make a few phone calls and see what I can do." Not being happy with Ally's oncologists from the beginning, my sister was enraged by the little communication and lack of empathy from Ally's oncologist. Without my approval, my sister took it upon herself to help Ally find a more suitable, compassionate provider. Someone who was more interested in ridding Ally of the disease versus merely extending her life with ultimatums instead of offering other possibilities and outcomes. My sister reached out to the CEO of the cancer center and told him about our current oncologist's bedside manner and his refusal to consider immunotherapy. He told her we would be assigned a new provider immediately.

Being this far into the race, I wasn't interested in starting over with a new oncologist, especially when we had one of the top mesothelioma doctors in the country in our back pocket overseeing the case from afar. We were still hopeful of enrolling Ally into her clinical trial immunotherapy treatment, which showed promising results. The only problem was that we needed two failed chemotherapy treatments to be considered a candidate for the clinical trial that could be performed in Seattle versus traveling all the way to Chicago. Ally's past three chemotherapy treatments were considered successful, with a 4th round scheduled in her regular three-week cycle.

At our follow-up, it seemed that Ally's oncologist was not very open to PM HIPEC or immunotherapy for treatment and stated that his end goal was simply chemotherapy to sustain her median life expectancy. This was extremely frustrating to hear for me and my sister. It seemed that Immunotherapy wasn't even on our oncologist's radar for consideration. All I knew was that Ally's overall health was deteriorating fast, and her pain was rapidly increasing. I felt like I had to do something and tried to broach the subject again with Ally's oncologist.

(Email to Onc)
From: Minh Vo
To: ▮
April 3, 2017: Follow up Questions from Ally's Appointment (email)
Hi ▮,

Hope you had a good weekend. Definitely, using Carboplatin vs Cisplatin has seemed to reduce the severity of her nausea to only one really bad night. Today after hydration, she was more so on the mend and feeling less pain and nausea after the help of the PA-C on Sunday.

I just wanted to ask a few questions in regards to Ally's Friday appointment. After given the findings of the CT scan, although nothing miraculous with no major

shrinkage and further discussion with you, we left the appointment feeling less encouraged and not very hopeful. This left Ally in a high emotional state in which she felt you have already classified her as median life expectancy for her cancer, which made her very distraught.

I fully understand and am aware that her cancer is rare and the success rate is very low, and that as mentioned you did not want to promise her something that might not be achievable. But when asking about an end goal, it seemed that your plan and solution was to maintain her on chemo for however long her existence shall be. When asked about possible HIPEC surgery, you had mentioned that it was not really an option. When asked about possible immunotherapy with Keytruda, you also referenced that this was not really an option as well. So just to be absolutely clear, what is your end goal, prognosis, and or possible solution and or alternatives for Ally's treatment plan?

With Ally quite possibly being the youngest to have this cancer. Having the right attitude and confidence in your provider is extremely important. Feelings of fear and hopelessness, although normal, can be a detriment to a patient's recovery. Fighting emotional stress and anxiety is a must for anyone hoping to overcome their disease. So, we feel that we need to have or regain confidence in your treatment plan for her, being her provider.

Blessings,
Minh Vo

(Email from Onc)
From: ▮
To: Minh Vo
SUBJECT: (RE) Follow up Questions from Ally's Appointment (email)
Hello Minh Vo,

I am glad the Carboplatin was much better tolerated. I am sorry that Friday's appointment was less encouraging. Though there are statistics for how people do (e.g. with peritoneal mesothelioma), there are no statistics for how Ally will do. My goal is to provide the care that will get the most for Ally. I have not classified her in anyway. The initial steps are going to be chemotherapy. The expected initial steps are chemotherapy. Surgery is most likely not a helpful option at this time.

I did not mean to write off immunotherapy. Right now, we are starting with chemotherapy, we will be trying immunotherapy at the right time. Most people get 6-8 cycles of chemotherapy and if a superb response is ongoing the clinical trial doctor recommended, we treat for 2 cycles beyond maximal response. We would continue the Bevacizumab. There is less data on maintenance pemetrexed in this diagnosis. If Ally's cancer was stable for over 6 months after stopping chemotherapy, we would resume this chemotherapy if/when her cancer subsequently worsened. We would consider at a time when chemotherapy is not working, something like Keytruda.

Ally is, somewhat by far, not the youngest of my patients with this diagnosis. Let me know if what I have said has been helpful. We have resources that may be helpful for her to talk about her fears and hopes. I will continue to do my best to help Ally and all of you through this.

(Email to Onc)
From: Minh Vo
To:
SUBJECT: (RE) Follow up Questions from Ally's Appointment (email)
Hi ,
Thank you so much for taking the time to respond to my questions and concerns. I did research the youngest peritoneal mesothelioma patient, thanks for bringing it to my attention.

Being so new to all this, I was basing it on what people have told me thus far. We remain hopeful.
   Blessings,
   Minh Vo

CHAPTER 17

FORGIVENESS

    Now with Julian's mother gone, I had to recruit help from family members and friends to stay with Ally while I was at work, even if it was only for a few hours. I didn't want Ally to be alone for fear that something might happen to her or that she would lie around, afraid and in pain, slowly wasting away. The care team at the cancer center added Fentanyl patches along with a maximum dose of 8 mg of Dilaudid every 8 hours to help ease Ally's pain, but the agony continued to worsen to the point where her pain felt just as bad as it had prior to using any pain meds. In the middle of the night, she'd wake me up with a scream as she writhed, clutching at her stomach while lying next to me. After speaking with the on-call fellow practically every night that week and exhausting all of our options, he recommended that Ally be admitted to the university's ER for further evaluation and pain management.

I rushed Ally to the ER and checked her in as fast as I could with the attending physicians on staff. Nurses began to prep her as the ER doc read Ally's notes and evaluated her for emergency treatment. IVs were immediately applied with a fentanyl drip to help control the pain, along with an assortment of other meds within her current arsenal from past treatments. Once stabilized, they wheeled her in for a CT scan to assess the current condition of her tumor. I immediately informed both of our families that Ally was back in the ER. My sister showed up shortly thereafter, receiving my texts that we were in the ER at UMC since she was usually on the university's campus early for work. "How is Ally doing?" she asked.

"I don't know. Good, I think? I am just waiting for the CT results that they took earlier," I told her.

"Well, keep me updated, and let me know if she is staying at the hospital. How are you doing, Vo?"

"As good as it gets. I am just glad Ally is finally getting some pain relief," I sighed. With a big hug, she left for her office to start her day. 4 hours had passed before the doctor came in to go over Ally's CT report.

IMPRESSION: CT SCAN 04/19/2017

Peritoneal mesothelioma with mild interval worsening of multifocal peritoneal masses and hepatic metastases compared to 3/27/2017. Many of the peritoneal masses displace, abut, and have long segment broad contact with many loops of the small and large bowel, but no associated proximal dilation to suggest obstruction and no evidence of bowel perforation.

The smaller tumors were growing! Feeling panicked, I immediately began emailing Ally's oncologist and his team to let them know of our current situation:

(Email to Onc)
From: Minh Vo
To: ▮
April 19, 2017: UMC ER This Morning (Email)
Hello ▮,

Hope you are well. We had a setback in pain this week, where her pain and nausea kept increasing as the days went by. Last night, I made a few calls to the on-call fellow, and we were unable to reduce the pain with her current medication. As stated by Ally at 2 a.m., "the pain feels like how it felt before we knew it was cancer, constant sharp and dull pain." We agreed to admit her to the ER at 5 a.m. when 8 mg of Dilaudid did nothing for her pain.

As you will see, the results of the CT scan has shown an increase in tumor size from the last CT scan done 2 weeks ago. We will have to decide whether to admit her for pain management or try to control pain at home till our visit with you on Friday and what your suggestions for next steps to be. In the meantime, what do you recommend we should do at this current moment before making a decision?

Blessings,
Minh Vo

(Email from GI RN)
From: ▮
To: Minh Vo
Subject: (RE) UMC ER This Morning
Minh Vo,

I am sorry to hear that Ally's pain is worse. I think admitting her would be the best option to get her comfortable. Once her pain is controlled, we can come up with a plan of what to do next.

(Email to GI RN)
From: Minh Vo
To: ▮
Subject: (RE) UMC ER This Morning

Would we still be doing chemo Friday? Or is that on hold now? I will ask Ally about being admitted. I know she is very fearful of being alone in the hospital. Hopefully, they will know the increase in growth soon.
Blessings,
Minh Vo

(Email from GI RN)
From:
To: Minh Vo
Subject: (RE) UMC ER This Morning
I will have to check with her oncologist about the chemo and get back to you, but I think pain control is first priority.

Another 2 hours had elapsed since the swarm of doctors and nurses faded in and out of Ally's make shift room in the ER unit, adjusting her meds via her IV. A luxury we didn't have at home. It was a faster form of relief not bound by physical digestion or rejected by the irritation or inflammation in Ally's frail body. The ER team was finally able to get Ally's pain management under control as she was now waning in and out of sleep to the steady beeping sound of her IV unit. The head ER doc came in to inform me that the hospital was full, so he was getting the papers ready for Ally to check out so we that we could go home. I thanked him for their help in stabilizing Ally and emailed her Onc and his care team the update.

(Email to GI RN)
From: Minh Vo
To:
Subject: (RE) UMC ER This Morning

After speaking with the ER doc, he said that the hospital is full right now, so she would have to stay in an ER room till a room opened up, which could be a while or even a few days.

He felt that since we have all the pain management meds at home and that we will be seeing you on Friday, that we would be okay. Ally is at a 1-2 pain level. So I think, since they do not have a room for her at the moment, we will try to see how she is at home. They said we can always admit her again if things worsen. I would say yes to admit if there was a room available. Let us know about keeping everything the same with Friday's appointment. CT report shows mixed. Smaller lesions growing, bigger has shrank a little, so mix bag.
    Blessings,
    Minh Vo

(Email from Onc)
From: ▓
To: Minh Vo
Subject: (RE) UMC ER This Morning

Hello,
If she is well on Friday I would anticipate proceeding unless you all wanted to wait until your appt with her new oncologist.
▓

Reading the email from Ally's oncologist made me a little confused. New oncologist? When did that happen? Even if my sister went ahead and requested that change, no one had contacted me or Ally to approve it. At this point we were too far into this. I couldn't fathom switching oncologists right now. We needed to stay with her original oncologist and the supervision of the specialists on the tumor board to keep things moving forward.

(Email to Onc)
From: Minh Vo
To: ▓
Subject: (RE) UMC ER This Morning
Hi ▓
Ally is currently trying to rest, but her abdomen still feels crampy with mild pain and nausea in her left upper

quadrant. As far as I know you are still her oncologist and we are continuing as plan for Friday's appointment with chemo, unless you feel we should wait or have other recommendations and/or obviously she has to be admitted before then. Do the new CT results warrant any changes in treatment plan or this morning's incident cause any reason to pause or reschedule chemotherapy? The ER doc basically said the doctors at the cancer center are the specialists and would make the call to admit her to the medical center if things worsened. Thank you in advance for your time and expertise in Ally's care and treatment.
Blessings,
Minh Vo

(Email from Onc)
From: ■
To: Minh Vo
Subject: (RE) UMC ER This Morning
REPLY: Minh Vo
Hello,
I had not seen the CT results. Did they review the CT with you in the ER?

(Email from Onc)
From: Minh Vo
To: ■
Subject: (RE) UMC ER This Morning
   Yes, they gave me a copy after the radiologist read the findings. I have attached a copy for your review.
Blessings,
Minh Vo

(Email from Onc)
From: ■
To: Minh Vo
Subject: (RE) UMC ER This Morning
Hello,

As you see in the report, it indicates cancer increased. At this time, we would need to place orders for immunotherapy, get an insurance denial once to twice, and then we can get it from the company for free (of course, we get it sooner if insurance pays for it). I will work on notes and orders to justify it. This means likely no chemo this Friday.

Reading his email made my heart jump with excitement. Hearing that we were shifting gears and beginning the immunotherapy route that was showing great promise for healing mesothelioma patients felt like a dream come true. We were no longer just trying to sustain Ally's median life span, but now we are once again trying to cure her so that she could have a better chance of survival! I immediately emailed back with questions related to the clinical trials.

>(Email to Onc)
>From: Minh Vo
>To:
>Subject: (RE) UMC ER This Morning
>Hello ▮.,
>Thank you for your reply, and thank you for all the work that you do for Ally. Couple of questions:
>Since the smaller lesions are growing, roughly how long do you think it will take before we may get approval and begin immunotherapy treatment?
>Do you need us to do anything the help assist you? Do we retest Ally for the CA 125 marker to see if it has gone up or down, and or test her for the PD-1 to see if she has it for best results for the immunotherapy?
>What do we do in the meantime to manage the tumor and its increasing pain and nausea since we are no longer doing chemo?
>Do we still meet with you on Friday minus the chemo?
>Blessings,
>Minh Vo

(Email from Onc)
From: ▮
To: Minh Vo
Subject: (RE) UMC ER This Morning
Hello,

I will order it and then we have to wait and see on insurance and such, that can take 1-2 weeks. If denied they will be asking for financial information from you most likely, though not sure.

The last CA125 was normal. Bevacizumab has benefits in decreasing it and decreasing peritoneal inflammation which is what it really is a sign of at this point.

We continue pain management the best we can, possibly enlisting help from the Palliative Care or Pain Management team.

We can meet Friday to discuss management of other symptoms or not, that is up to you all.

I began texting both of our families the good news that Ally was finally starting immunotherapy and that Ally was on her way to being cured! Everyone was ecstatic hearing the news, considering how the day started. Ally's mom was scheduled to arrive for Ally's 4th round of chemo, but now that was on hold, and I wouldn't have to worry about trying to find someone to watch over Ally while I was at work. I also reached out to my sister to inform her that I had no interest in changing oncologists at this point and that our faith had led us to this moment. She reluctantly agreed and offered to take Ally and her mom to her follow-up with our oncologist.

(Email to Onc)
From: Minh Vo
To: ▮
Subject: (RE) UMC ER This Morning
Hello ▮,

Thanks for your reply. Ally will be accompanied by my sister and her mom to discuss anything that you recommend or suggest for pain management until we are able to begin immunotherapy treatment. They are scheduled to meet with you at 2:45 p.m. Hopefully we will get approval sooner than later, fingers crossed. Once again, thank you so much for your help in Ally's treatment and care.

Blessings,
Minh Vo

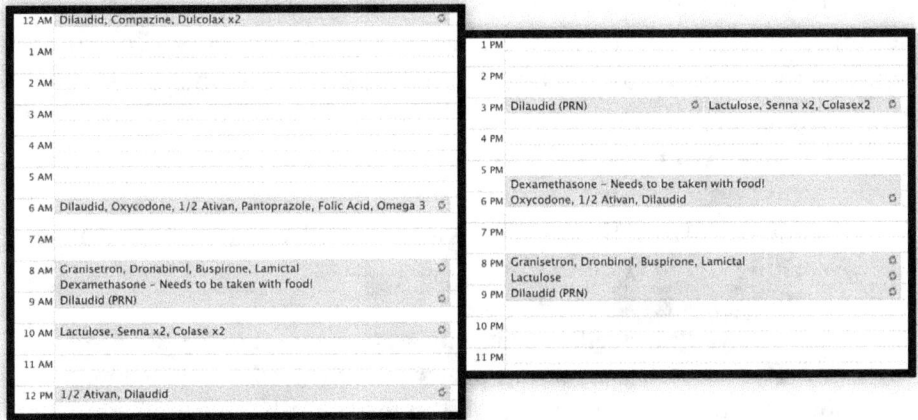

After the trip to the ER, Ally's pain and nausea had decreased to a level of 1-2, but Ally's pain had risen to a pain level of 4-5 within less than an hour of coming home. She lay on the bed writhing in pain as she clasped her stomach. I tried to subside her pain with the various meds that we were prescribed, but it was apparent that our current regimen wasn't working. After a few hours of trying to stabilize Ally with the given regimen without any luck, I called the cancer center to ask for advice so that she would be able to sleep. They said her pain dose was too low. They suggested increasing the fentanyl patches to 75 mg or taking 30 mg of oxycodone every 8 hours versus every 12 hours for her pain. I decided to go with the patch since Ally was so nauseous and couldn't really ingest anything without wanting to throw it back up. They also suggested Ally take promethazine (nausea) if needed with 8 mg of Dilaudid (pain) and 0.5 mg Ativan (anxiety), and lastly, to start taking dexamethasone (steroid) to hopefully help all her medications work better.

After being admitted to the ER and her past experience with chemo, Ally consistently needed more days on dexamethasone. UMC had her continue with 1 mg tablets daily for a week after she left and after previous chemo treatments. Ally was also prescribed to take an average of 6-8 4 mg tablets of Dilaudid a day spaced out. Things were obviously getting worse for Ally as the day progressed. Admitting her to UMC for pain management seemed inevitable. Ally's mom was scheduled to fly in the following day for the next round of chemotherapy, but now that was put on hold since Ally's oncologist decided to switch gears to go with the immunotherapy route. Ally would be assessed by her oncologist and their team that Friday to determine the next steps to manage her pain.

(Email to Onc)
From: Minh Vo
To: ▇

April 21, 2017: Ally Vo Pain Management Not Working Again (Email)

Hi ▇ & ▇,

Hope you are well. Ally has an appointment today starting at 1:20 p.m. Ally was doing pretty well yesterday. By evening she began to have some mild nausea with vomiting that escalated through the night. I left a message this morning with GI RN. Was wanting to get her into SCC to get her stabilized and have her meet her palliative care team early to help figure out how to stabilize her pain and nausea prior to meeting with her oncologist at 3 p.m.

Unfortunately, I have to go to work, but my sister can be reached by cell phone. She will be taking her in early if the cancer center can fit her in. I have included screenshots of her daily pain nausea management. Suggestions over the weekend by the on-call doctor at SCC was to increase her fentanyl patch from 50 to 75mg, which we had from previous prescription or shorten her 30 mg of oxycodone to every 8 hours versus 12 hours. We chose the patch due to not ingesting. They also suggested to start the dexamethasone twice a day, starting yesterday. Only other med is scopolamine patch once every 3 days.

Blessings,
Minh Vo

Later that day, the palliative care team at SCC recommended that Ally be re-admitted to UMC to figure out a way to help stabilize her pain that was, in essence, also causing her nausea. Ally's care team also sent orders for UMC to try to figure out a way to solve Ally's nutritional dilemma since she was no longer able to comfortably eat on her own. Marie now spent most of her time in Seattle, living at the hospital with Ally as they tried to figure out how to get her pain and nausea under control.

Instead of heading home from work that evening, I met Ally and her mother at the hospital to visit and check-in. Marie would stay the night with Ally since the inpatient room had only enough space for a single pull-out chair bed. In the morning, I'd come back to visit them before heading off to work again. On the weekend, I stayed as late as I could with Ally and her mom before going home to catch up on much-needed sleep after months of sleep deprivation. When the workweek began on Monday, my time to spend time with Ally was limited once again.

At work, I received a text from Ally's mom.

Marie: Ally fell while trying to go to the bathroom.

Minh: Is Ally okay?

Marie: She is doing ok. I notified the nurse to help Ally.

Minh: That is good.

Marie: I just wanted to let you know.

Minh: Thanks. I will see you two after work.

When I entered Ally's room that evening, I noticed extreme silence and uncomfortable tension in the air between Ally and her mother. The two of them had been confined together in a small room 24/7 for the past several days. With so much time alone together, it was only a matter of time before the many years of anger and strain on their relationship had to come out since it had nowhere to hide. It must have reared its ugly head and finally came out. Ally hadn't spent that much one-on-one time with anyone except for me in the last number of years. Already under a lot of duress and without being able to leave the confinements of the room, she got stir-crazy and said, "I need to do my walk, Minh."

"Of course, let me help you," I said as I unplugged her IV unit from the wall. She motioned that the bed alarm was armed and told me I had to turn it off and helped her out of bed. Marie then left the room, clearly upset. As we began to slowly walk down the hospital halls, I asked, "What was that all about?"

"Oh my GOD!" she said, "I don't know how much more of this that I can handle. She is always doting on me and won't leave me alone."

"Well, she is here to help watch and take care of you. We need someone to be with you so that you are not alone by yourself," I reminded her.

"I know, but you heard about my fall today, right?" she asked.

"Yes, your mom texted and told me you fell while going to the bathroom, and the nurses had to help you," I confirmed.

"It wasn't a big deal! I was fine! But she had to call the nurse. After that, they turned on the bed alarm to notify them if I got out of bed. Now I can't do anything without their assistance!" she exclaimed. "Also, I am your wife, and I should be the one to inform you if anything happens to me, and not my mom!" This made Ally extremely irritated. In essence, Ally, being my wife, felt that she should be the one to tell me anything important that was happening to her and blew up at Marie for texting me what had happened. Although Marie' heart was in the right place, Ally wanted to hold onto any dignity of herself and our marriage.

"Ally, your mom was just trying to help. You shouldn't be mad at her about that. You are going to be stuck with them for who knows how long until they finally release you. So, you are going to have to figure out a way to forgive her until then," I suggested to her.

"Fine! I will try," she said as she wrapped her arms around me to give me a kiss. "I just wish everything was back to normal again like it used to be."

"I know. Me too, but soon! Hopefully, you will get approval right away for the immunotherapy to begin, and you will be cured, babe," I told her.

"Yes! I hope so, too," she smiled. Seeing that Ally was beginning to breathe a little heavily, I suggested that we walk back to her room so that she could rest a little. I had to leave a little earlier that night because I had to meet up with a friend who wanted to personally give me his donation for Ally. When we arrived, Marie had returned and was sitting quietly in her chair. Ally kept her focus on me, still deciding to ignore her mom's presence till she could figure out a way to let go of the anger that she was holding on to. I gave Ally a farewell hug and kiss and wished the both of them a good night before having to leave.

I drove to meet my friend at a nearby pub, where he offered me food and a beverage as we caught up on all the mayhem that had happened to Ally thus far. Halfway through our conversation, my phone rang. It was Ally's mom. I excused myself for a moment, thinking something bad might have happened to Ally after I had left. I stepped outside to answer the phone. "Hey Marie, is everything okay?"

Marie answered the phone, sounding extremely upset, "I… I can't believe how horribly mean Ally is to me. She is blaming me for every little thing I am doing," she sobbed. "All I have done was fly all the way over here to be with her and help her!" Ally must have continued to rip into her mom about anything and everything, purging years of suppressed anger toward her.

After a while of listening, I finally had to stop Marie from spewing her feelings and gave her a reality check: "Regardless of whether Ally is right or wrong, or how mean or how hard she is being on you for whatever reason, you just have to sit there, swallow your pride and your emotions, and take it." I told her. "You have to understand that what Ally is going through is a thousand times harder than anything that she is doing to you. And I hate to say it," as I began choking my words, "but there is a real chance that Ally might not make it through this cancer. The one thing you don't want to live with for the rest of your life is the regret of leaving anger and resentment between the two of you if she were to pass away. So as hard as it might be for you to do this, you must go back and apologize to Ally, no matter whether she is right or wrong, and just be there for her through this incredibly difficult time. This is the time in her life when she needs us the most; she needs her mother the most."

Marie soaked in every word intently and said, "You are right, Minh. I am sorry. I was just having a moment. Thank you for putting everything into perspective."

"Of course, you don't have to say sorry to me. Just be there for Ally. I will see you in the morning," I said to her before I hung up the phone to return to my friend, who was waiting for me back at the restaurant.

The first time Marie visited Seattle prior to the wedding was the first time we officially met. Leading up to her mom's visit, Ally fretted over meeting her mom again after seeing her for the first time in a long time in Oklahoma on her niece's birthday. Everything seemed a little scary at first, but once she was actually with her mom, it wasn't as bad as she had originally imagined it to be. Ally and Marie's time together was about getting to know each other again to re-establish rapport since it had been so long since they spent any real-time together. It was a good starting point, and Ally was willing to be open to see where their relationship could go from there. Marie spent most of her time with Ally and getting to know a little more about me and my family.

Near the end of her visit, we planned a picnic at The Arboretum with Richard and Lisa. As we settled in on a nice spot in the park, we talked about each other's life experiences and what we had witnessed over the years. As the conversation grew deeper, we discussed relationship dynamics between parents and children during separation and divorce and how it affected one another. The reality is that sometimes life gives us things we can't handle, and we have to make decisions that are right for us at the time, even though they may not be right for others. But in the end, we have to live our truth and learn to accept and forgive those who are involved. At that moment, we witnessed a breakthrough in Ally and Marie's relationship as tears began to fall from the eyes of both mother and daughter. The words, "I am sorry," fell from Marie's lips, and a great healing took place that day between the two of them. We all hugged one another in honor and support of what had just occurred. From that day forward, Ally and Marie's relationship strengthened. Marie left Seattle with a stronger bond with her daughter, and they parted with plans of Marie visiting again the following year, which would be our wedding.

When I arrived the next morning, I saw Ally and her mother talking and laughing about some old stories together. Marie must have listened to every word I said to her the night before. She regretted the day that she made the most difficult decision of her life when she chose to leave her girls back in Gainesville and has carried the guilt ever since. It was time for her to make amends and be there for her daughter. She told Ally that she was sorry. Afterward, there was a big shift in their relationship. The two of them had smiles on their faces, and Ally was no longer angry and resentful at her mother.

You and Me,
No Matter What

CHAPTER
18

Waiting

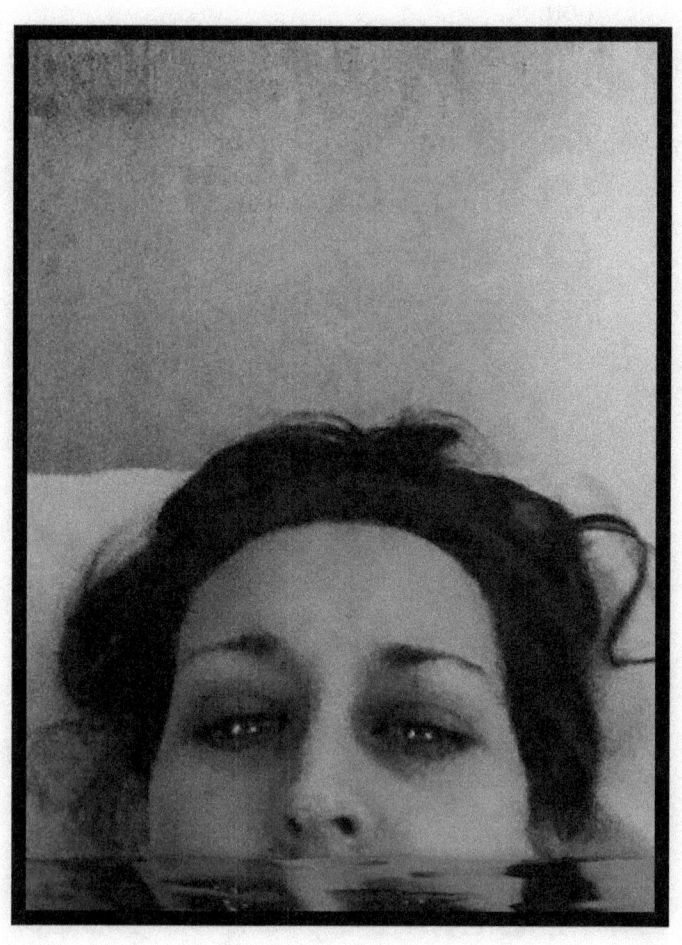

April 24, 2017 (Ally's Healing Circle)

Admin Apr 24, 2017

Hi everyone – just an update. There's a lot that's been happening with Ally since her third round of chemo on March 31.

Ally was scheduled to receive her fourth round of chemo this past Friday (4/21), but her doctors decided not to move forward with chemo and pursue Immunotherapy instead. (This is the treatment plan mentioned on Ally's ▮▮▮▮ page which remains in clinical trial. You can read more here: http://bit.ly/2oAx4ji.)

The last couple weeks have been very difficult for Ally. Her pain and nausea have been extreme due to the larger tumor and the smaller cancer lesions interacting with her bowels. Ally has lost 15 pounds in this time span, and we have been in and out of the hospital, working with her care team to manage her pain. Currently, Ally is 100 pounds and has been at ▮▮▮ Medical Center since Friday.

These two developments – Ally's weight and the growth of the smaller lesions – caused Ally's doctors to decide against moving forward with chemo.

There is some administrative work that needs to happen with insurance, but the hope is for Ally to begin Immunotherapy this Friday, April 28. To make sure Ally gets the right level of nutrition and calories, fluids will also be administered into bloodstream daily (i.e. TPN – Total Parental Nutrition).

Friends, this is an absolute critical time for Ally's prognosis going forward. Please keep Ally in your thoughts and prayers as often as you can. You can also pray that Ally and Minh receive "compassionate access" to move forward with Immunatherapy at an affordable cost, since this treatment is extremely expensive and isn't expected to be covered by insurance.

As always, for those who wish to help in a more tangible way, you can support them financially by giving at Ally and Minh's ▮▮▮▮▮▮ site:

Also a huge shout-out to ▮▮▮▮▮▮▮▮▮▮▮▮▮▮▮▮▮▮▮▮▮ who have already raised $5000 for Ally's medical costs through their Tips for Cancer Program!

Minh and Ally are deeply thankful for the generosity of all of you, and the way you have continued to rally around them.

Much love to you all.

A lot of things took place during Ally's stay at the medical center that would change her life going forward. With pain management being UMC's top priority, Ally was transitioned from fentanyl pain patches and pills to a portable patient-controlled analgesia (PCA) fentanyl pump, a device commonly used in hospitals that administered a constant low dose of liquid medication to help control pain levels. This device also allowed patients to self-administer an additional limited dose whenever their discomfort began to spike. Trying to figure out the right dose that Ally needed to stay at a lower level of pain was the main focus of her care team. Ally would need to stay connected to her new PCA around the clock.

The second priority was Ally's nutrition. They needed to feed her to sustain her energy levels and enable her to gain some weight now that she was down to 100 lbs. Since Ally could no longer eat any decent portion of solid foods without them causing severe pain and nausea due to the blockage from the main tumor, Ally was placed on Total Parenteral Nutrition (TPN). The majority of her nutrition, protein, and calories would be received through a liquid feeding bag administered via an IV pump a few times a day. In order to do this, Ally had to have a dual Peripherally Inserted Central Catheter (PICC) line in her right arm to allow her to use both her PCA and TPN when needed. Having another full-time piece of equipment attached to her body didn't sit well with Ally. We didn't have much choice, but we hoped it was temporary. Our faith now rested on the success of the immunotherapy treatment.

I became even more anxious and concerned. I tried to think of other options now that Ally didn't have anything in her system to combat the growing tumors. I kept thinking about how quickly the tumor had grown within the time that we had waited for her diagnosis before she was able to receive any treatment. These fears caused my anxiety to skyrocket as I kept visualizing the tumor rapidly doubling in size. I felt like the only solution was to expedite the process of immunotherapy treatment. I wanted to use all the donated money from Ally's cancer fund and whatever monies we had to get things started immediately until compassion access was granted.

(Email to Onc)
From: Minh Vo
To: ▮
April 27, 2017: Pembrolizumab Treatment Questions (Email)
Hi ▮.,
Thank you so much for all your help and the update of where we are at in the process. A few quick private questions:
Is it realistic to get approved for compassion access by next week (5/5/17) or the week after (5/12/17)? Or do you think it would take even longer from your experience?

How much is pembrolizumab to administer one treatment if we were to pay out of pocket?

Since there is no line of defense in place, would it make sense if we can afford one treatment to pay for it until we receive compassion access? Obviously urgency is always the best result and I would do everything in my power to make sure she gets the best result.

And would it hurt us acceptance-wise if we paid out of pocket for one treatment in getting compassion access? Thank you for your time in answering my questions. I am very thankful.

Blessings,
Minh Vo

(Email from Onc)
From: ▉
To: Minh Vo
Subject: (RE) Pembrolizumab Treatment Questions
Hello,
These are all great questions that I am going to pass on to pharmacy.

We didn't hear back from the pharmacy department till the next day. Our oncologist forwarded their reply.

(Email from the pharmacist)
From: ▉
To: Minh Vo
April 28, 2017 – (FW) Subject: (RE) Pembrolizumab Treatment Questions

I am the clinical pharmacist with our GI Service – but I am not an insurance expert and would defer further questions to our specialists in PFS and Pharmacy Billing. Given the high urgency of this matter, I have tried to do the best of my ability to help with your questions:

Answers to pembrolizumab questions:

Is it realistic to get approved for compassion access* by next week (5/5) or the week after (5/12)? Or do you think it would take even longer from your experience?

Your insurance may take up to 7-10 business days to approve or deny a high-cost drug referral. The referral was entered on 4-24. If the referral is approved by your insurance, she could be treated as soon as she is scheduled. If the referral for pembrolizumab is denied by your insurance, then a patient assistance program could be applied for.

However, I cannot tell you how long the Keytruda-Pembrolizumab Assistance* program is taking once an insurance denial is obtained. For that information, you could contact our Pharmacy Billing Department – Assistance Specialist.

How much is pembrolizumab to administer one treatment if we were to pay out of pocket?

A very general "ballpark" figure for one dose of pembrolizumab would be around $18,000-20,000 dollars. Please note that I do not have access to the actual cost at SCC.

Since there is no line of defense in place, would it make sense if we can afford one treatment to pay for it until we receive compassion access? Obviously urgency is always the best result and I would do everything in my power to make sure she gets the best result.

I would suggest calling your insurance to request that they expedite the approval. We have already done this. However, an urgent request from you may also help. Also, please see the answer to the next question.

And would it hurt us acceptance-wise if we paid out of pocket for one treatment in getting compassion access?

I was told by our Pharmacy Billing Department – Assistance Specialist that paying for pembrolizumab out-of-pocket may greatly hinder your chances of being considered for patient assistance by the manufacturer.

*Please note that the sponsored patient assistance is different than FDA-defined "compassionate use or access," which relates to the provision of drugs outside of clinical trials, not insurance coverage.

Please know that several people at the cancer center have been working to convince your insurance provider to approve this coverage urgently.

Thank you,

■

(Email to Onc)
From: Minh Vo
To: ■
Subject: (RE) Pembrolizumab Treatment Questions

,
Thank you so much for your reply. The answer to the last question says it all. We have enough money raised through savings and our donations to pay for one time, so that was my thinking. Anything to help Ally get a better and faster chance of succeeding, but if doing so greatly hinders, then we must stay the course. I will get on the phone again today and try to push. Thank you so much for your help. Seeing her in constant pain is very emotionally trying, but I still have hope and faith.

Blessings,
Minh Vo

I quickly called my insurance and stated Ally's dilemma to the case manager, who was also a nurse that handled insurance requests. Seeing that time was of the essence, she was very compassionate toward Ally's cause and immediately sent it for expedited review. I quickly forwarded the news to Ally's oncologist.

(Email from Onc)
From: Minh Vo
To: ■
Subject: (RE) Pembrolizumab Treatment Questions

■,
Update: I just got off the phone with my insurance. It is in expedited review. The nurse said she had received the file today and will hopefully have an answer by Monday. Thank you so much for your assistance.
   Blessings,
   Minh Vo

Time suddenly became our new nemesis, as we had to wait roughly two weeks for our insurance to deny the immunotherapy drug before we could be considered for "compassion access" that would allow us free access to pembrolizumab based on our current income. Without it, each dose would cost $18,000- $20,000, performed every three weeks. It was something that we certainly could not afford. It would take an estimated five weeks if we were lucky enough for all this to be approved.

A week passed before Ally was released home with a new set of hardware and a new set of skills for me to learn in my growing arsenal of nursing skills and patient caregiver duties. The first week of learning how to deal with the PCA pump was a constant nightmare as the fentanyl line would set off an alarm reading "high pressure." This meant that Ally wasn't receiving her pain meds. This often happened in the beginning, especially while giving Ally her evening TPN, which needed the PICC lines to be flushed with saline syringes to clear the stickiness of the nutritional concoction that nourished Ally. I spent many days and nights on the phone learning from the on-call pharmacist about increasing or decreasing the levels of her fentanyl in order to find an appropriate balance that provided Ally with maximum pain relief without making her overly high or incoherent. We also began to receive weekly visits by traveling nurses to change Ally's dressing for her PICC line to make sure it was working correctly before cleaning and sterilizing it to avoid contamination or infection. Bathing time was also a challenge now that we had to disconnect her PCA and wrap her lines in saran wrap so that nothing would get wet or become infected, as there were open lines leading into her body that could allow bacteria or viruses to enter. Everything had to be constantly sterilized and disinfected. It was a whole new world for not only Ally but also for me.

Sure enough, my new fears began to manifest. Not having had any preventive treatment for the tumors in over four weeks, it had begun to cause Ally's hematocrit (HCT – red blood cell volume) to drop, which meant that she'd need to receive a blood transfusion. We didn't necessarily know what caused this, whether it was the cancer feeding on Ally's blood supply or if she was leaking blood from her intestinal tract. Her oncologist wanted to do another CT scan to see what the tumor was doing now that Ally was losing blood. It had now been over five weeks since her last chemotherapy treatment.

All I knew was that life had become a steep learning curve with nursing, patient caregiving, and multiple weekly visits to the cancer center while simultaneously maintaining a full-time job. Ally and I had to lean even more on our friends and family to help during the times I couldn't be there, especially now that she was completely dependent on her PCA for pain relief. I had to give mini lessons to those who volunteered to help us when I wasn't around on how to clear the line if the PCA ever buzzed the dreaded "high pressure" signal. The instructions were so complicated to grasp within a short 20–30-minute teaching session that I would often receive multiple phone calls during work from our volunteers to walk them through the steps again on how to clear the lines, as the sound of the dreaded high-pressure signal screamed in the background. Without me physically being there to attend to Ally personally, the stress became almost too much, to say the least, as I turned to my own doctor for prescription drugs to deal with the many sleepless nights and the massive anxiety I was feeling. And then, we got the results of her latest CT scan.

IMPRESSION: CT SCAN 05/08/2017
1. Short-term interval progression of intrahepatic metastases, perihepatic implants and multiple peritoneal masses.
2. Small to moderate amount of ascites, worse, when compared to prior.
3. Progressive mass effect, on the stomach, rectosigmoid colon. Some contrast transit, into the small bowel however is seen.
4. New right moderate hydronephrosis, ureter ectasis with a transition point in the mid abdomen, due to mass effect from the extensive peritoneal lesion.

Ally's oncologist went over the CT with us as he compared the current scans to the previous ones, measuring the size difference, and stated that essentially all the tumors were growing and getting bigger, her largest one growing from 13.7 cm x 8.1 cm to 15 x 9.3 cm. The smaller tumors came close to doubling in size. While fluid from the inflammation was increasing in her abdomen, and her kidneys were swelling due to fluid buildup inside, that was most likely due to the tumor's mass pressing on her organs, not allowing them to function normally. What could we expect since Ally hadn't had any sort of treatment in over five weeks since her last chemo?

Things couldn't seem to get any worse for Ally, especially with her 39th birthday just around the corner. It was all so heart-wrenching. On May 9th, Ally received an early birthday present. We received a phone call from the pharmacy department, "Hello, Mr. Vo. I wanted to personally inform you that Ally was granted compassion access to begin her immunotherapy treatment." My heart jumped as a smile lit up my face. I couldn't believe what I was hearing. "We have taken the liberty to schedule her today for a 10:00 a.m. infusion at SCC, along with a follow-up with her oncologist afterward. Then she will meet with her Palliative Care team shortly afterward."

"Yes! We will be there! Thank you so much!!" I screamed elatedly into the phone.

"Details of Ally's schedule will be emailed to you. We will see you soon," the pharmacist said as he concluded the phone call.

I immediately looked at Ally and yelled, "Ally! Ally! We got approved for your immunotherapy! You are getting a treatment today at 10 o'clock!"

Ally looked at me and smiled, "That is great news, babe." Ally was happy in her own way, but the daily grind of pain and nausea was definitely taking a toll on her and her body. She slowly gathered her strength to get ready for her appointment.

I immediately texted both families to tell them that Ally would be starting immunotherapy today. We all cheered and celebrated with immense joy from hearing the incredible news. Ally and I were so thankful that we had several dozen cupcakes specially made; they were the same cupcakes we served at our wedding. I personally delivered them to her oncologist and his team, as well as the pharmacy team, on Ally's birthday to show our appreciation for all of their hard work. Ally received the greatest gift of all: the ability to fight for her life again. We were so incredibly thankful. All we had to do now was wait and see the results of the immunotherapy treatment.

Nothing would have made Ally happier than for us to have a normal life again. To hang out with our friends and family, have people over for dinner, snuggle up to watch movies while having a glass of wine, or simply cook and eat together. All of this was just a fleeting memory in our not-too-distant past. It killed me inside to see Ally this way. So, when it came time for her actual birthday, I wanted to take her out to a nice restaurant by the water where she could try to eat a few French fries or have a little something to nibble on. Something to resemble some sort of normalcy. Jules purposely booked his flight for later that night so the three of us could celebrate her birthday together, and Julian could spend a week helping out and spending time with his dear friend.

Earlier that day, Ally's pain levels spiked uncontrollably, and the visiting nurse was given authorization to increase her PCA to a new recommended fentanyl dosage. Ally finally felt manageable pain relief within an hour after the adjustment, but as the day went on, the dosage proved to be way too strong for her body. During a FaceTime call with her sister's family, Ally began rambling on about things she did that never took place. This seemed strange and alarming to me and her sister's family on the other end of the phone. We both went along with her delusion so as not to disturb her mood till I could get her home to try and figure out what was happening to her.

Once at home, Ally's demeanor was similar to a drunk person, wanting to move around wildly, which was so far from her normal demeanor and energy levels. Soon after, there was a knock on the door. I motioned Ally to come to see who it was. As the door opened, Ally was so surprised to see it was Julian. They embraced each other, and Julian put his luggage into his room as we waited at the dining table. Suddenly the lights went out, and Jules came out holding a chocolate-frosted cupcake with a lit candle. He then placed the cupcake before we began to sing happy birthday to her. Mid-song, Ally grabbed the cupcake and proceeded to scarf it down till there was nothing left. This was the most Ally had eaten in one sitting in such a long time.

Glazing over the bizarre incident, Julian then presented Ally with Tiffany's blue bag, something Ally truly adored so much. She immediately reached into the bag and pulled out the little blue box, and stripped away the white bow. Julian presented her with a special necklace that he chose just for her, a double-hearted green and black jade pendant to reflect what the two of them meant to each other. Ally simply said, "Thanks Jules," and disregarded it as some little trinket.

After this obscure incident with Ally, I knew something was definitely wrong with the increased dosage, especially when she no longer needed additional pumps of medication from her PCA to control her pain levels. Normally, you are not supposed to change dosages within 24 hours, but I didn't care what the rules were anymore. I just needed Ally to get back to normal and proceeded to lower the dose to the previous level prior to the adjustment. Within a few hours, Ally was much more coherent and aware. When I asked if she could recall anything from her birthday, she admitted that she couldn't remember anything. Not talking to her sister's family, not blowing out the candle, and eating a cupcake, let alone when Julian arrived. The special birthday that was planned for Ally was forever erased within the gap of her euphoric delusions from an excessively heightened drug overdose.

May 13, 2017 (Ally's Healing Circle)

 is with **Minh Vo**.
Admin May 13, 2017 ·

Hi everyone - just an update. This past Tuesday, in a miraculous series of events, Ally's care team at SCC worked as quick as possible so that Ally could be approved for ▇▇ "Patient Assistance Program" (subsidized treatment cost) to begin immunotherapy. This was a major exception that allowed for same day infusion, since Ally has had no defensive treatment since her last chemo roughly 6 weeks ago.

This was also a great encouragement to us because it has been a difficult waiting period with insurance. Since the drug is in clinical trial, insurance did not need to pay for this extremely costly drug. However, this past week Minh and Ally received the insurance denial information that they needed, and were approved to begin this treatment.

These continue to be delicate and trying times for Minh and Ally. Ally continues to struggle to find her appetite, is nauseous, has lost significant weight, and sleeps very little due to pain and nausea. She also continues to receive TPN and her pain meds via IV at home.

The latest CT scan performed on Tuesday May 9th, showed another increase of 3 cm to her largest tumor, as well as more increases with her smaller lesions. These new growths have caused the tumors to put pressure on her kidneys and intestines, which causes extreme pain and discomfort, as well as difficulty eating. Pain and nausea will continue to remain a struggle with the new treatment plan, but we are thankful that there is now something in place to help her fight back and move towards healing.

We are thankful for the support that Ally's mom, ▇▇, was able to provide for Ally at ▇▇ while Minh was working, and the daily care that their friends and family are able to provide during the weekdays moving forward. We also thank ▇▇ and her father ▇▇ for coming out this week to help take care of Ally.

We also celebrated Ally's birthday yesterday! Please join us in celebrating Ally's life, love, and friendship, and also in prayer for the gift of sharing many more birthdays and memories together with her in the years to come.

Thanks to everyone for all the love, support, and donations that all of you have provided in these last few months. Special thanks once again to ▇▇ store with their "Tips for Cancer" program that raised a total of $6437 for Ally during the month of April.

We know that many of you have tried to reach out to Ally without response, but be assured, she has seen and heard of all the love that you have given her and is so thankful to have all of you in her life.

(Note: this picture was taken on April 9 at the University of Washington which was the last time Ally was able to go out and walk for a significant amount of time.)

I was beginning to think that we could finally be headed in the right direction with the immunotherapy running through her body, destroying every cancer cell in its path. Ally's dad flew in to pick up the reigns as Jules readied his departure back to San Francisco. As Jules stood at the door, Ally leaned and wrapped her arms around him as if she never wanted to let him go. Jules held Ally close to him as they embraced affectionately. They then both looked at each other, and they said their goodbyes. It was reminiscent of when Ally left San Francisco to move to Seattle to be with me. When Ally decided, she was going to move, one of the first people she told was Jules. He was shocked that she would even think about moving since San Francisco was considered her home. He knew she didn't want to be in Seattle, but she wanted to be with me. Her way of spending quality time with him and easing the fact that it might be a while before they saw each other again was by living with Jules in his 300-square-foot studio during the past few months. It was also a sort of celebratory way to honor their deep bond. Before she left, they said their goodbyes, and Jules put her in an Uber headed for the airport to close a big chapter in her life. With everything that he had witnessed and had seen Ally go through since the start of her cancer, Julian knew that somewhere deep in his heart that this would probably be the last time he would see his dearest friend.

CHAPTER 19

MY WISH

JB flew in the same day to help take care of Ally and to have his own belated birthday celebration with his baby girl. The next morning, I dropped Ally and her dad off at the cancer center for a series of appointments before heading to work. Ally had extra difficulty breathing, which I assumed had something to do with her asthma, but instead, we received grave news from her oncologist. The chest x-ray showed that Ally developed pneumonitis in her right lung due to fluid backup from the tumor pushing on her stomach backflowing up her esophagus and into her lungs causing the lumen cells in her lungs to be infected and inflamed. Ally was immediately rushed to the medical center's cancer wing. Instead of a peaceful, quiet birthday celebration at home, JB spent the following week at the medical center with Ally as more life-threatening complications began to arise.

May 26, 2017 (Ally's Healing Circle)

is with **Allyson** and **Minh Vo**.
Admin · May 26, 2017

Dear friends and family - it's been less than two weeks since our last update, yet each day seems to bring new challenges in Ally's condition and the time since our last update has been no exception.

Last Wednesday 5/17, just a week after Ally began immunotherapy she began experiencing increasing levels of pain, nausea/vomiting, and shortness of breath. With her oxygen levels decreasing, the doctors discovered that Ally developed a serious infection in her right lung (luminitis) that was the direct result of the large tumor pressing in on her organs, causing fluid to back up into her stomach, her esophagus, and ultimately her lungs.

After being rushed to ███████ ER, the doctors were able to treat the infection with antibiotics. They also tried to address the drainage issue using an NG tube, and performing minor surgery to insert a stent for better drainage due to the tumor blockage that was created in her GI tract. Yet after all this, Ally was still vomiting.

This past Sunday, Ally began vomiting blood. After further tests, the doctors determined that's Ally tumor had ulcerated and that she is internally bleeding out. Apparently, this wasn't the first time Ally experienced an ulceration, but the issue is that there is no surgical way to stop the bleeding.

On Monday 5/22, we learned that the doctors are only giving Ally hours, days, up to a week to live, due to the fact that she is bleeding out faster than she can take in (after giving her four pints of blood). Her family and closest friends were notified immediately and have flown into Seattle to be together to surround Minh and Ally during this extremely difficult time.

Ally's last resort is to give her Octreotide injections to help slow down her fluid production and hopefully slow down or miraculously stop the bleeding of the ulcerated tumor. They caution that this is only a temporary band aide and is not considered a curable treatment for what they consider is inevitable. But there is always hope.

Since being on Octreotide, she has been able to maintain some stability with her hematocrit levels. For how long, we don't know, but it is currently moving her in the right direction. If a miracle happens and she becomes stable and strong enough, she will resume her immunotherapy on 5/30. But even immunotherapy isn't an immediate curable treatment.

Words are failing to express the deep sadness we feel right now for Ally and Minh. We love Ally so much, and her loss will be devastating. In the days ahead, we will cherish these remaining moments we have with Ally - every word, every glance, every touch, every opportunity to be with her.

We are truly thankful for you -- family and friends -- who have supported Minh and Ally on this journey. We know that many of you would like to see her, but due to the criticalness of her condition, the doctors at ▉▉▉▉▉ have limited visitors to family members only, so as not to place any additional stress on Ally. Her condition remains critical day to day. Please do not send flower or gifts, but please do keep her in your hearts and prayers for a miracle.

Once she was admitted, doctors worked quickly and diligently to resolve the lung infection. They tried to figure out a solution for the blockage and drainage in her stomach and intestines so this same issue wouldn't occur again. I spent the weekend with Ally and her dad at the hospital, JB and I took turns watching over her. Everything seemed to be moving in a good direction again when I left for work on Monday morning. I hadn't been at work long when the phone rang. It was one of the head doctors of the Palliative Care (PC) team at UMC, "Mr. Vo, I am one of the PC doctors assigned to Ally. I wanted to inform you that Ally's tumor has ulcerated, and she is losing a lot of blood." My heart stopped as tears began to fill my eyes. "We are giving her blood transfusions, but she is bleeding out more blood than we can give her. I think you should come to the hospital right away. I honestly don't know how much time she has left."

"I am on my way!" I screamed into the phone. I immediately dropped everything and yelled to Sydney, "Ally is bleeding out and might die. I have to leave for the hospital right now!" As I ran towards the door.

"Oh no! Go! I will shut down the office. Don't worry about anything. Just go be with her," she said just before the door closed.

I sped down the freeway as fast as I could, as I began calling my sister. Choking the words, "Minh! Ally is dying!"

"What?!!" she screamed back.

"Her tumor has ulcerated, and she is bleeding out. They don't know how much time she has left!" I screamed.

"I am so sorry, Vo. Are you on your way to the hospital?" she asked.

"Yes! Can you please let everyone know?" I asked. Not really wanting to talk to anyone. My only focus was getting to Ally as soon as possible.

"Of course. I will be there soon," she said as she hung up the phone.

I rushed to the hospital and ran as fast as I could up to Ally's room. When I arrived in the hallway leading to her room, JB stood outside her door waiting for me. As I approached closer with raw, overwhelming emotions coursing through my veins, I just collapsed into his arms and wept uncontrollably as JB held open his arms and pulled me in. We stood there for what seemed to be an eternity, leaving all my emotions at the door with him before standing in front of Ally, who lay unconscious in her hospital bed. I sat there holding her hand as I prayed for a miracle to happen, that she would just wake up and everything would be okay again. I just couldn't accept in my heart that Ally was about to die.

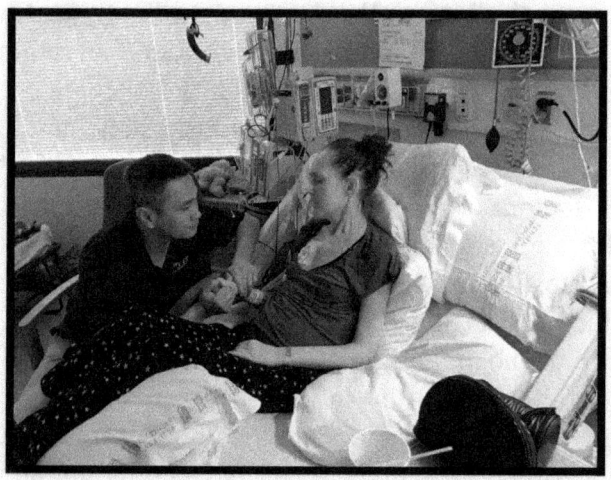

Thanks to my sister, all of my family immediately came to see Ally that day. Even my mother and her Buddhist companion Daisy flew to Seattle to perform a sacred Buddhist prayer and ritual just in case Ally was to pass so that she would find her way to the other side. Ally's family and closest friends were notified immediately of the direness of her situation. They were recommended to visit as soon as possible if they wanted to see Ally, possibly for the last time. The following day, Ally's mom and her husband, along with her two aunts, her sister and her husband, AT, and her friend Michelle from San Francisco, all flew in to see her. We were brought into a room in groups, immediate family, then friends, as the PC doctor explained the seriousness of her present condition, "As you may already know, Ally's tumor has ulcerated, split opened, and she is bleeding out internally. We are basically sustaining her life with blood transfusions, but unfortunately, she is losing more blood faster than we can give it to her. We will eventually have to stop."

I was becoming increasingly angry hearing his words. In my mind, I thought to myself, *'Well, keep giving blood to her! You can't just let her die!'*

He went on to say, "Sometimes it is better to let her go so that she can be in peace and no longer in pain. Now is the time to make your peace with her and tell her your final goodbyes."

Again, I thought, *'What the fuck is wrong with him! She is not going to die! You can't let her just die!'*

He then prepared us to see Ally. "Ally is drifting in and out of consciousness. Her condition is still very critical. It is very important not to alarm or over-excite her. So, I think it would be best if only two people enter at a time to say their goodbyes, and then the other two can leave as the next two enter." He then led us quietly to her room.

When Ally finally regained consciousness long enough to be alert and awake for visits, the PC doctor motioned for two people to enter and reiterated not to trigger anything that could excite or accelerate her condition. Of course, that didn't go over too well with everyone so anxiously waiting to see Ally. It wasn't more than 30 seconds before two more rushed in and then followed by everyone else. Ally was soon surrounded by all her family and close friends. Ally looked around the room and said, "What is happening? Why are you all here? Is there a surprise party or something?

The PC was in the room trying to some way control all of the commotion that had just occurred. He then went up to Ally and said, "You have been in and out of consciousness for a while now due to the fact that your tumor has split open, and you are losing a lot of blood internally. We are doing all we can to save your life, but we don't quite know the outcome yet."

When her family and friends left the hospital, and we were alone with her and her doctors, she looked at the doctors and said the crushing words, *"Please don't let me die."*

I tried comforting her. I told her, "The doctors are doing everything they can to make sure that wouldn't happen. Try not to worry babe."

"I don't want to leave you." Her words destroyed me. I had to remain strong for her, for us, so that she could get through all of this.

"You are not going to die babe. They will find a way to stop the bleeding, and everything will be okay," I told her. I knew that I wasn't being completely honest with her, but I didn't want her to be afraid, even if it was possible.

The only course of treatment that the doctors had at the moment was to feed her body pints of blood to keep her alive long enough to try to figure out a solution to this critical life-or-death stage. Then one of the doctors standing in the room said, "I remember a similar incident when I worked in ICU. It is sort of a long shot, but we used Octreotide to slow down the bleeding in hopes that it will allow the body enough time to clot and seal the wound." The doctors agreed, and orders were placed immediately to begin intravenously injecting Ally. Now it was up to her and God to let us know what would happen next. We all waited day by day, moment by moment, hoping and praying for Ally to miraculously heal.

As the news spread among my friends, I received a call from Derek, my long-time college friend. He helped Ally and me find a place to live in Seattle, as well as catered for our rehearsal dinner. He asked, "Would it be okay if I could swing by the hospital?"

"I am a little bit busy with everything going on with Ally," I told him.

"I am actually already here. Take your time, I don't mind waiting. I will sit in the visitor's area when you are ready," he said.

"Okay, I will pop down for a moment and say hi as soon as I am free." It was a while before I finally broke away to see Derek in the visitor's area. As I approached, I told him, "Hey Derek, thanks for coming, but unfortunately, Ally can't have any visitors outside of family because of the severity of her condition."

"I am not here to see her. I am here to see you, my friend." I stood there a little shocked and confused. "I know how hard it is to lose someone close to you. I went through it when I lost someone close to me to cancer growing up. So, I just wanted to come by and make sure you were doing okay and see if there was anything you needed that I could do for you."

It surprised me a little to hear this. With everything that was happening to Ally, Derek wanted to be there for me. We spent the few moments I could spare talking about how I was feeling and everything that was going on with me. I was deeply thankful for his thoughtfulness and was at a loss for words after Derek had to leave due to visitor's hours coming to a close.

During the next few days, without my knowledge, Ally was psychologically evaluated by the palliative care team of doctors. The head PC pulled me aside into a room and said, "We have been talking to Ally about the possibility of dying, just in case that was to happen. After our conversations, we have concluded that Ally has a tremendous fear of death." This wasn't any news to me. I thought to myself, *'Why wouldn't she want to live? Heck, I want her to live.'* He continued, "I know you probably don't want to hear this, but we are suggesting that maybe it would be best if we let her go versus trying to continue to save her life. We can only give her so much blood before we will eventually have to stop."

I was enraged, especially since I wasn't willing to give up on Ally's life. I had made her a promise to do everything I could to save her, and I didn't want to hear what he was telling me. "No, I won't do that. There is still a chance that Ally can survive this," I firmly told him. I just knew in my heart that she was going to somehow make it through this. He nodded and walked away.

Later that day, the doctor who had suggested using the meds to slow her bleeding walked into the room as he was looking at Ally's chart notes and smiled, "I don't know how this happened, but the Octreotide must be doing its job. Ally's bleeding must have finally stopped. She is not losing more blood than they were putting into her." We all screamed with excitement upon hearing the news.

"Thank you so much for saving Ally!" I told the doctor. Everyone in the room cheered and hugged each other as we spread the news to the waiting family in friends still in the hospital. Miraculously, the bleeding finally stopped.

Hearing all the loud noise and commotion from the excitement, Ally woke up to what seemed to be the Ally we all knew and loved. The first thing that came out of her mouth was, "Man, I am starving. Can I have a sub sandwich?" We all laughed and were so excited about the turn of events.

When Ally fully stabilized, we were finally able to take her home. I waited alone with Ally in her room. Ally's oncologist came to the hospital to visit her before her final checkout. He entered the room and said, "Congratulations Ally, you gave us a pretty good scare, but you pulled through and are alive and well again." Ally was somber and quiet, not really looking at him during his visit. He sat down next to her and said, "Ally, is there something on your mind? You can tell me if you'd like." Her oncologist looked concerned for her well-being, and I was so grateful for his help.

"I guess I just feel like I've disappointed everyone, "Ally said. "I did everything you asked me to. I did the chemo. It didn't work. I am doing immunotherapy, and it doesn't seem to be working. And now I almost died," she said as she continued to look down towards the floor.

"But you didn't die, Ally. If anything, you overcame huge odds. That's hardly a disappointment. In terms of the immunotherapy, it takes time for it to work," he told her.

"I guess," she sighed, not letting go of the disappointment so easily.

He then said to Ally, "If things did go south again, is there anything you might want to do before you leave this earth? We had a patient who really wanted to see Australia before she died, and the Make-a-Wish Foundation made it possible for her. SCC works with them, so we could make this happen for you if you'd like."

Ally sat there for a moment, thinking before she responded, "If she could have just one wish before I die, I want to know that I made a difference in just one person's life," she paused, "That is all I want." Ally wanted no trip, no money, no material things. She just wanted to know that she made a difference in other people's lives.

I immediately looked at her and told her, "Ally, you have made all the difference in my life, and I am so grateful to have you in it."

Her oncologist smiled and then turned to me, "What about you, Minh? Is there something that you and Ally weren't able to do that you think Ally would enjoy?"

"Well... we didn't really have a honeymoon, and Ally has always wanted to go to Paris," I said, looking to Ally for some sort of agreement or confirmation, although we both knew Ally was unable to fly anywhere for any period of time. Then I said, "No," as I shook my head, "I guess if I could have only one wish, I wished that I could spend the rest of my time with Ally with whatever time she had left."

He smiled at the both of us, "Well, if you change your mind. Just let me know. We will resume immunotherapy treatment as scheduled. Congratulations, Ally, on beating the odds. You are still here with us. I will see both of you again."

Now that Ally and I were alone for a moment without family or doctors around, I turned to her and held both of her hands. "Ally, there is a reason why you survived what you just went through. The chances were slim to none, but you beat the odds, and you are still here with me today." She smiled. "The immunotherapy is going to work, and you will be cured, and then we will live a long life together. You just need to believe that this is all true."

She put her arms around me and drew me close, "I love you so much."

I told her, "There is nowhere I would rather be than here with her. We are very close babe. Just don't give up hope."

"I won't," she whispered. We lay there in her hospital bed as we held each other closely. "it's been so long since we have been able to hold each other. It feels so good" I smiled and gave her a kiss as we drifted off to sleep.

I woke to the buzzing sound of my phone. It was my supervisor Tiffany from work, "I just wanted to call you to check to see how Ally and you are doing. Sydney told me everything that happened."

"Oh hey. Yes, it has been a hectic couple of days. I am so sorry that I missed so much work, but I had to be here just in case something happened to Ally," apologizing profusely.

"Stop it," Tiffany said, "I spoke to Dr. Kris, the boss, about everything that was going on with Ally and you. We agreed that based upon all of the recent events that you two are going through, we decided that we didn't want you to work anymore so that you could spend whatever time you had with Ally."

I couldn't believe what I was hearing, "What about the clinic and the patients? I still need to work for money and be able to maintain our insurance for Ally. I don't know how long this thing can last," I pleaded.

"Don't worry about anything. Take as much time off as you need to be with Ally. You will continue to get paid your normal salary, and we will pay for your insurance to remain active. I will take care of everything. Just focus on Ally," she told me. I couldn't believe my ears as I sat there and wept.

I asked one last time, "Are you sure about this?"

She replied, "Dr. Kris told me to tell you that you had more important things to worry about than working at the clinic. We want to fully support Ally and you. Don't worry about anything. The clinic will be there waiting for you when you are ready to return."

"I just can't believe this. Thank you so much, Tiffany. Please tell Dr. Kris to thank you so much as well." My one wish came true.

After we arrived home, I threw a mini celebration with her visiting family in honor of Ally's victory in beating death before they all departed the following day for home. JB was the last to leave Seattle and paid a final visit with Ally before his flight to Florida. As JB stood there in the doorway saying his goodbyes to his baby girl, Ally quickly ran to the bathroom to throw up. Out came a pool of bright red blood. JB didn't want to acknowledge that this was not over yet and that Ally hadn't beaten death just yet. He gave her one last hug and a kiss before catching his ride to the airport. I stood there looking at all the blood sitting in the toilet, and I couldn't help but wonder about what would happen next.

The next few days seemed fragile with everything that had taken place. Every time Ally needed to throw up, the fear of seeing a bowl of pure red blood haunted me. The looming question still remained: What if Ally didn't survive the cancer? Especially since Ally had been knocking on death's door less than a week prior, but by some miracle, she survived.

As much as I didn't want to broach the subject, I asked Ally if she would create a will for the "unlikelihood" that she might not make it. I had to fight back tears, but I was able to keep a stoic face. I didn't want to further upset Ally. She reluctantly agreed. I got out a notepad and began asking her a few basic questions.

"Do you want to be buried or cremated?"

"Cremated."

"What do you want to do with the ashes?"

"Spread them."

"Where?"

"In the water."

"Where? San Francisco, Seattle, Gainesville?"

"I don't know."

"You don't have to decide this moment," I told her. "What would you want to leave and to whom?"

Ally walked over to her drawer, grabbed her jewelry box, and began laying things out on the bed. She began separating a few different items that were precious to her and started making small piles.

"This will go to my sister, and this to Jules…" and then she stopped and shook her head. She looked up at me and said in a scared voice, "I can't do this right now."

I told her that creating a will didn't mean that we were not going to find a cure to save her life, but we just needed to do this just in case. I tried to encourage her to do a little bit more, but then she began to well up, and tears slowly fell from her beautiful blue eyes. That was enough for me to know that I needed to just listen and be there for her. I held her in my arms. "It's okay. We don't have to do this right now."

"Sorry, Babe," she whispered, "It's just too much for me right now."

I told her that we could try again a little later. "We will find a cure, and everything will be good again."

She nodded with her head buried in my chest, and I continued to hold her for as long as she needed.

June 9, 2017 (Ally's Healing Circle)

 is with **Allyson** ▆▆▆ and **Minh Vo**.
Admin · 9 June 2017 ·

Dear friends and family - Just two weeks ago during our update, Ally was experiencing internal bleeding, was vomiting blood, and her doctors at ▆▆▆ feared for the worst. However, on May 29, Ally stopped vomiting blood and her condition began to stabilize and so her oncologist decided to move forward with the second treatment of immunotherapy on May 31.

After this second treatment, Ally continued to show signs of stabilizing -- still struggling with nausea and pain, but her hematocrit levels are stablized, and she began to show more signs of moving in the right direction.

This past weekend, Ally began running a slight fever so Minh took her to SCC on Tuesday to run some tests and blood labs. Although her scans came up normal, Ally's white blood cell count (WBC) was extremely high, registering at 52,000 and increasing daily-- normal ranges are 4,500-11,000. It appears Ally has a serious infection, but the doctors don't know exactly where it's coming from because all of her other tests are normal.

For this week, the doctors plan to give Ally IV antibiotics to treat the infection. If it doesn't resolve within 1-2 weeks of treatment, Ally will have to be admitted again to ▆▆▆ or they will need to consult with an infectious disease specialist. Until then Minh will be taking Ally to SCC daily for treatments.

Ally's next immunotherapy treatment is scheduled for June 21. And, since it's been over a month since Ally has eaten solid foods, Ally and Minh will be meeting with a nutritionist to discuss possible food options. (Ally continues to be on TPN to receive the necessary calories she needs on a daily basis.)

With daily injections of Octreotide to slow down Ally's internal bleeding, we continue to pray and hope for a miracle. And, Minh and Ally continue to hope and pray one day at a time with gratitude and thankfulness. Please continue to keep them in your hearts and prayers as her care team treat this serious infection.

Special thanks to Dr. ███████ ████████, and ████████████ for their generous support -- allowing Minh to have this time off to be with Ally during this critical time period.

As always, for those who wish to support Minh and Ally in a more tangible way, you can do so on their ████████ site: ████████████████████████████████

Another long stay at the hospital brought more skills that I was required to learn to sustain Ally's life. Now I had to give her daily octreotide injections into her abdomen every 8 hours on top of TPN twice a day for food, PCA fentanyl replacements, and whatever meds she needed to deal with pain and nausea. But now I was able to be with her around the clock. To make sure everything was done properly and on time, I could also be there for all of her appointments and get all the information firsthand rather than email or by word of mouth. I'd no longer need to be dependent on other people to watch over her while I was at work.

Ally needed a blood transfusion almost every other week to combat the blood leakage. I assumed it was due to what the octreotide wasn't preventing or the fact that the cancer was still changing and growing and creating little microtears that caused her to bleed out slowly. With her immune system weak and fragile, Ally began getting spikes in her white blood cell (WBC) count. This could have been due to the immunotherapy fighting cancer, or it could have been due to the fact that she previously had a serious lung infection that made her prone to more infections. All her labs were normal, minus the WBC. So this meant having more visits to the cancer center for daily IV antibiotics. I just hoped that these side effects were from the immunotherapy doing its job, especially now that Ally received her second round.

At this point, I could pretty much do everything that Ally's visiting nurses were doing for her. I had no choice but to learn to be a full-time nursing caregiver. Ally was practically immobile and needed help with just about everything. I was more than happy to do all of it as she was the better half of my heart. This was my wife, this was our marriage, she was my present and future, and this was the promise I made to her: for better or for worse, til death do us part. I didn't want to ever leave her side. I wanted to make sure she was comfortable and had everything she needed, and was well taken care of. All my efforts would be more than worth it if the immunotherapy was doing its job to shrink Ally's tumor. All I could do for her was to try to make her as comfortable as possible so that she could live to fight another day.

CHAPTER 20

ONE LAST STAND

On May 31, 2017, Ally received her second round of immunotherapy. More infections, more fevers, more IV antibiotics, more visits to the cancer center, more tests and scans, and more complications followed. The stent installed in Ally's stomach wasn't really doing its job of draining into the lower intestines. This caused Ally to constantly vomit a brownish mixture of what was considered an array of stomach juices and old blood. As long as it was not fresh red blood, we were considered safe from anything considered serious or fatal. With Ally constantly needing to vomit whenever her stomach became too full, the suggestion of installing a peg tube in her stomach was recommended. This way, we could empty the contents of her stomach via an installed tube instead of her constantly throwing it up. Once installed, Ally wouldn't be unable to eat any sort of solid food again, given the chance that it could get stuck in the tube. The thought of this was life-changing since good food was one of Ally's passions in life. It took Ally a few days to consider this option. In the end, we decided to go through with the procedure to give Ally some relief, especially since it had been so long since she'd eaten any sort of real food.

The last time I saw Ally eat solid food was when I brought her to her favorite spot on the water at Richard and Lisa's condo. I stopped off at the local market and picked up organic popsicles and an overly ripened donut peach. I carefully peeled away the skin and cut the flesh into tiny bite-size pieces. "Ally, be sure to chew completely before you swallow it," I told her before I put it on a spoon and fed it to her. But as she ate the first piece, the peach just slid down her throat. It was so soft and juicy.

"Mmmm ... This tastes so good, Babe," she said and squealed with joy. As concerned as I was, Ally was so happy since she hadn't tasted food in a very long time. I decided to let her enjoy her moment of happiness since they were so few and far between.

After the peg tube evaluation, Ally was not considered a good candidate for the surgery. The space that was left on her abdomen was barely large enough to allow this procedure to take place. Even if they were to perform a successful surgery, the placement of the tube exiting Ally's body would rub and irritate her rib cage. This would cause her additional discomfort on top of the constant pain that she already had. I honestly can't recall if I was happy or upset when I heard this news. The idea of Ally no longer being able to eat solid food was already hard for me to accept, but I didn't want her to constantly vomit, either. Ally would have to continue to empty the contents of her stomach by vomiting. To try and help reduce this, she was switched to a low-residue diet with no hard or fibrous foods. This would prevent food from getting stuck in her digestive tract, and it wouldn't affect the stent that was in place for drainage. Ally now had to receive most of her nutrition via TPN and small sips of water or juices whenever she felt parched.

During this time, I did my best to give us some sort of normalcy. I took her to various parks where we could sit and look out at the water; we'd drive to Snoqualmie Falls to enjoy the scenery. In Snoqualmie, I'd wheel her up to the nearby hotel restaurant so she could enjoy something to drink while looking at the majestic waterfall outside the restaurant's big scenic windows. I'd ask her if she wanted to go somewhere for the night and have a romantic getaway together, but knowing all the stuff we would have to bring along with us to make that happen, she always opted out and was content with being home alone with me.

Our friend visitation request list was long. We had to narrow it down to how much energy Ally had for visits and who she really wanted to see. We'd try to reenact the times when all of us hung out together. It would last until she got too tired and had to go lie down to rest. Ally did this because she, too, also wanted me to have a somewhat normal life in the midst of this chaos. She always tried her best because she wanted to see me happy. Ally preferred one-on-one time with no more than two people and became overwhelmed when there were too many around. This pretty much meant no more family gatherings. Ally especially enjoyed visits with friends who came to see her from out of town. They would reminisce about the past and the good times back in San Francisco or in Florida. Far away from the current nightmare that we were living.

On June 21, 2017, Ally received her third round of immunotherapy. Shortly before receiving the treatment, all of the infections and antibiotic treatments finally subsided but were now replaced with a new complication: Ally's body was beginning to react to the immunotherapy treatment. At first, she noticed a few small red spots forming on her neck and chest. These began to itch a little, but after a few more days, the spots grew larger, covering most of her body and legs. When she was finally seen by her oncologist, we asked him about the large red blotches that Ally kept getting. As he began examining Ally's face, her limbs, and other parts of her body, he said, "Ally is developing what we call an immunotherapy rash, and by the looks of it, it is pretty advanced. Basically, Ally's body is rejecting the drug." He then began typing on his computer to put in orders and went on to say, "We need to stop her treatments for now. Any further treatments with the drug could cause her severe problems. We need to begin treating her with corticosteroids to calm the inflammation." Ally sighed as she sat quietly in her wheelchair, deep in her thoughts.

My heart sank upon hearing this news. I immediately asked, "Once the rash is under control, could we resume treatment?"

"Unfortunately, no, because it would likely happen again and could cause something worse. Ally has another CT scan coming up that will give us more information, and then we can figure out the next steps," he said as we concluded our appointment.

"Let's go home," Ally murmured. I couldn't imagine what was going through her head since my own thoughts were racing, looking for answers to even just one single question. What are we going to do now? We had to wait for the results of the next scheduled CT as we began her corticosteroid treatments to see whether the immunotherapy drug was killing the cancer cells.

IMPRESSION: CT SCAN 07/11/2017
1. Dominant necrotic intraperitoneal/omental mass unchanged in overall size and involvement of the surrounding bowel compared to prior examination. Slight decrease in size of the mass in the left inferior abdomen. Unchanged omental/peritoneal nodularity.
2. Significant progression of diffuse hepatic metastases, which have increased in number and size of the index lesions.
3. Stable bilateral small pleural effusions.

The following day we went over the results of the CT scan with Ally's oncologist. To me, the scan seemed positive since there was no increase in her largest tumor, and the smaller ones were shrinking. Unfortunately, Ally's original oncologist didn't agree. He told us, "If the immunotherapy had worked, all of the tumors would have reduced in size. The fact that the liver tumors are multiplying in number means that it has spread in the liver. Unfortunately, at this point, there is nothing more I can do."

Tears began rolling down my face as I began to plead, "Can we try to continue the immunotherapy again? Are there, not any alternative solutions we could come up with to help Ally heal? What about surgery?"

He replied, "I already asked the tumor board about the possibility of surgery and removing the tumor. They told me that she wouldn't be strong enough to survive the surgery." Knowing that there was no better way of saying things, he finally said, "I am so sorry, but there is nothing else we can do for Ally. I think it is best to begin hospice care to make Ally as comfortable as she can and enjoy whatever time you have left with each other."

Ally sat there calmly and grabbed my arm. "Babe, let's go home. I just want to go home."

During the car ride home, I was unbearably sad yet angry at the same time. *Why is all of this happening to us?*

Ally sat quietly and stared out the window. My mind was racing as I tried to figure out what I could say to Ally to raise her spirits and how I would tell our family about this news that was just given to us. To tell them that we had to start hospice so that they could make Ally as comfortable as possible and enjoy whatever time we had left together.

When we arrived home, Ally went into our room and began calling her family to personally let them know how the appointment ended. I could her crying softly as she tried to inform them that we had exhausted all of our options and that there was nothing more that the doctors could do to help her.

An hour had passed as I sat out in the living room, deep in my thoughts. Then all of a sudden, it dawned on me. We still had one option left: Mexico! I rushed into our bedroom, where Ally was still talking to one of her family members, and yelled, "We are not giving up! We still have a chance! We were going to Mexico to find you a cure!" This was a recommendation that was suggested when all of this started, but we couldn't afford to do it since it cost so much, and none of the clinics down there took insurance. Now, we had raised enough money, and I had already done all of the research necessary -- deciding on the best clinics in Mexico for Ally's treatments if and when the time came down to this.

"Do not lose hope!" I texted everyone. We are going to continue our fight in Mexico. Tears of sadness became tears of hope and joy as I shared the news with our families. Later that night, while lying in our bed, knowing everything that we had been through earlier that day, I turned to Ally and asked, "How are you doing with everything that happened today? Are you ready to go to Mexico?"

She looked at me and said, "I am a little nervous, to be honest with you."

"Why are you nervous, Ally?" I asked.

"I don't know. You heard what the doctor said. What if the treatment in Mexico doesn't work?" she said fearfully.

"It has to work, Ally," I emphasized, "It is the only thing that we have left. They will find a cure for you."

She just smiled as she caressed my face with both hands and said, "I don't want to leave you, Babe." Then she kissed my lips.

"You won't. I won't let that happen," I told her as I held her hand as I fell asleep.

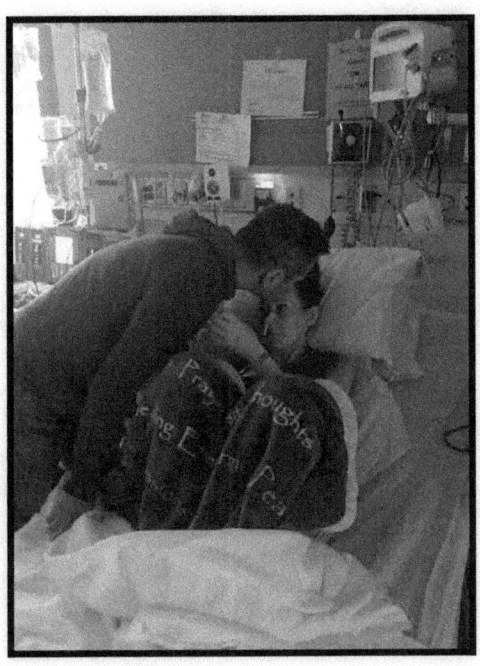

July 16, 2017 (Ally's Healing Circle)

 is with Allyson ▮▮▮ and Minh Vo.

Dear family and friends,

It has been a little over a month since our last update, and a little over two months since Ally began her immunotherapy treatment. Ally seemed to be responding well to the treatment overall, with the exception of an infection that lasted a couple of weeks. Ally received her third immunotherapy treatment on June 21.

Shortly after her third treatment, Ally began to develop a severe rash that spread all over her body. It was originally thought to be related to a new medication, but continued to spread even after a round of steroids. This led her oncologist to suspect that the rash was the result of the immunotherapy.

On July 11, the results of the long-awaited CT scan began showing some improvements -- the large tumor in Ally's abdomen showed no new growth, a smaller one had shrunken, and there was less swelling.

Unfortunately, the results also showed that the tumors on her liver multiplied significantly and increased in size. In April, there were 4-5 small lesions, but this number has tripled.

Based on the CT scan results, Ally's oncologist concluded that the immunotherapy was not effective. The treatment should be reducing the tumors on her organs (not multiplying them). Due to these findings and the severe rash, Ally's care team communicated that the best course of action is to discontinue treatment. They also communicated that they have no other treatment alternatives, and suggested hospice care for better quality of life, for however long that may be. Their rationale is that they don't want to cause Ally more pain and suffering, and continue this treatment just to do something.

Needless to say, we were shocked and deeply devastated when we heard this news. However, the first thing Minh told us was, "DO NOT LOSE HOPE!" He has been researching alternative treatment plans since the beginning after reading about Paul Kraus' battle (the longest peritoneal mesothelioma survivor of 20 years), who accredits his survival to diet, mental state of mind, and ozone therapy. Minh's research led him to consider Mexico, where they are conducting some of the most advanced alternative therapies for cancer treatment without the administrative hindrance of the FDA.

Minh found a treatment center based in Arizona whose cancer hospital resides just across the border in Mexico near Yuma, administering an immunotherapy program that focuses on comprehensive experimental treatments consisting of ozone therapy, dendritic cell therapy, and various I.V. therapies. This combination of treatments work to boost the immune system to attack and shrink her tumors. Mexico was always on the back burner for Ally and Minh if Keytruda would fail them.

Minh and Ally are preparing to fly to Arizona this Friday, 7/21, to begin their final option for Ally's fight against cancer. This comprehensive immunotherapy treatment program is costly, and is not covered by insurance. We anticipate that the cost of this program to be well over $30K, with additional costs for follow up visits, labs, and diagnostics for the following 6 months. But this will all be worth it, if it gets Ally the results that we have been desperately seeking.

While words cannot express how deeply saddened we are by the results of the recent immunotherapy and current prognosis, we, too, are not going to lose hope.

For those who wish to support Minh & Ally in some tangible way, you can continue to do so by sharing and visiting their ▇▇▇ site ▇▇▇▇▇▇▇ ▇▇▇▇▇▇▇▇▇▇ Thank you for your constant love and support throughout this journey – Ally and Minh love you all so very much, and are so thankful for the support and encouragement they have continued to receive from all of you.

Special thanks to ▇▇▇▇▇▇ for hosting a volleyball tournament fundraiser, ▇▇▇ ▇▇▇▇▇▇▇▇ for donating her fees for services, and continued thanks Dr. ▇▇ ▇▇▇▇▇ and ▇▇▇▇▇▇▇▇▇ in supporting Ally and Minh during this extremely difficult time, so that Minh can spend his time focusing on Ally's health and wellbeing, as they search for a cure.

(Photo was taken May 24 when Ally was admitted to ▇▇▇▇ for internal bleeding as result of her ulcerated tumor.)

Over the next few days, I arranged everything necessary after we had chosen what we thought was the most successful and comprehensive treatment facility for Ally. I called up my friend Todd, who lived in Arizona, and told him of our plans to fly into Phoenix to allow Ally to rest a few days before heading down to Mexico for the 12-day intensive treatment. He offered to drive us down to the Mexico border, where we would be picked up the following day by shuttle to cross the border.

At Ally's next follow-up visit with her oncologist, I informed him that we were going to Arizona to get away for a little bit and do some alternative treatments, such as high-dose vitamin C and a few others, since there was nothing else that the cancer center could do for us. He told us that it would be fine and cautioned us that it was experimental and not to spend a whole lot of money on it. The fact was, we had used all the money raised to pay for Ally's Mexico treatments. For some unknown reason, I didn't want him to know about our plans to resume her cancer treatment in Mexico. Maybe I was still mad at him for telling us to go home and enjoy the rest of our time together. Maybe I just wanted to prove him wrong that we were going to cure Ally. Regardless, I felt that it was none of his business. Especially now, since I felt they had given up on us.

With the corticosteroids Ally was given to treat her rash, her energy level was unusually similar to that of the days in between chemo treatments. Ally was strong enough to actually walk short distances on her own without the use of a wheelchair. We took advantage of her newfound strength as we prepared her for the heat of Arizona and Mexico, which were hitting 100+ degrees during the August months. We went shopping at various stores, that Ally had chosen to pick out shorts, T-shirts, and loose dresses for her to wear. She would try them on to make sure she liked them, and they had to fit properly and make her feel good about herself.

When we were at H&M, I picked out an array of clothes for her and suggested that she try them on in the handicap dressing room that provided an extra-large place for her to sit. When I headed back to the dressing rooms and saw that the handicapped room was empty, I became immediately became anxious and called out, "Ally! Ally!" in hopes that bad nothing had happened to her.

She opened the door from a small stall and called, "I am over here."

"Why are you in the small changing room? What happened to the handicapped room?" I asked her.

"They told me that I had to use this room," as she pointed over to the gentleman that was cleaning out a stall nearby.

I was furious as I walked Ally over to the attendant and screamed, "Why did you not let my wife use the handicap changing room?"

He looked at me and said, "Sir, that room is reserved for our handicap customers."

I grabbed Ally's hand and showed him her PCA pump that was attached to her arm and yelled, "She is handicapped. She has terminal cancer. Is that good enough for you?" He quickly escorted Ally to the room and apologized for his ignorance in not recognizing Ally's frail condition. We were finally all set and ready to make our one last stand.

August 11, 2017 (Ally's Healing Circle)

 is with **Allyson** ▇▇▇ and **Minh Vo**.
Admin Aug 11, 2017

Dear family and friends,

It's been almost a month since Ally was told by her doctors that immunotherapy wasn't working, and that they had no other alternatives to offer but hospice care. Since her liver lesions multiplied, Ally sustained a severe immunotherapy rash all over her body, as well as swelling and edema in her abdomen and limbs. Another dose of Keytruda wasn't an option since it could cause her more harm.

Not giving up hope, Minh and Ally researched alternative therapies when she was originally diagnosed. Rather than hospice, they decided to go to ▇▇▇▇▇▇▇▇ in Arizona for a 12-day intensive cancer treatment program. Since most advanced alternative cancer treatments are not FDA approved, their cancer hospital was located in San Luis Rio Colorado Mexico – a location unrestricted by the FDA.

Everything went smoothly and Ally was feeling fine; however, due to other unforeseen factors, her treatment was not utilized to its full benefit. Prior to the trip, Ally was given a two-week high dose of prednisone to treat her immunotherapy rash, which seemed to be very effective. After her medication was done, she began to feel weaker and her nausea and vomiting began to increase.

Ally and Minh flew down to Phoenix a few days earlier to visit close friends and allow Ally to acclimate to the weather. On July 24th, they were picked up from a hotel in Yuma and transported to their new temporary home for the next 12 days. The doctors did a comprehensive physical (and labs) to determine Ally's baseline prior to beginning treatment. We were shocked to find out that Ally's hematocrit had dropped from 25% to 19 % in less than 5 days, which translates to an immediate need for a blood transfusion. The last time she was this low, she was internally bleeding out at ▇▇▇▇ back in May, which caused Minh much alarm and emotional stress. The doctors ordered the blood and performed an ultrasound to confirm that there wasn't any internal bleeding.

In the nights to come, Ally was plagued by bouts of severe nausea and vomiting that lasted anywhere from 4-6 hours. The doctors at New Hope brought in an internist specialist for evaluation. The internist concluded that Ally was experiencing adrenal shock, due to not being tapered down from her high doses of prednisone. He immediately gave instructions to taper her down, which slowly began to stabilize her system.

Despite all of these challenges, Ally's continued treatment. Every day she went through a combination of 8-10 treatments to help rebuild her immune system. (This ranged from ionic foot bath, hyperbaric oxygen chamber, far infrared heat, IV high vitamin C, IV albumin, IV vitamins and nutrients, homeopathy, coffee enema, as well as the most important treatments of IV ozone therapy, dendritic cell therapy, stem cell therapy, and the creation of a cancer antigen from her own blood on day one.). At times, this ranged from 8am till 10pm at night. With such an aggressive schedule, along with all these other complications in the background, Ally was ready to come home after the 12 days.

In Ally's exit interview, Ally's hematocrit had dropped once again to 19% after a little over a week since her last transfusion. Instead of spending a restful night in their hotel the day before they were to head back to Seattle, they spent another 6 hours in the ER in Yuma so that Ally could get another infusion. On Saturday August 5th, Ally and Minh were finally home. Only thing left was to go to SCC on Sunday for her routine once a month Octreotide injection.

During Ally's visit to SCC, it was discovered that one of her PICC lines was full of blood clots. After several attempts to clear them, the PA decided to pull her PICC line to reduce the risk of giving Ally a stroke. A few days later at ▓▓, Ally's nurse concluded that her veins were too small to place a new PICC line, due to lack of hydration and no TPN for several days. Ally lost 10 lbs. in the 3 days, since she was unable to receive TPN without a PICC. For now, Ally will be using her port to provide her the nutrients she needs to sustain her nutrition and increase her weight. Ally will be monitored closely for increased internal bleeding, but the fact remains, there are no other options to stop the bleeding, except for the Octreotide, which seems to be lessening its effects.

As daunting as these last few weeks have been, Ally and Minh still remain hopeful and are waiting patiently for her cancer antigen to be sent. Once they receive the antigen, Ally will be injecting it into herself over the next four months. Ally's cancer antigen is perceived as the biggest game changer within her journey to Mexico. With ▓▓▓▓ most advanced and complete cancer program in the world, they have an 84% success rate of sustaining life in cancer patients based on the ▓▓▓▓ Cancer Institute's stage 4 calculations of remission (stopping the progression of cancer). Ideally, this antigen will be able to stop the progression of Ally's cancer and shrink it enough so that it can be removed and put her into remission. Ally and Minh continue to hope and pray that this path lies ahead of them.

We too will hope and pray for Ally and Minh -- that remission will not be a dream, but a reality that comes true. For those who wish to support Ally and Minh in some tangible way, you can continue to do so by sharing and visiting their ▓▓▓▓ site ▓▓▓▓ ▓▓▓▓▓▓▓▓▓▓▓▓▓▓▓▓.

Thank you for your constant love and support throughout this journey – Ally and Minh love you all so very much, and are so thankful for the support and encouragement they have continued to receive from all of you. Our continued thanks to Dr. ▓▓▓▓, ▓▓▓▓ ▓▓▓▓ and ▓▓▓▓▓▓▓▓▓▓ for supporting Ally and Minh during this extremely difficult time, so that Minh can stay focused on Ally's health, as they continue their journey for a cure.

I wish that I could say that everything went smoothly during our stay in Mexico and that Ally's treatments were a miraculous success, but with everything that had transpired, we were only met with more and more complications as Ally's health began to fail. Ally had long hard days of around-the-clock treatments that quickly wore on her. During one of her routine blood labs, the results showed that her hematocrit was below normal. Ally was losing blood. Reviewing her notes and her current medications, the doctor concluded that Ally wasn't properly tapered off while on her corticosteroids. Instead of slowly weaning her body off her steroids, she was instructed to stop her high dosage when her prescription was finished, causing her body to rebound, and she began losing blood. Since the local hospital didn't have blood storage, we had to travel to a different city in Mexico for her to receive blood transfusions to keep her above the deadly 18% hematocrit mark. Although I stayed with her in the same room during the entire treatment program, Ally was not allowed to take breaks in between treatments. She was not allowed to leave the clinic to visit the small town or experience a moment of peace. The only thing that was remotely close to rest was at nighttime when we'd watch television together while she was hooked up to an IV to receive some sort of treatment for the evening. After about a week into the program, Ally was ready to end all of her treatments and go home. As much as she wanted to give up, I kept encouraging her to do her best because this was all we had left. This was our last hope.

When we finally finished the 12 days of treatment, we were told that the miracle antigen they had been preparing since we'd arrived would be sent to our home in a few weeks. It was, in essence, their version of stem cell therapy to rejuvenate and grow new cells to fight cancer. It was prized as the miracle cure and was the most important part of the program. Ally was so tired and worn down from all the constant treatments during her time in Mexico. She asked me to promise her that there would be no more treatments until we got home. The night before we were to fly back to Seattle, Ally began throwing up blood again and faded in and out of consciousness. Her hematocrit was barely at 19% before we checked out of the clinic in Mexico. I began to panic and decided to rush her to the local hospital's ER to receive another blood transfusion. While we were there, Ally kept repeating, "You promised no more treatments. No more hospitals until we got back home!" I told her I was sorry, but she was throwing up too much blood, and we didn't have a choice. When she was finally admitted to the ER, her hematocrit dropped to 17%. We spent most of the night at the hospital before her levels were safe enough to leave in the morning. With only a few hours of rest at our hotel, we were shuttled to the airport. We finally left Mexico and were on our way home.

We were relieved to be back in Seattle. The fear of Ally losing blood kept playing like a broken record over and over again in my mind. Luckily, we already had an appointment scheduled for the following day at the cancer center to make sure everything was okay with Ally. The cancer center was like our second home, where we knew she would get the best care possible. During the visit, we wanted to make sure that Ally was back to normal with her theoretically improved immune system from the alternative treatments in Mexico. The PA made a gut decision to pull the PICC line. Ally's port was the only feed left in her body to sustain her PCA for pain relief. With the PICC line no longer available, Ally's body began to shrink even further as she was unable to receive hydration or nourishment via TPN. Ally went hungry for the next few days as they tried to figure out how to resolve this new problem. Things couldn't get any worse. By the following week, another nightmare unfolded. Ally's tumor ulcerated again.

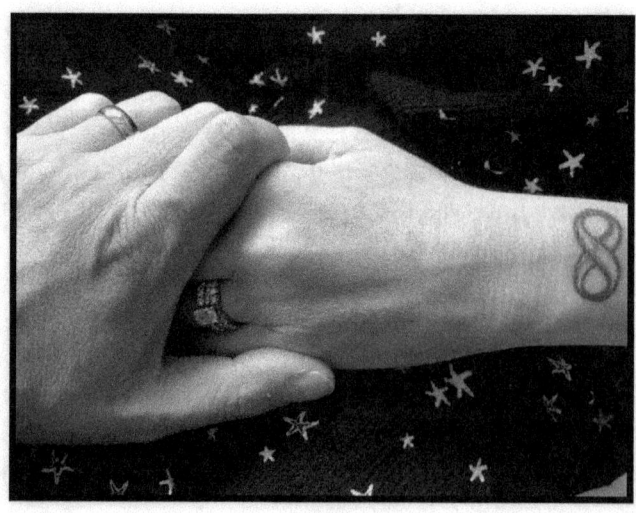

August 13, 2017 (Ally's Healing Circle)

■■■■ is with **Allyson** ■■■■ and **Minh Vo**.
Admin · 13 August 2017 · 🌐

Dear family and friends,

Although we had just posted an update on Ally's journey to Mexico, we hoped for fruitful returns. As you know, Ally had several difficult hurdles along that journey, and still these hurdles are ever more present.

Ally started bleeding internally again at the end of last week. Her visit to SCC on Friday showed her hematocrit had dropped from 27% on Sunday to 17% by Friday. This required immediate action, so Ally was sent directly to ■■■■ ER to be assessed and evaluated. The news was extremely shocking and disheartening to hear.

The GI and ER team communicated that based on how fast she was dropping in hematocrit levels, most likely Ally's tumor ulcerated again. Our options were disheartening - either go home and enjoy whatever time she had left or they could try a ventilation endoscopy to see where the bleeding was. For the latter option, there was a 90% chance they could still do nothing about it and the chances of her waking up from the procedure were slim to none.

Overwhelming sadness and fear consumed Minh and Ally, until the ICU doctor stepped in and said that Ally beat the odds before, so why not try again. We can hope for the best and do everything we can, but know the worst can be moments away.

With that said, they immediately gave Ally 3 pints of blood and placed her on IV Octreotide, IV Pantoprazole, IV Cipro, and other clotting factors on Saturday, and then Ally was admitted for a 72-hour observation.

As in moments past, this is a critical time for Ally and Minh. Please carry these two in your hearts and prayers in the days ahead so that Ally can continue to live and fight another day. They are not accepting visitors and ask to limit inquires so that they can focus on Ally's health and wellbeing.

All hope was lost as Ally's prognosis quickly became fatal. Even if they could confirm where her tumor had ulcerated, there was nothing they could do to stop the bleeding. Upon hearing the news, Ally's mom flew in the next day to be with her daughter just in case it was the last time she'd be able to see her. Upon Ally's request, we flew her sister in to give Ally additional support and strength to carry on her fight for her life. Ally's condition was beyond critical, and the doctors told us that we had to limit her visitors. I told JB to wait a day or two since he was scheduled to come out to Seattle to help and would notify him if things went south quickly. As Ally was prepped to go to the ICU for what seemed to be her final days left on this earth, the head of the ICU decided to do one last Hail Mary and tried the same treatment that had worked on Ally previously when her tumor ulcerated. All we could do was wait, hope, and pray that another miracle would take place and Ally would be able to live and fight another day.

August 16, 2017 (Ally's Healing Circle)

Dear family and friends,

We are pleased to announce that Ally's hematocrit is stable at 23% and was released from ▇▇▇▇ yesterday evening. She is safe at home resting.

It has been a tumultuous several weeks for Ally, with her two week intensive treatments in Mexico and numerous visits to various hospitals.

Ally and Minh aren't taking visitors at this time and ask to limit inquiries so that they can both get much needed rest.

But, they did want to thank everyone for continuing to sustain them with your love and prayers - your support gives them strength for each day in this journey, and inspires their hope to share many more days together in love and marriage.

Ally miraculously beat the odds and healed once again from her fatal internal bleed-out. With a new PICC installed, fully hydrated, and nourished once again, all of us were so happy and thrilled with the outcome. Ally was once again stable and among the living. As we prepared to check out, Ally sat on her hospital bed, all sad and glum. I asked her, "What was wrong, babe?"

"Nothing is working, and every day it seemed to be getting worse," she said, frustrated. Ally was losing hope, something that all cancer patients desperately needed to win their fight.

I took her hands once again and pleaded, "There is a reason why you survived two fatal bleed outs when you should have died twice now. There is a reason you are still alive today. You are meant to be cured. We still have the antigen coming. It has a high success rate in curing cancer, and it will work. We will beat the odds, you will be cured, and we will be able to spend the rest of our lives together."

She looked at me a bit more renewed. "Yes, you are right," she smiled. My words somewhat restored her faith, given the logic and reasons as to why she was still alive.

"Everything is going to be alright, Ally. You just got to have faith. We will get through this," I reassured her.

"You promise?"

I kissed her and held her close to me. "You and me, no matter what. I promise we are going to beat this thing."

CHAPTER 21

A Broken Promise

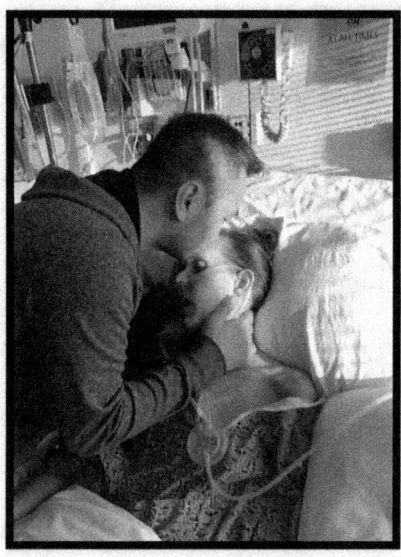

After the hospital, we had the next several days by ourselves. We were finally home alone, where Ally could have a little peace and quiet away from the hospital and constant treatments. Things seemed back to normal for once. After this last brush with death, I spent time reinforcing Ally's belief that she would be healed and made sure to tell her every day about how much I loved her and that there was nowhere in the world that I would ever rather be. I needed her to know how much I loved her and how much I needed her to be with me. I wanted her to have a reason to continue the fight.

It wasn't long after being home that Ally started getting infections and fevers again. Now that we were no longer in active treatment, I had to administer her IV antibiotics at home to save her the trouble of daily trips to the cancer center. We had it set up so I could administer her IV antibiotics and hydration packs around the clock. Her visiting nurses would come by to check in on her every once in a while. Ally had weekly visits to the cancer center for labs and to make sure she was doing okay. The following week, the antigen finally arrived from Mexico. "It's here! It's here Ally!" After reading the directions, I immediately began to administer her daily dosage. This consisted of a small vile of antigen that I had to inject into her thigh. We were ecstatic and hopeful that Ally finally had something that could fight her cancer again. All we could do was hope and pray that she would miraculously heal with this antigen.

    I wish I could say that the antigen went immediately to work on Ally, and she began getting stronger every day. I wish I could say that Ally's pain lessened with each new dose. I wish I could say that Ally no longer needed to vomit and that she was able to eat again. Instead, Ally grew less alert and even more exhausted. She was soon unable to stand on her own and often needed to be wheelchaired around in from one room to the next in our small apartment. I set up a makeshift bed for her on our couch in the living room while I slept on a gel mattress pad near her on the ground. She would usually wake up at around 5 or 6 in the evening, and we would spend time talking and watching our favorite shows together until I could no longer stay awake to keep her company. In the morning, I would wake to find her curled up, soundly asleep on the couch again. When I had to run errands for food or for medical supplies, I often recruited Lisa or other women friends that lived close by to look after her. Ally was too embarrassed by the way she looked and didn't want any male friends around to help look after her, especially when she needed help going to the bathroom.

    After a week of sleeping on the couch, Ally finally wanted the comfort of our bed. I moved everything back to the bedroom and set everything up the way she liked it. She would have to lay on a wedge since the massive tumor in her abdomen took away the ability for her to lay flat several months ago. She would want her pillows surrounding her, propping up her head just right so that she was comfortable while resting or watching her iPad. I hadn't been able to hold her in my arms while resting next to her since she almost died from her first bleed out. Either way, it was still nice to lay next to her, even if all I could do was lay there and hold her hand.

As we sat there talking a bit before it was time to sleep, Ally leaned forward, grabbed her stomach, and let out a big yelp. I quickly asked her, "Are you okay? Where is the pain? Do you want me to increase your pain meds on your PCA?"

She sat there for a moment, trying to catch her breath until she finally said, "Whoa, that was intense, Babe."

"What can I do to help you, Ally?" I asked.

"I don't know babe. This pain is completely different from the normal pain I feel. It was so much deeper and more intense." After a moment longer, she said she started to breathe normally again. "I think I am fine now. You don't have to worry about anything. You should get some rest, babe."

The next morning when I woke, she said she was still feeling an increase in her pain levels. She had trouble breathing and asked for her inhaler. I quickly ran to the bathroom to retrieve it and assumed she was having an asthma attack, which wasn't uncommon or out of the ordinary. I then increased her meds on her PCA to help ease the pain she felt from the night before. I moved everything back out to the living room, where she could rest and watch TV as we started our morning. As the day went on, I could tell that something was definitely off. Ally was losing strength to the point where she could no longer push herself up in order to sit, and she needed my full assistance with almost everything she did. After a few more times of helping her up and down, Ally finally broke down and began sobbing profusely. "I am so fucking tired of being sick all the time. I just can't take it anymore!"

I tried to soothe her, "I know you are frustrated, Ally, but we got to be patient. The medicine needs a little bit more time for it to work. Then everything will get better soon," I pleaded. "We just needed to wait a little longer for your medicine to do its job."

"I hate this. I just hate this babe," she cried.

"I know. I know. I hate this too, but we will get through this. I promise. You and me, no matter what!" I told her. "I love you so much, Ally. We are going to get through this. I am not going anywhere." She was my heart, my everything. All that mattered was curing so that she could live. After she finally calmed down, she dozed off to sleep. The day continued as normal with IV antibiotics, hydration, TPN, and me providing additional help to get Ally around. I then emailed Ally's oncologist and her care team with an update on Ally's condition.

>(Email to Ally's Oncologist and care team)
>**From: Minh Vo**
>**To:** ███, ███**, Etc…**
>**August 28, 2017: Allyson Vo Update**
>**Good Morning,**
>   **Just a quick update. Ally's pain level in her abdomen had increased quite a bit last night through this morning. At 9 a.m. we raised the PCA basal rate to 1.0 mL/hr (50 mcg) from at 0.8 mL/hr (40 mcg) to see if that would help. She described it as a sharp stabbing crampy pain.**
>   **Vomiting still remains at 3-4/day, 200-400 mL volumes. The last one last night was probably closer to 500 mL with a more reddish tinge during this increase in pain. She did have a bowel movement yesterday.**
>   **We are on our last two days of Flagyl. Due to being bed-bound the first 3-4 days since it made her extremely tired and wiped out, she is definitely a lot weaker. Yesterday was the first day she was more awake and alert. Urine is brown, but it's a side effect of Flagyl.**
>   **Hopefully everything is still working and on track. I know Friday's labs were good with 9.0 hemoglobin, and 27.5 hematocrit. Hopefully cultures on Wednesday will show everything resolved.**
>   **Blessings,**
>   **Minh Vo**

At nighttime, Ally wanted to sleep in the comfort of our own bed again. So, I moved all of our supplies back to our bedroom and got Ally all comfortable and situated for the evening as we chatted a bit before I finally fell asleep. It wasn't more than a few hours when I awoke to Ally gasping and violently coughing. "Ally! What's wrong? Is everything ok?"

"I am having a hard time breathing," she said as she gasped for air.

"Why didn't you wake me up and tell me?!" I yelled, panicked.

"I did this morning when I asked you for my inhaler."

The way Ally was coughing and gasping for air, I immediately thought to myself that fluid must have backed up in her lungs again, making it hard for her to breathe. "I know you don't want to do this, but I have to take you to the ER so they can figure out what's wrong."

She just nodded in compliance as she continued to cough and gasp. I quickly put on some clothes and grabbed a few things to prepare for another long night at the hospital as I wheeled her out the door to get her into the car.

At 4 AM, I drove us as quickly as I could to the ER. After we checked in, the nursing staff and doctors immediately wheeled her into a room and began hooking her up to IVs, putting on an oxygen mask to help her breathe, and switching her to the hospital's PCA machine to better regulate and control her pain. They then drew blood to run labs and other noninvasive tests and began to review her extensive medical history to get a better picture of who and what they were dealing with. After the review, they called in a special team of doctors onsite who were aware of Ally's case to help assist. I called my sister, knowing that she would be at work soon and would be nearby. I then immediately began texting Ally's family about her current situation. I promised to keep them informed if anything serious were to happen. Then I emailed her oncologist and care team.

> (Email to GI RN)
> **From: Minh Vo**
> **To:** ▮
> **August 29, 2017: Allyson Vo – ER UMC (5:22 a.m.)**
> **Good Morning,**
>
> **I had to take Ally to the ER this morning around 3:30/4 a.m. Last night, 30 minutes prior to giving Ally her 11 pm IV dose of Flagyl, I noticed her legs and body becoming blotchy and red. Called her pharmacist and the cancer center's on-call Fellow, and they both suggested not giving her the dose and give her Benadryl instead.**

> In the middle of the night, I noticed her coughing and wheezing. She said she couldn't breathe, so here we are now. So far ER doc had done chest x-ray, blood labs + cultures, and hydration to determine why she has a rash and if it was because of antibiotics. Their main concern also is her heart rate at 138-140. Seeing if hydration will help since she is due today for some, and she vomited 4-5 times yesterday. Will contact infectious disease to see what they have to say.
> Blessings,
> Minh Vo

Several hours passed, and Ally began to stabilize somewhat and was trying to communicate to the attending doctors what she was feeling and experiencing. I noticed that she was having some trouble forming her words and communicating what she wanted to convey. I tried my best to fill in the gaps with everything that had happened and helped Ally express what she wanted to tell them the best I could.

> (Email from GI RN)
> From: ▮
> To: Minh Vo
> Subject: (RE) Allyson Vo - ER UMC (10:34 am)
> Hi Minh,
> I'm thinking about you and Ally. I'm guessing Onc is in touch with the ED team. I'm glad she is there and getting good care.
>

One of the specialists who was called in to assist with Ally's case walked into the room and asked if she could speak to me for a moment in private. She introduced herself and let me know that she was very familiar with Ally and everything that had occurred in the last several months while Ally was in and out of the hospital. She asked if I understood medical terminology or had a medical background, knowing that I did something in the healthcare field. I nodded. This allowed her to cut straight to the chase and get to the heart of the matter of Ally's condition. She walked me into a private room and began discussing what they had discovered in Ally's labs. "When reviewing Ally's labs, everything was relatively normal considering Ally's current condition," she paused for a moment, "but the one thing that was most alarming was how low Ally's oxygen levels were in addition to the increase in lactate levels in her blood work. This combination in a person's blood work is usually a good indication that Ally is experiencing sepsis." My face immediately went blank as tears began to fall from my eyes upon hearing this information.

Sepsis, that was a word that I was very aware of and didn't ever want to hear. Back in chiropractic school, we had to study clinical diagnosis, differential diagnosis, and infectious disease. We had to know what was good, what was bad, and what was fatal. Sepsis was a life-threatening condition in response to a usually fatal internal infection.

Looking at my expression, she had to ask, "Do you understand everything I am saying?" I slowly nodded. "In Ally's case, part of her intestine must have ruptured, allowing fecal matter to enter her bloodstream, sending poisonous toxins throughout the body and organs. The poisonous toxins are now taking over, which explains why she began experiencing extreme weakness and is losing mental clarity due to a lack of oxygen in the bloodstream." She went on to say, "If we could have caught it within the first 6 hours of it happening, then we could have performed emergency surgery to stop the spread of poisonous toxins in her body." She looked at me again, "Even if we did catch in time, I don't think Ally would have been able to survive the surgery in her weakened condition."

In Ally's case, based upon what they gathered, most likely, her bowel had perforated and had torn open from the weight of the tumor the night before. This was likely the cause of her intense pain the night before. It would have also explained the sudden weakness and decreased mental acuity she was experiencing. Given the time frame, we were way past the 6 to 8-hour mark. Even if they wanted to perform the surgery, the chance of survival was unlikely in Ally's present condition. Knowing the horrifying news, I had just received, she asked again, "Do you understand everything I just said?" I slowly nodded again. She then went on to ask, "Would you like me to relay this information to Ally?" My heart had just shattered into a million pieces, knowing that we had finally reached the end and that there was no longer any hope left. Ally was going to die.

I gathered every bit of strength I had left to compose myself. I could only stare at the floor as I slowly shook my head and whispered, "No, I need to be the one. I need to tell Ally myself."

"I am so sorry, Mr. Vo. We will run some more labs to confirm, but I am almost certain this is where we are at with Ally." She could see and feel the tremendous pain that I was going through and asked, "Can I give you a hug?" I nodded as she reached in to hug me and then walked away. I slowly walked back to the room to find Ally sitting alone on the ER bed, still lucid and somewhat alert. I pulled up a chair so I could be close to her and held both of her hands. As I began to speak, tears welled up in my eyes.

"Babe, I don't think we are going to make it out of the hospital this time." I squeezed her hands, trying to keep my voice steady. "The doctor just told me that you probably have sepsis and that your tumor has torn the lining in your bowel open and is leaking toxins into your body. There is nothing they can do about it."

She just nodded, then took off her oxygen mask and tried to lean forward to kiss me.

"I am so sorry, Babe, but there is nothing we can do this time. I love you so much." I sat next to her on her bed and held her for as long as I could, sobbing uncontrollably before alarms started going off, and nurses rushed in to attend to Ally.

My sister arrived and asked me what was happening. "Ally's bowels tore open, and now she has sepsis, and there is nothing that they can do. She is dying." I told her as I was crying uncontrollably.

She reached out to give me a hug, "I am so sorry, Vo," she paused for a second, "I have to check in with work really quick and will return as soon as I can. I will let the family know what has happened to Ally," before needing to rush off.

I slumped into my chair and pulled out my MacBook and began to give an update to her oncologist and her care team at the cancer center.

(Email to Onc)
From: Minh Vo
To: ▮
Subject: Allyson Vo – ER UMC (10:54 a.m.):

This time does feel a lot different, and not in a good way. Ally is not doing well at all. She is barely lucid, and her body is really weak and struggling. I spoke with her team. They don't expect her to last the night. We are doing a CAT of the chest and abdomen to rule out an embolism in the lungs and to see what is causing all of these problems. Based upon her blood lab results, they think she might have sepsis, possibly from a perforated bowel due to tumor growth and there is nothing they can do to stop it. But let's hope they are wrong and that she will be home soon. Will let you know what the CAT scan says after they get the results. Always hopeful.
Blessings,
Minh Vo

Another hour had passed before the doctor who spoke to me earlier returned and brought the results of the latest blood labs. Ally's oxygen was falling even further, the lactate levels were rising, and Ally's blood pressure was dropping. They concluded that Ally had sepsis and that the only thing left to do was to give her morphine to ease her pain, supply her with oxygen so she wouldn't suffocate to death, and keep her as comfortable as possible as they would begin to move her to a room in the cancer center wing of the medical center. Finally, they told me that she'd most likely not last through the night. My heart sank to its deepest depths, knowing that I would now have to break the news one by one to her family.

Minh – *'As you know, I had to admit Ally to the ER early this morning because she had trouble breathing. The doctors informed me that the weight of her tumor caused her bowels to split open, causing sepsis in her body, and there is nothing that they can do about it. Ally is dying. I am so sorry I couldn't save Ally's life. I am so sorry that I failed you.'* I broke out into uncontrollable tears as I typed the last few lines.

Texts from various members of Ally's family immediately chimed in:

~It's not your fault Minh!
~You did everything you could to save Ally!
~Ally was so lucky to have you by her side.
~We love you Minh

Once they heard the news, they all wanted to take the next plane out first thing in the morning to be with her during her final hours. I had to tell them that the doctors didn't think she would last through the night based on her current condition. Ally would most likely have passed by the time they arrived in Seattle. The amount of guilt and pain I felt finally reached full force within me. In the end, all I could say was how sorry I was that I failed them. I had failed to save Ally's life.

I typed my final email to Ally's oncologist and Ally's care team.

> (Email to Ally's Oncologist and Care Team)
> **From: Minh Vo**
> **To: ▓▓▓ , ▓▓▓ , Etc…**
> **Subject: Allyson Vo – ER UMC (3:37 p.m.):**
> **The doctors at the ER has decided to forgo the scan, because it is evident that Ally has sepsis and her blood pressure and oxygen are dropping based upon her lactate levels. Once again, she is not expected to make it through the night. Thank you everyone for giving her your best.**
> **Ally fought as hard as she could, but sometimes things don't always go as planned. We both are extremely grateful for all that you have done.**
> **Blessings,**
> **Ally + Vo**

CHAPTER 22

FINAL GOODBYES

    I walked alongside Ally's bed as they transported her to the room where she would spend the last moments of her life. Ally was now motionless, unable to move or talk. My sister and brother arrived shortly afterward and sat in the room with me in silent support and solidarity. The nurse that was prepping the room said to me, "She is still here. She can still hear you."

    I sat next to Ally so I could be by her side until her final moments. I grabbed her hand and whispered to her, "I love you so much Ally. I am so proud of you and all that you have done. I am so proud to be with you." I paused for a moment to catch my breath. "I am so sorry we couldn't find a cure, and I am so sorry that I failed you. I love you so much Ally." I stroked her hair, played her music, and oftentimes, just sat there and cried to myself. Soon, other members of my family began to filter in to show their love and support. They, too, wanted to share their final words and prayers with their aunt, sister-in-law, and family. The only other person who I let visit that day was Leo. He wanted to come by to drop off food, check in to see how I was doing, and see if there was anything else he could do for us.

The evening finally came, and Ally was still breathing with the help of the ventilator. I told my sister and brother that they should go home and rest as I wanted to be alone with her when it was time for her to pass. They hesitantly agreed since they really didn't want to leave my side. They said they'd be there first thing in the morning if they didn't hear from me, which would indicate that Ally had lasted the night. When I was finally alone, A nurse came in to check Ally's vitals and check on the morphine that was being administered to her for comfort from any pain. I asked, "Could I possibly see the blood labs that were used to assess Ally's condition throughout the day?"

She looked at me and smiled, "Let me see what I can pull up from her charts." Ally was still alive and breathing on assisted oxygen. In my mind, I was hoping that this was all a big mistake and that Ally would soon wake up and we'd be able to go home. After reviewing the labs that showed a definitive increase in lactate, I asked, "Do you think Ally is in any pain?"

She smiled once again, "I can assure you that she isn't feeling any pain with the amount of morphine that we are giving her. She will probably pass soon. Most people usually don't last the night."

I then asked her, "How will I know when it will happen?"

She said, "It will be pretty obvious when it happens. You will definitely know when it is her time to pass." I situated my cot next to Ally's bed so I could be next to her. I then reached up my hand and interlaced my fingers with hers so I could hold Ally's hand throughout the night as we often did at home. I wanted to let her know that I was still there right beside her the whole time and was never leaving her side as I had promised her. In the morning when I woke, my hand was still holding Ally's. She was still breathing, but now it was a more labored breath. As promised, Minh and Billy returned to the room at around 7:00 a.m. to take their seats next to me.

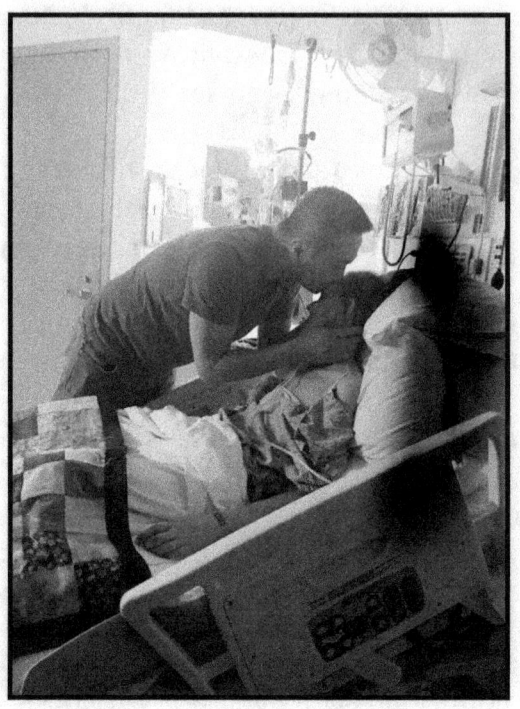

August 31, 2017 (Ally's Healing Circle)

 is with **Allyson** ▮▮▮ and **Minh Vo**.
Admin Aug 31, 2017 ·

Dear family and friends,

It is with a heavy heart and deep sadness that we share today's news.

It has only been two weeks since Ally miraculously survived another fatal internal bleeding incident. This was not without consequence. Following her discharge from ▮▮▮ Ally experienced an infection. The infection caused a fever and an increase in white blood cells which SCC treated with antibiotics.

Near the end of her treatment, Ally experienced several acute symptoms: intense abdominal pain, severe weakness, an allergic reaction, and difficulty breathing in the middle of the night. This prompted an immediate visit to the ▮▮▮ ER.

After obtaining labs and test results, things took a massive turn for the worse. The ER doctor pulled Minh aside and told him that Ally had sepsis; that is, harmful bacteria and toxins spilling out into her body that was the result of an ulceration.

> The severe pain (and sepsis) was determined to be the result of new tumor growth that ulcerated her small intestine. The doctors told Minh that there was nothing that they could do to stop it except to ease her pain in the remaining hours of her life.
>
> Ally has been at ▮▮▮▮▮ since early morning yesterday surrounded by loved ones. Minh has been right by Ally's side during these final hours and was able to sleep next to her, holding her hand throughout the night.
>
> In these final moments we are reminded that this heart wrenching sadness we feel is ultimately the result of the immeasurable love that we feel for Ally.
>
> We are so blessed to have shared the gift of life, friendship, and love with you, Ally. We couldn't be more proud of you. You fought till the bitter end with hope and strength. And, you touched all of us with your love for life, compassion for others, and strength in the face of the unknown. We will always love you, and you will always remain in our hearts.
>
> Please take this moment to remember Ally as we cherish these remaining hours that we have together. Thank you so much for all your love and support along this journey.

With the release of the news on Ally's Healing Circle, several close friends began to text me, asking if I needed anything or if they could come to say goodbye to Ally one last time. I told them I would think about it and get back to them. Ally had once again defied the odds of the doctor's predictions and lasted through the night. Ally's family could only see or talk to her through my phone so that she could hear their voices as they all said their final goodbyes. I decided to let a few of our closest friends who had helped us during Ally's fight do the same. The doctors and nurses emphasized that Ally could still hear me even though she couldn't move or speak. I wanted her to hear how much she was loved by everyone and what a difference she had made in everyone's lives. By evening time, there were just my sister Minh, Billy, and Leo left in the room. Leo stopped by to bring us all dinner for the night and to say his last words to Ally.

At one point, I looked over at Ally and understood what the nurses meant when they said, "You definitely know when it was time for someone to pass." I immediately yelled for everyone to leave the room, knowing full well that my final selfish wish was to be alone with Ally when this moment came. As Ally's life left her body, I sat beside her, holding her hand and kissing her face as I cried, "I love you so much Ally. I am so sorry that I failed you. I am so sorry that I have broken my promise to find you a cure. I love you so much." And just like that, she was gone.

The attending doctor came into the room to confirm and record her time of death, "It is 8:00 pm. Allyson Lenay Vo has passed. I am so sorry for your loss, Mr. Vo. Unfortunately, I have a few medical questions to ask you before I am able to submit Ally's death certificate." I nodded. She then said, "I can see Ally was an organ donor, but due to cancer, most of her organs are not viable. But there is one thing that she can still donate with your permission." I looked up at her again. "She can donate her eyes."

Those eyes. Those beautiful blue eyes. The same ones that triggered the start of our whole relationship, I thought to myself. And now here we are. "No," I told her. "I don't want to donate her eyes."

"I understand," the doctor said. "Once again, I am so sorry for your loss Mr. Vo. The nurses will be coming in shortly to wash and prep Ally's body for transport to the morgue."

"Would it be okay if I could stay and watch?" I asked. I used to bathe Ally every night during the months leading up to this.

"Of course, I will inform the nurses," she said before she left.

I watched as the two nurses sponge-bathed Ally's lifeless body and dressed her in a clean gown. As they finished, they told me that I could stay as long as I needed to be with her.

Alone once again, I stood beside her bed and stared at her as she lay peacefully. To me, it seemed as if she was just there lying quietly asleep. I finally mustered up the courage to say my final words to her.

"Ally… Babe, it is time for you to wake up and open your eyes. It is time for you to get up now so that we can go home." I had to take a short pause to wipe away the tears streaming down my face as I murmured, "If you don't wake up soon, then I will have to leave the hospital without you, Babe. Ally, please wake up so that we can go home. Please wake up for me. It's time for us to go home now."

August 30, 2017 (Ally's Healing Circle)

 is with **Allyson** ▇▇▇ and **Minh Vo**.
Admin · 30 August 2017 · 😊

Dear friends and family,

At 8pm tonight, Ally breathed her last breath, and is finally at peace, and free of pain and suffering.

As Minh said, "Ally is in a better place now. Love her in your hearts and your memories. I am so thankful for her and thankful for all of you."

When Ally was asked by her doctors about the one thing she wished she could do before she passed away, she didn't talk about some specific place to travel, or some other experience. Rather she said that she wished could make a difference in someone's life.

As a way of honoring Ally's life, we invite you to share your favorite memory or picture of Ally, and/or any way she made a difference in your life.

"This life will not be the same without you in it. The Universe will surely pair us up again, but until then know that I'll miss you dearly and you can come visit me anytime. If nothing else than to show off your kitchen dance moves in my dreams. Love you girl. ~"

"September 2013 was my first time meeting Minh and Ally in Seattle! We laughed, drank, laughed some more.. oh and ate a ton! Minh and Ally took us on this ridiculously amazing express Seattle food tour. We must have hit up 7-8 spots in 2 hrs or something crazy like that 😂🙌 I will never forget that trip, and the time we spent together."

"We love you, Minh and Allyson 😊🖤 Cheers to the many laughs, smiles and good times you have given us, Ally! We will never forget you 😌🖤🙏 ~"

"Ally, we had a good run love. I feel so grateful and blessed to have spent a little time with you in Seattle this summer. It was tough to see what cancer had done to your body but the beautiful fun-loving spirit you've always possessed was still on display. You lost your battle last night but you won the war. Thank you for bringing your light into the world even for just a little while. Safe travels sweet girl and go gators. You will be missed but never forgotten. ~"

"My Ally, I can't pick just one favorite memory; there are far too many. We once told each other that we were one of each other's closest friends, and it stayed that way for years. I treasure every memory of you. ~"

"Every Monday for a few years Allyson and I met up after work to chat, give each other a pep talk, hug, vent and make plans for the future, right before she moved to Seattle we were mulling around over starting a kids clothing line together...she was so inspired by & crazy in love with her nieces and would text me pictures of every *little thing they did 😄😄 the line was called "Swimsie" it was all her idea & I had the patterning and sewing skills. I always thought we made a good team if only we could concentrate on not laughing at each other's craziness 🤣🤣. We spent a few months, almost everyday brainstorming and making samples and doing research. During that time she was lit up with creative ideas and just so happy. She spent so many nights at my home with her laughter ringing through the house, I loved waking up to her chatting with my daughter in the morning...I was sad when she moved to Seattle but so happy she'd found love and a partner Minh Vo to spend her life with. Minh, you gave her exactly what she wanted, what she needed and deserved, you loved her just as she was, you took care of her heart, you made my friend so happy!!! I have a lifetime of great memories with Ally, and I'll always be grateful she took me into her heart and gave me the gift of her friendship! She was a true genuine friend. Love you so much Ally. ~"*

"Remembering the good times with you and Minh. Sad to see you go before your time Ally. You gave it a hell of a fight. I hope you are at peace and forever surrounded by love. ~"

I had no choice but to finally leave the hospital. Ally was no longer there, and I had no reason to stay anymore. I left the hospital without Ally this time, and I was now alone. They say that when a loved one or a married partner passes, oftentimes, you can feel or even see their presence at home. As I walked through the door, I felt as if I saw Ally waiting there with a great big smile and a hug to greet me. I tried to speak to her, but I couldn't hear a sound. I took out one of our white votive candles that Ally always loved and lit it on the coffee table in our living room. Then I sat and began meditating to try to better connect with Ally's spirit. I tried to talk to her, hoping to hear her tell me that she was okay and that she was in a better place. But still, nothing was heard, only seen. Afterward, I left the candle to burn through the night until I went into our bedroom and cried to sleep.

As news of Ally's passing circulated, I was bombarded with calls and texts from several friends asking if I was okay and if there was anything they could do for me. Some took it upon themselves to book my airline tickets to get away from Seattle for a reprieve, while others planned trips to come to see me. Several wanted to schedule alone time with me to see how I was holding up and to make sure I wasn't suicidal or alone. There was no shortage of love and support shown to me after Ally passed.

It wasn't long after that I began receiving inquiries about her funeral. It wasn't out of the ordinary to have a funeral during the weekend of her passing. Yet there was already so much to do after Ally's death, with no real downtime to mourn appropriately. On top of all this, I had to return back to work soon. That was the least I could do since my company granted me so much leave to care for Ally. I thought about funeral proceedings for a moment since that was all so foreign to me. I thought to myself that since most of her family and friends lived far away and would need to request time off, book plane tickets, and arrange accommodations, having a last-minute funeral would make it tough for anyone to easily attend. So, I thought, why not have it on what would have been our one-year anniversary and celebrate her passing on the happiest days of our lives?

September 1, 2017 (Ally's Healing Circle)

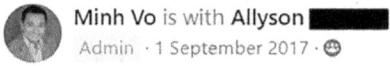

Minh Vo is with **Allyson**
Admin · 1 September 2017 ·

Thank you everyone for all the condolences and wonderful memories that you have shared about Ally. I know she is so happy to see all the love that you have for her. I know a lot of you have asked, and are wondering about funeral/memorial plans. We plan to have Ally's memorial on October 14, 2017, to celebrate her life on the same day that we celebrated our lives together as one. This was one of the happiest days of her life. Details will follow when everything is confirmed.

Although greatly appreciated, please refrain from sending any flowers. The many memories that you have shared of Ally overflows my heart with joy. Thank you so much for all the support that you have provided us along this difficult journey. Ally and I are truly grateful for all of you. Thank you for listening. Cheers!

Every morning, I woke up to meditate and look for signs of Ally. I'd sit there, allowing whatever thoughts, images, and emotions needed to express themselves within my body to help release any sort of grief or guilt I was experiencing. Sometimes, I would see her but still could not hear or understand what she was trying to tell me. Soon, I received a random phone call from one of my psychically inclined friends. "Hey Vo. A weird thing happened to me earlier today. Ally came to me and gave me a message. She said she was scared and alone in the dark." This troubled me and added to the mountain of grief that I held inside. I recruited the help of people experienced in helping loved ones move on into the light where they were surrounded by loved ones and/or a higher power. I wanted to know that Ally's spirit was in a good, safe place in the afterlife, so I sought out the help of a medium. I wanted to talk to Ally and know that she was fine. In our conversation, a lot of it didn't quite make sense, but a few things rang true to me. I was told that the candle that I lit for her after she passed helped guide her to where she needed to be. She was in the light and was safe from all harm. I was relieved upon hearing this and was satisfied with what I was told.

You hear many stories as to why some spirits or souls don't cross over to the other side. Usually, it is because they have unresolved reasons as to why they want to stay. This could be the fact that they don't want to leave their loved ones, or they were wronged or trapped by anger or rage. We hear and see these stories all of the time in books, movies, and sometimes in real life. Whatever the reason, we all want what is best for the ones we love. We want them to be safe and with those who love them. That is all I wanted for Ally, to know that her spirit was safe and not tormented by her own death.

I spent the rest of my days leading up to the memorial dealing with all the red tape of Ally's cremation. I sorted through her belongings and kept a few things of hers that I couldn't part with just yet. A multi-set of bands formed a ring that she wore at the beginning of our relationship. Ally used to always worry about losing one of the bands, but eventually, she did lose a few bands on one of our adventures together. An old yellow and grey striped cardigan that she would always when we lived in San Francisco. Her coveted Louis Vuitton suitcase, which she never used because she was too worried about scratching it up. And the necklace that Julian gave her as a wedding present to be adorned at our wedding. The rest of her belongings were first offered to her family, so they could take what they wanted to keep or remember her by. Whatever was left was offered to my family, with the remaining items donated to Goodwill, the place where Ally received her first employment after graduating from the Art Institute in San Francisco.

At the same time, I had to look for a venue to hold Ally's memorial. I finally chose a place that overlooked Puget Sound, and I decided to make it a mini-reception similar to our wedding since Ally had always loved a big party. I reached out to our caterer who catered for our wedding and asked if he would cater to Ally's memorial. Hearing the shocking news, he waived all of his fees and offered his services at his cost.

A close friend of mine invited me to a Seahawks game to keep me company and to have a respite from dealing with grief. As we roamed through the plethora of tailgating parties, I ran into the DJ from our wedding. He high-fived me when he saw me and asked, "Where's Ally?"

With a somber look I told him, "Ally passed away earlier this year due to terminal cancer."

He was floored at hearing the news and asked, "Will there be a memorial?"

"Yes. Ironically it will be on the day of your wedding anniversary," I told him.

"I would love to help out and dee jay the event for you, for free. Anything you need," he said. I accepted and thanked him for his kind offer. Everything fell into place as we prepared for Ally's memorial.

September 18, 2017 (Ally's Healing Circle)

Minh Vo ▶ Ally's Healing Circle
Admin · 18 September 2017

This will be a formal event. Memorial will start prompt at 1pm. Celebration of Ally's life will follow with accompanying hors d'oeuvres and beverages. Although much appreciated please do not bring flowers. We will toast her life as she would have wanted us to do so.

90   1 comment

Roughly six weeks after Ally's passing, on what would have been the day of our first anniversary, instead of celebrating our first year of marriage together, we were having a celebration of life for my beloved Ally. Family and friends from all around came to Seattle to honor and celebrate Ally's life, as seats many seats filled the small auditorium. Old friends, new friends, and family friends piled in as staff and family members prepared the stage for the memorial to begin. I asked her family members who felt able enough to give speeches in honor of her life and recruited my family to speak, pray, and create a visual story for all of us to remember her by. I also asked Rose, her childhood best friend, AT, and Jules, who she was closest to and who stood by her side at our wedding, to contribute. I wanted to tell the story of her whole life through stories from those who knew and loved her most. One by one, we all stood before the auditorium and reminisced about moments in Ally's life. Then it was finally my turn to tell the story of us leading up to our last moments together.

You could hear whispers in the crowd. People wondered if I would be talking today and whether I was strong enough to deliver such a speech, knowing that not much time had passed. I stood before the audience and began my eulogy:

> *"For those of you who do not know me, some people know me as Vo. Some people know me as Minh. But I am both. I know some of you are probably wondering if I was going to serenade you guys like I serenaded Ally on our wedding day, but I am not going to pain your ears today. I woke up this morning and realized that it was our anniversary. Thinking back, I was like, wow, we didn't even have a year. But we do have stories, and I am here to tell the story about Ally. And I will try not to mumble.*
>
> *I remember the first time we met. It was at a gay bar in San Francisco. I took one look at you and said, 'You have the most beautiful blue eyes that I have ever seen.' Then you said to me, 'I am a lesbian.' I replied, 'No, you are not.' You then turned to Julian, and he nodded - yes. We exchanged a few more words, and as I was walking away, you tapped me on the shoulder and said, 'You are*

right. I am not a lesbian.' That was the beginning of our story. A story that was filled with much laughter, adventure, heartache, but most of all, love.

You always said to me a good relationship is built on the foundation of how many good stories one can tell about their life together and that we started ours off with a great story. There are countless stories that I can share about our life together, just like I am sure many of you in this room can do the same. That is what made Ally so special, the way she could impact someone's life no matter how long or how short you may have known her. But I am willing to bet that almost everyone here in this room has a few good stories about your time with Ally.

To Ally, life wasn't worth living unless it had meaning. With every thought, word, and action, she always made sure it counted, even down to the very smallest details. Because to her, the details mattered most. To her, each and every one of you mattered most. And she did that by making sure that everyone was important and was always included and that no one ever felt left out, alone, or abandoned. And that everyone in her life felt loved.

Love. That was the thing that meant so much to her. Ally wasn't born with a silver spoon in her mouth. Nothing was ever really given to her or always went her way, but that never stopped Ally from experiencing life. In fact, it motivated her to exude life. Whether it was overcoming the struggles of a broken home during her childhood, uprooting her life from Gainesville, FL, to start a new life in San Francisco, traveling across the globe to run a marathon in Greece, or moving here to Seattle to start a new life with me, she has faced various challenges. With each obstacle and challenge that she faced, she laughed, she cried, and you know, she probably yelled and screamed a lot, but in the end, she learned and grew a little bit more each and every day because every day would bring her one step closer to what mattered most. Love.

When I first met Ally, we were an identical match in many ways. Like two peas in a pod, we were instantaneously inseparable. In fact, on our very first date, we were approached by another couple who asked us, 'How long have you two been married?' and we replied, 'This is our first date.' And they were shocked because they thought we had been together forever by the way we acted. I was so in love with her, and she was with me. I remember telling her, 'I will give you the world if you give me enough time.' But for Ally, even time wasn't on her side.

In the beginning, we often didn't have much, but it never stopped us from always dreaming big and living our life to its fullest. Believing that one day we would achieve everything we had ever imagined because we believed in ourselves. Ally was always there to encourage me whenever I was feeling down. Support me when I didn't have a leg to stand on or anything to offer. Believed in me when the road got tough. She was my greatest cheerleader and my best friend. 'You and me, no matter what.' That was our mantra this year. Especially after we found out she had cancer.

Cancer... That was the word that changed the rest of our life together. I remember getting a call from Ally on Wednesday, January 18th. Ally was crying and choking and could barely breathe, but was able to muster the words, 'I have cancer, Babe.' I immediately dropped everything to be by her side. Words could not express what she must have felt, what we must have felt. All of our dreams were quickly becoming nightmares.

And after the dust settled, I picked her up and told her, 'We can do this. We will find a cure, and everything will be OK. We just have to believe in ourselves.' And she said, 'OK, we can do this.' And Ally was ready to face the biggest challenge that she had ever experienced in her life. I wish I could stand here today and say that Ally's final story was a story of miracles and that she had overcome and survived her cancer, but we wouldn't all be here today.

So let me share with you this one last story. As a child, I wasn't raised with a silver spoon in my mouth, and my childhood and life weren't always so pleasant either. I remember lying there in the middle of the night and often dreaming about my one true love. A person that I could give all my heart to and who would love me back infinitely, and we would spend the rest of our lives together so happy in love.

The day I met, Ally was the day I met my heart. Ally, you are my heart, the love of my life, my one true love. There isn't a day that goes by that I don't wish you were still here. To hold you, to kiss you, to tell you how much I love you each and every day. My heart continually breaks not having you here by my side. I am so proud and honored that you chose to love me and that we chose each other. If I had to do it all again, I would because I would still be able to be with you. You were the only one who accepted and loved me unconditionally as I loved you. Soul mates for all eternity. As the great philosopher Rumi says, "Lovers don't finally meet somewhere along the way. They're in each other all along." And in my heart and soul, you will remain for all eternity.

When asked by her oncologist, 'If I couldn't cure you, what is the one thing that you would like to achieve in this life before you leave?' Ally said, 'I want to know that I made a difference in just one person's life.' Ally, I know you are here with us now, and as you can see looking out into this room, how many lives you have impacted and made a difference with your love, especially mine.

2nd Timothy 4:7 says, 'I have fought the good fight, I have finished the race, I have kept the faith.' Ally, you have fought the good fight, there is no more pain and suffering, and you have finished the race. It is now time to celebrate. You are a winner in my eyes because you are my hero, my heart, my wife, and my best friend. And I am so, so very proud of you for all that you have done. We gave it our best, and you did your very best. And this is not the end of our story. Goodbyes are for those who love with their mind and their eyes, those who love with their heart and soul. There is no such thing as separation. And I promise you that one day, I will see you again.

I want to thank everybody, as well as everyone who couldn't be here, that has supported Ally and me through this journey. I have always said that it takes a village to support a couple, and we are so grateful that with all the generous support, love, and *donations that you were able to provide Ally for her battle, I am very thankful for everyone here, especially those who traveled a long way because every single one of you is very, very important to Ally and important to me. And it means a lot to me that everyone is here. So, with that said, I would like to spend the rest of the time celebrating her life as she would want us to celebrate and toast to her big heart that could never give enough. The one thing that I have learned the most from Ally is that there is really nothing more important than love. We have all these different struggles every day, and when we take away those layers of struggles at the heart of it, we can always find love. So instead of looking at life as a journey, look at life as being able to not only love yourself but love each other and remember why we are all here on this earth together. Ally will always be in my heart, and I will always love her.*

Thank you for listening."

CHAPTER 23

Facing Grief

The weight of guilt and sorrow enveloped me, suffocating my spirit, as I grappled with the overwhelming grief of Ally's absence. Every corner of my world echoed with her memory, a constant reminder of the love we once shared. Hours turned into a blur of tear-stained cheeks and aching sobs as I traversed the lonely landscape of my shattered heart. The burden I carried extended beyond the depths of emotional pain. My physical well-being suffered in the aftermath of Ally's passing, manifesting as skyrocketing blood pressure that demanded an increase in medication just to regain a semblance of normalcy. The toll was not only internal but also external, visible in the weariness etched upon my face and the exhaustion that consumed my being. Well-intentioned voices attempted to lift my spirits, offering words of solace and encouragement. But their words, however genuine, felt like mere whispers in the face of my profound anguish. No external comfort could fill the void left by Ally's departure. It was as if a part of me had been mercilessly ripped away, leaving behind a raw and bleeding wound that seared with unyielding pain. Amid others' attempts to console and advise, I often found myself lost in a world of numbness, staring into the void as their voices melded into an indistinguishable murmur. Healing, I came to understand, was a deeply personal journey, one that required me to confront the depths of my pain and slowly mend the fragments of my shattered soul. In the realm of grief, I became an unwitting member of a heartrending club, an exclusive gathering where we bore witness to the anguish of watching our loved ones endure agonizing and merciless deaths. The lyrics of the haunting melody "Hotel California" by the Eagles echoed in my mind, a somber reflection of the unyielding grip of grief held upon me. I yearned to escape the clutches of this desolate space, yet its grip remained unyielding, a constant reminder that I could never truly leave its realm. But as the days turned into weeks and the weeks into months, a sliver of resilience flickered within me. I realized that healing was not about checking out or abandoning the pain but about finding the strength to carry the weight of loss and gradually rediscover joy amidst the darkness. Though scars would forever mark my soul, I vowed to honor Ally's memory by navigating the labyrinth of grief with courage and grace, embracing the love we shared, and weaving it into the tapestry of my healing.

Every day I would do my best to confront the multiheaded beast of grief. Some days I would be filled with immense anger at the thought of Ally being taken from me. On other days I would be riddled with guilt, not knowing if we had made the right choices in trying to find a cure for her. But most days, I would sit with this new visitor of mine that called himself 'Grief.'

Every day I would wake up and attempt my daily meditation and emotional releasing techniques. Afterward, I would have long periods of being alone in our apartment, where everything reminded me of Ally. I often turned to alcohol to numb my senses. I tried desperately to find brief moments of peace but frequently drank to create a chemically induced false state of happiness to mentally and emotionally check out of my own reality. When people are bereaved, they often need to take a break from grief. Some people may choose to run away on trips or vacations; some people may bury themselves in work; some people may turn to drugs or alcohol, and some may be lucky enough to find love again.

In the depths of my sorrow, I yearned for respite from the ceaseless torrent of thoughts and emotions that threatened to consume me. Numbing my senses became my refuge, a familiar and temporary escape that allowed me to navigate the labyrinth of each day. Thankfully, I was surrounded by a network of understanding friends who, without judgment, supported my coping mechanisms and offered solace amidst my self-imposed exile. Their unwavering presence provided a semblance of comfort, assuring me that my struggles with alcohol were not perceived as a weakness but as a desperate attempt to cope with the overwhelming loss of Ally. The ache of missing her was an unrelenting force that often pushed me to the precipice of desperation. In fleeting moments of despair, I contemplated actions that could sever my journey, if only for a brief, agonizing moment. Yet, deep within the recesses of my heart, I clung to the deep-rooted belief that Ally would implore me to persevere, to find solace in life's unyielding embrace. It was this steadfast conviction that propelled me forward, even when the weight of her absence threatened to shatter my resolve. To fill the void, I immersed myself in a whirlwind of activity. Work became both a refuge and a distraction, providing a semblance of structure and purpose amidst the chaos of my inner turmoil. And when the day waned, I sought solace in the company of friends, seeking their silent companionship as I mourned, allowing me to drown my sorrows in the fleeting numbness that alcohol provided. Their understanding presence, void of judgment or expectations, became the balm that soothed my wounded soul, an unspoken affirmation that I was not alone in my grief. Seeking solace in the ephemeral, I embarked on countless journeys, traversing different cities and states during weekends and holidays. Each new destination served as a temporary refuge, an attempt to outrun the relentless grip of emotional anguish that I was not yet prepared to confront. It was a desperate dance between numbing the pain and fleeing from the depths of my vulnerability. Though my actions may have appeared as avoidance, I knew deep down that this was merely a temporary respite. The journey of healing could not be evaded forever. It awaited me patiently, ready to unfold its lessons when the time was right. For now, I clung to the crutches that helped me navigate the darkest corridors of grief, acknowledging that the path to healing was a complex and nonlinear one, where moments of numbing and escape were woven into the fabric of my survival. In the depths of my longing, I held onto the glimmer of hope that someday, when the tumult of grief had receded, I would find the strength to face the pain head-on. Until then, I treasured the fleeting moments of solace, cherishing the support of friends and the temporary respite that numbing provided. It was a delicate balance, a fragile dance between survival and surrender, as I journeyed toward the eventual reunion with my own emotional truth.

The fact is, I needed to take breaks, which is okay to do as long as it is done intentionally. I was aware that I was doing it for a specific reason. I needed to take a break from grief, and numbing is acceptable for a period of time. It is what is needed just as much as working on letting go of grief itself. It is a way of acknowledging the loss, no matter how fucked up it might seem to others. I needed to be gentle with myself and not let other people's judgments and opinions get to me. I am the one who has to work through this grief, and no one can do this for me. This was my own personal journey and no one else's. It may not have been the wisest choice, but it was what I thought I needed, and it was what I could handle after Ally's death.

My sister quickly noticed what I was doing to myself and the downward spiral that I was taking. "I am concerned for you, Vo. I think you need help. I think you need to start seeing a grief counselor," she said. "You have been drinking way too much, and it just isn't healthy for you. I can get a referral for you at UW. They have a great bereavement program there for people who have lost their loved ones, and it is free to you."

"I know I need help, but I don't know if I want to go there," I told her.

"Why?!" she asked.

"I am just so mad at them for not being able to save Ally," I replied.

"It is not their fault Vo. They did everything they could," she told me.

I took a breath to calm myself. "I know... I know... I guess I am just so mad at everyone right now. I don't know if I could go back to the place right now," I admitted.

"I already got a referral from the head of the Palliative Care Program. She is the best. I need you to see her for me, and if not for me, you need to do this for yourself and for Ally," she said before hanging up the phone and emailing me the information.

I wasn't quite ready to step back into the place where I watched Ally take her last breath. I was afraid to return to the place where Ally and I spent our last moments together. The thought of walking through those halls again and being reminded of all the horrible memories of Ally's illness just seemed too much for me to handle at the moment. But I knew I had to do something. Meditation, running away, and alcohol weren't healing me. So, I took a deep breath and booked my first appointment to see Cara, one of the medical center's palliative care social workers and bereavement counselor.

Fear and anxiety overwhelmed me as I turned into the familiar parking garage at the hospital. As I entered the building, memories came rushing back. I slowly walked down the long corridor. Memories began to flicker in my mind; running as fast I could through the same hallways to get to Ally after her first brush with death, coming here daily to see Ally before and after work when she was ill, and of course, leaving here for the last time after Ally had passed.

When I arrived at our intended place to meet Cara for our first visit, she stood near the entrance of the main hospital and greeted me warmly before leading me upstairs to a private room where we would begin our first session. As we sat down, she began to tell me how sorry she was for my loss and commended me for making our appointment so soon after Ally's passing. It had only been a little over two months since her death. She began to tell me that it wasn't uncommon for people who experienced the passing of a loved one to not leave their house, let alone their bedroom, for a good 3-6 months or even up to a year. The fact that I was upright, functioning, and presentable was a very rare occurrence. In a low, quiet voice, I began talking, "I always tried to face and deal with my fears instead of being afraid of them or running away from them. I knew that I was failing at this, and that's the reason why I am here." Tears fell from my face as I admitted, "It was very hard for me to come here today. I really don't want to be here. I almost didn't show up because I am just so angry," I paused for a moment to fight back my tears, "I am so angry that they failed to save Ally's life, even though I know it wasn't their fault."

Cara looked at me with her sympathetic demeanor, "Vo, you have every right to be angry, and you are right. We did fail you and Ally." Knowing a bit about Ally and me through the Palliative care team, Cara noticed that I was still wearing my wedding ring and told me, "Just because Ally had passed doesn't mean that she is not here with you now. It isn't like you broke up or got a divorce. You are still married to her in your heart and in your mind, and that bond that the two of you share will always remain for the rest of your life." She then went on to say, "Ally was a big part of your life, and you shared many experiences and created many memories together, including your vows as husband and wife, until death do you part... You didn't expect that in such a short period of time, she would be facing a life-threatening disease that would rob you of your future and your wife. So, of course, you'd still feel like you are still married to Ally because you still are." She also stated that it was likely even more difficult for me, given the short period of time we had together after our marriage before she passed.

"Your life and your future with Ally were robbed and taken away from you. The word 'bereavement' itself is an Old English word meaning 'to be robbed,' and unfortunately, now, this is your life. The ring that you wear is a way of acknowledging and honoring the loss of Ally."

Cara then relayed the story of a bereaved older man whose wife had recently passed. He said, "It took me 50 years to figure out how to be married, and now, six months after my wife's death, people expect me to know how to not be married." She then relayed another story about a man whose wife had passed away some 30 years prior, and for 30 years, he never once took down any of her pictures from the wall. When a friend asked why, he inquired why he would because he was still married to her.

She then handed me a series of pamphlets to look at and explained the 4 Tasks of Mourning identified by J. William Worden, PhD.:

Task 1: Acknowledge / Accept the reality of the loss.
Task 2: Work through the pain or experience the pain.
Task 3: Adjust to the environment in which the deceased is missing.
Task 4: Find an enduring connection with the deceased and embark on a new life.

Cara then asked about some of the emotions I had been dealing with since Ally passed. I was obviously dealing with a number of them, grief being the first, but the greatest emotion that screamed the loudest in my head was the amount of guilt I carried inside. I told her, "I broke my promise to Ally. I promised her that we would find a cure and save her life, and then everything will be all right. I keep thinking to myself whether or not we made the right decisions for Ally. If we had chosen to seek treatment in Houston, would Ally be alive today?" The pain and anguish of my guilt began to rise inside of me. I told Cara more of our story, "I thought I did everything right. I researched everything I could about Ally's cancer, but none of it worked. I was with Ally throughout the entire illness and hospitalizations, and after witnessing everything, there was nothing I could do."

Cara looked at me and told me, "None of this is your fault, Vo. You did everything possible to help Ally get through her battle with cancer. Everyone did, and now we are here. Now you are here."

Cara began talking about Bob Deits' work from his book *Life After Loss*. The way out of grief is going through it. Grief is very hard work. The worst kind of grief is your own. You are the only one who truly knows what and how you are feeling. Unfortunately, it must be done alone. Although only you can resolve your own grief, it need not be done alone. It is okay to ask for help along the way, just like we are doing now.

She then went on to say that grief has many heads. One moment you might feel sad, numb, angry, depressed, or, in my case, guilty. There is no right or wrong way of dealing with grief, and the only way out of it is to go through it. Grief constantly changes throughout life, and the best thing that I could do for myself was try not to run away from it, avoid it, or try to get over it too quickly. Grief is very hard work, and the worst kind of grief is your own. But acknowledge the pain and allow yourself to feel it. Feeling the pain was the second grief task that I needed to take on for a lifetime.

It was nice to be able to talk to Cara. She didn't judge me, she didn't correct me, and she didn't tell me I was doing anything wrong unless I was bullying myself. She just listened to everything I had to say. Things that I couldn't talk about with my family or friends. It felt easier talking to this caring stranger than anyone else. The reality was I was grief dumping, and instead of keeping it all bottled up in my mind, Cara was a sounding board who sat with me and listened to me. Cara would never use the term "grief dumping." Instead, she would see a bereaved person sorting out different emotions and then identifying those that are most challenging at that moment. She then allowed the bereaved to work through these emotions openly and expressively, feelings of anger, guilt, relief, and depression. Allowing a bereaved to "grief dump" makes for a caring place to gain perspective on all they've lost and how much pain they're in.

Cara then went on to suggest that one day when I start dating again, the person I find would be someone special. She only brought that up because she'd hoped to put the idea in my head and heart that there could be a future in which joy and sorrow could live together. That my life was not over, even if the life I wanted and worked hard for with Ally was. She said when I met that special person, she would not just be dating me, but dating Ally and me. She would have to understand and be okay with the fact that I could be in love with two people: one being Ally and the other being her. "Because, once again, you and Ally were still married when she passed away, and your love for her will most likely never go away. Find a way to stay connected while remembering your relationship with Ally." A lot transpired that day in our first session, and a big part of me felt hope. Given everything I was thinking and feeling, I knew I wasn't alone. I booked my next appointment, knowing that doing so meant taking another step forward in my journey with grief.

A friend from the ayahuasca circle called me up and invited me to come down to California and sit with him to journey with the medicine. Three and a half months had passed since Ally had passed, and I already had five sessions with Cara by this time. Although it was extremely helpful to talk to someone about my grief, I knew I had to go much deeper. I agreed to join him and called up JR to come to sit with us as the three of us did back when I first initiated him into the healing world of ayahuasca. Back then, he was the new kid on the block, but now his spiritual journey has led him down the path to becoming a healer. He prefaced with the shamans about what I had been through in the past year, so they paid extra attention to my needs and offered me additional prayers and medicines to help with my healing. My intentions leading up to the meditation with the medicine were, first and foremost, to clearly see and speak to Ally; second, to help remove as much grief as possible; and third, to show me things that I needed to know and what was next for my life.

As we settled ourselves in our space for the evening, the head shaman greeted me with a warm embrace and asked me how I was feeling and if I needed any additional assistance. I told him my intentions and was ready to do the work. He smiled and offered me a little prayer prior to starting the ceremony. Ironically, my first intention was granted not by way of ayahuasca but by way of rapé, which is a sacred tobacco that Amazonian shamans often used as a powerful healing medicine. It clears the sinuses to open and stimulate the pineal gland, which to some is considered where the psychic third eye lies in the brain. It allows you to enhance your ayahuasca journey and increase your own psychic abilities for a short period of time. When it was suggested and offered to me, I immediately agreed to take medicine. I would do anything to see, hear, and speak to Ally again. As I closed my eyes and sat there in a meditative position, the tobacco medicine was administered to me via a special tool that shot the medicine deep into my sinuses. It burned intensely and caused me to become teary-eyed as it penetrated the sinuses and made its way up my pineal gland. My mind and spirit were immediately uprooted and launched into a sacred white space where I could see Ally's spirit waiting for me.

I started crying when I saw her sitting before me. Our two souls immediately embraced each other. I immediately told her, "I love you, Ally. I miss you so much." I then asked, "Are you in a safe place?"

"Yes," she replied.

I then told her, "Ally, I don't know how to live my life without you."

She smiled at me and said, "Love yourself as much as I loved you. I will always be there for you. Live your life in honor of me." I later realized that Ally was showing me how important Task 4 of mourning was: to remember the deceased. Live your life and form new relationships while never leaving the deceased behind. And then I was back in my body. If the ceremony had ended right at that moment, I would have been happy knowing that I could, for the first time, clearly see, hear, and speak to Ally. That was really the only thing I ever wanted after she passed.

Dusk had arrived, and it was time to go deeper into my subconscious to face the new demons I created. I drank the medicine and sat patiently in the dark. I waited to see what was before me. As soon as I was catapulted to the other side, I immediately called out for Ally and searched for her, hoping to see and talk to her again. Instead, I was greeted by spirit guides that immediately began the hard work of trying to heal me from the inside. In the depths of my anguish, haunting visions plagued my mind like relentless ghosts, each one a harrowing reminder of Ally's suffering. The walls of my consciousness trembled as I witnessed vivid scenes unfold before me, cruel images of Ally wracked with pain, disgorging pools of blood that tainted our shared existence. The tumor that held her captive was inflamed and devoured, threatening to tear her away from my desperate grasp. Helpless and overwhelmed, I found my voice erupting in a guttural scream, a plea to the universe itself: "NO! STOP!" During this torment, I beseech the cosmic forces to release me from the grip of these harrowing memories. I yearned for respite, for a reprieve from the relentless assault on my senses. The spirit guides from the other realm responded to my anguished pleas. With a surge of ethereal power, they extracted the thick, suffocating tendrils of darkness that had entwined themselves with my very being. The energy that had stagnated within me, heavy and viscous like tar, was now subjected to their unearthly intervention. The spirit guides, with their otherworldly wisdom, delicately unraveled the knots of anguish, painstakingly removing the residue of torment that clung to my spirit. As they worked, the weight of the memories lifted, gradually relinquishing their hold on my consciousness. Faced with this profound spiritual intervention, I experienced a tumultuous mixture of relief and vulnerability. It was as if a portal had been opened, allowing me to release the anguish that had been festering within. Though the process was agonizing, it was a necessary purging, a shedding of the remnants of pain that had intertwined itself with my very essence. As the thick, dark energy dissipated, I felt a newfound clarity emerging within. The tormenting memories faded, losing their power to haunt my waking hours. In their wake, a space was carved for healing and restoration. Through the transformative intervention of the spirit guides, I glimpsed a glimmer of hope, a flickering light amidst the encroaching darkness. Though the scars of those harrowing visions would forever mark my soul, I now carried within me the seeds of resilience and the unwavering determination to honor Ally's memory. I understood that healing would be an ongoing journey, one that required courage and an unwavering commitment to confronting the pain that dwelled within. In the aftermath of this cathartic experience, I emerged with newfound strength, ready to navigate the intricate dance between remembering and healing. I would honor the spirit guides that had come to my aid by embarking on a path of self-discovery and self-compassion. Their intervention had opened a doorway to release some of the torment that had plagued me, allowing me a little space to rebuild my shattered world with renewed purpose and a deeper understanding of the fragility of life. No longer bound by the chains of relentless memories, I would seek solace in the healing embrace of time and compassion. With each step forward, I would honor Ally's legacy by embracing the light that still shone within me, a testament to the enduring power of love amidst the shadows of grief.

As the group delved deeper into the recesses of their subconscious, a ripple of laughter erupted, cascading through the room like a symphony of joy. Each chuckle intertwined with another, growing in intensity until the collective laughter filled the air. In the grip of my anguish, I felt myself descending into the abyss of my sorrow. Tears welled up, threatening to spill forth, yet my screams remained locked in the confines of my being, unheard by those around me. Desperately, I sought solace in the depths of my consciousness, silently beseeching Ally, my beloved, to come to my aid. With every fiber of my being, I longed for the torment to cease, yearning for a glimmer of respite. And then, unexpectedly, a shift occurred. A member of the group reached for a guitar, its gentle strums reverberating through the room. With each melodious note, the enchanting lyrics of Joni Mitchell's "Both Sides Now" filled the space, offering a fleeting moment of solace. In this interlude of music, my heart found a brief layoff, catching its breath before the next wave of emotional work beckoned.

Within the tapestry of my subconscious, I found myself transported to a heart-wrenching scene: standing by Ally's bedside during her final moments in the hospital. Once again, the life drained from her fragile form, etching itself into my memory with indelible clarity. Overwhelmed by grief, I held her close, my voice quivering with remorse as I whispered my apologies for my perceived failure to save her. The weight of the world pressed upon my chest, and my silent cries reverberated through my mind, echoing the anguished plea, "It's just not fair... It's just not fair." I was submerged beneath the surface as if baptized in the waters of catharsis, a symbolic rebirth beckoning me toward healing. Looking up through the crystalline depths, my eyes locked onto a vision that both startled and comforted me. There stood Ally, ethereal and serene, accompanied by the spirit guide entrusted with purging my soul of the burdensome grief that had taken root within me. I yearned to hear her voice once more, to feel her presence, yet my cries were met with the silence of the spirit world. Slowly, the journey began to fade, its ethereal tapestry unraveling, and I found myself drifting in and out of consciousness, suspended between realms.

As I gradually emerged from the depths of this profound experience, fragments of the spirit world mingled with the reality before me. The weight of my grief remained, but a newfound understanding blossomed within me, nourished by the transformative journey I had undertaken. Though Ally's physical presence was forever lost, I carried her essence within, intertwined with the wisdom and healing bestowed by the spirit guides.

In the haze of my awakening, I resolved to honor Ally's memory by embarking on a path of self-discovery and healing. Through the ebbs and flows of consciousness, I would forge a connection to the spirit world, drawing strength from its ethereal whispers and finding solace in the ever-present love that transcended the boundaries of life and death. And as I stepped forward into the unknown, my heart embraced the light of remembrance, forever entwined with the ethereal realm that had offered me both pain and healing.

As people began to regain hold of their realities and started to walk around and prepare for bed, I asked for a bucket to physically release the remains of what was left of the metaphoric grief burdening my soul. It was probably one of the toughest journeys I have ever experienced thus far.

The next morning, I felt something had changed inside of me. My grief was no longer blaring or screaming in my head. As the days passed, instead of needing to weep several times an hour, it lessened to almost once a day. I felt like I was finally able to breathe again. The medicine had made a little room in my grief-filled heart, but even that only lasted for maybe a month before a new face of grief slid in.

I busied myself with work and friends again. To protect myself at work, I put up a sign at the clinic asking patients to respect my privacy by not asking questions, but that didn't stop some of my patients. Some would still inquire, "Sorry to ask, but are you doing okay? Is there anything I can do for you?" I would just smile and thank them, saying that I was doing fine to put an end to any further questions.

Then one day, a patient who lived over on the peninsula with his wife walked in alone. They were some of my first patients when I started with the chiropractic franchise. They would come together once a month for their maintenance adjustments. They believed in a healthy lifestyle and raised their own livestock, and had a flourishing garden. Everything was organic and pure.

I asked him, "Where is his wife?" He stood there staring back at me and began to break down.

"She had passed away during the summer after she had been diagnosed with a rare form of terminal cancer. She didn't survive the past four months when we found out." I stood there, and we embraced. We both knew what the other was experiencing. I kept thinking to myself that her life was cut shorter than Ally's after they found out. I offered my personal number and let him know some of the things I was doing to deal with the loss. And similar to my response toward others who extended themselves to me, he just smiled and said, "Thank you." Advice is not always the best thing to offer someone fresh into grief.

In the same month, another patient who was a proponent of health came to see me on a weekly basis to get her maintenance adjustment. Before work put me on a forced sabbatical so I could take care of and be with Ally during her final days, we worked on alleviating a sudden onset of low back pain radiating down her leg. After each visit, she would receive only momentary relief from the treatment. I strongly suggested that she get an X-ray and an MRI at the very least to see what was happening with her spine and if there was anything else that might be causing her pain. She resisted at first, blaming the cause due to her age, but eventually, the pain became bad enough that she reluctantly agreed.

Several months had passed before I had finally returned to work. When she walked into my office, she was using the assistance of a walker, which was not out of the ordinary when her condition worsened. As she slowly worked her way to the back office, she said, "Hello, Dr. Vo. I wanted to personally come by and tell you how sorry I am to hear of the death of your wife."

"Thank you so much," I told her.

"I also wanted to tell you that I finally got some X-rays done of my lower back. The doctors told me that I had terminal bone cancer and that I don't have a lot of time left," she said.

"Oh no. I am so sorry," I told her.

She sort of chuckled, "It's okay. I guess I should have taken your advice a lot earlier, but here I am for now."

"Please let me know if there is anything we can do for you," I told her.

"I am fine. God has a plan for me. I just wanted to tell you and see how you were doing." We hugged one last time before seeing each other for the last time. I stood there in shock. It was like a door had opened to the disease, and now everyone was getting it or knew someone who was going through it. Luckily, some would survive. But many others would not. Who decides who gets to live? No one really knows the answer to that, but sometimes faith is all you have to get through your pain and lead you to the other side.

For me, taking the medicine and facing my subconscious head-on was the greatest relief that I had experienced thus far. This time, I would journey to southern California to partake in a new circle with my friend JR for a different style of ceremony. One that neither of us had experienced before, and it was completely opposite of what we were used to with our own meditation circle. There were no prayers, no rituals, no opening or closing ceremonies, and no vomiting after drinking their ayahuasca medicine. It was bottoms up, find a comfortable spot in the house where they held their sacred space, and prepare yourself for the ride.

In comparing the differences in the ways Shamans practiced Ayahuasca ceremonies, you have to look at pre- and post-Christianity influences. I learned that vomiting was a result of having too much bark in the mixture versus pure leaf; the vomiting represents the sin, or as we called it, up north, the gift that we expel from our physical healing. This is considered a post-Christian influence. The one we were experiencing here was similar to pre-Christianity influence, where shamans sat around the fire, drank the medicine, and waited to connect to the spirit world.

Unfamiliar with this style and not knowing what to expect, I was happy that there were no buckets or vomiting involved. I took medicine in the light of the sunset and, within 10 minutes, was immediately launched to the other side of reality. My heart raced and immediately began pounding as the adrenaline raced through my body. The spirit guides immediately went to work on me, ripping and tearing the grief from my energy, one after the other. It seemed like a sprint. At the same time, it felt like I was running a marathon, and I was barely able to catch my breath. This journey was all hard work and gave me little information. Yet I kept searching for a glimpse of Ally as I moved through various dimensions, but she was nowhere to be found. When the medicine finally let up and night fell across the clear sky, I laid out on a patio chaise lounge and began crying to myself. I didn't know if it was the work, the grief, or the fact that I didn't get to see or speak to Ally as I had in my previous journey, but I found greater release. From then on, I only broke down and cried once a week versus once a day. Maybe it was because it was my second time journeying, maybe it was because it was a different medicine, but it helped me release much more of the grief that I held.

CHAPTER 24

A NEW YOU

The following week, I had a follow-up appointment with Cara at the medical center. It had been a little over two months and two shamanic journeys since I last saw her. I told her of my experiences and what the results of my journeys were. She was amazed and ecstatic for me. I was able to come up for air and receive moments of relief. No judgment, no criticisms, no opinions. She just listened and accepted what I shared with her as truth and was happy for me. Being able to breathe easier, I began to see what she meant about discovering the new me and how I evolve with grief versus stuffing it down or pushing it away. Evolving with your grief is Task 3, where you adjust, cope, and learn to be with grief and your new life. I felt like I was gaining some ground in my grief work, but at the same time, I started feeling guilty for how quickly this was moving within the last five months since Ally's passing.

Crying all the time felt like something I was supposed to do, like a badge that I was carrying to validate and honor the death of Ally. Task 4 encourages the bereaved to be in a relationship with the deceased as a continuing bond with them. The bereaved do not have to cry or be sad to have permission to talk about the deceased or to still love the deceased. I asked Cara, "Is it normal that I no longer need to cry all of the time? Do you think there is something wrong with me?"

"Vo, you are working so hard on releasing your grief. You are what I would call a 'unicorn' for coming as far as you have come with your grief work. I wish most people were as strong as you are, but unfortunately, they are too afraid to even take the first step," she sighed. "Sometimes it would take years for people, if ever at all because it is too painful for them to begin. You are willing to embrace grief so that it can evolve into something greater. You are learning how to morph grief into love. Remember, it was okay to have breaks from grief. It is the reward for all the hard work I have done. And yes, it is okay that you don't need to cry all the time to prove that you still grieve for Ally."

Life took on a new normal since my last spiritual journey. I didn't feel the need to always run away for the weekend or replace my sorrows with booze. I was actually beginning to feel a little normal. That is until tax season came around. My accountant told me that I needed to itemize all of our medical bills from the year before so we could assess what we could deduct for a better tax return. No one really enjoys doing tax stuff, but I needed to get it done, and I was finally in a place where I could focus on it.

As I pulled out our file of bills and started to go through each item one by one, it dawned on me: each medical bill was a memory that documented Ally's cancer from beginning to end. This copay was for the meds when she went in for her first visit with Dr. Tony. This copay was for when she filled her prescription at the cancer center for the very first time, and this one was for the amount owed after her CT scan diagnosed the beginning of our nightmare. Then there was the first chemotherapy treatment bill and the bill for Ally's first stay at the medical center. It was like reliving each vivid memory of Ally's cancer journey but through the lens of Ally's medical bills.

I had to stop several times as I began to wail in tears remembering all the things that had happened to her. When I was finally done, the first thing I did was call up Lisa and Richard to say, "I need a drink." For a moment, I thought that giving in to alcohol would be a huge setback in my forward progress with grief, but instead, it was more of a reminder that a deeper pain was still there waiting to be uncovered.

When Ally was alive, I had always wanted her to take me back to Gainesville, Florida, her hometown, to show me where she grew up. I wanted to connect images to all of the stories she told me about her former life. She hemmed and hawed, not being too enthused about the whole idea but did agree that we should go to the Florida Keys someday. As Ally's 40th birthday was approaching, I thought to myself, what better way to celebrate it than to fulfill the two things that we hadn't been able to do when she was alive? This way, I would be able to visit her dad in Naples, jet ferry to the Keys with AT, then make a pit stop in Tampa to visit Ally's sister's family before heading to Gainesville to celebrate Ally's 40th in her hometown.

When I had finally arrived in Gainesville, JB and AT drove me around the town, showing me all the houses that Ally used to live in, 'The Swamp," where Ally worked during school, and they pointed out various places where they shared special memories with Ally growing up in Florida. On her birthday, we went out to her favorite sushi restaurant. Afterward, we headed back to The Swamp to have a final drink before calling it a night. Unbeknownst to us, a few of Ally's old friends from way back showed up at the bar. They joined us for a drink, and we had a mini-birthday party for Ally. It wound up being the best way for me to celebrate her 40th birthday together.

May 11, 2018 (Ally's Healing Circle)

 Minh Vo ▶ **Ally's Healing Circle**
Admin · 11 May 2018 · 😊

Happy Birthday Babe. Today would of been your big 40th, and we would be having a big celebration in honor of you. There would be eating, drinking, maybe a little dancing, and a whole lot of love between us, family, and friends. But instead the angels are singing in heaven and you are dancing amongst the brightest stars. Much grander than anything that anyone has ever seen.

You are the greatest gift that I have ever received. And there isn't a moment that goes by that I wish you were still here next to me. To hold your hand, kiss you, and tell you how much I love you for years to come till we are all wrinkled, old, and still so madly in love.

I wish I could be celebrating your birthday with you up in the heavens above. Fly me too the moon so that we could play amongst the stars, would be what we would be doing right now if I were with you at this moment. I love you and miss you so much. Happy Birthday. You are and will always be in my heart and the love of my life for all eternity.

I don't know if celebrating Ally's 40th birthday back in Gainesville was a good thing or a bad thing, but it was something I felt I needed to do to honor her. After I returned home, it catapulted me into another cycle of running away and numbing my feelings with alcohol and activities. I made an excuse that it was summertime, and it was a good reason to travel and party with friends from all over the US, fulfilling promises one by one that I would come to visit them. But the true test to determine if I was healed was how much time I was able to be around people before I would have to retreat somewhere secluded. That way, I could be alone with my thoughts, or in essence, be alone with Ally in my thoughts. Although I was physically present, oftentimes, I was not mentally or emotionally present. And when it was time, I would often need to retreat to a quiet place. Somewhere I could be alone for a moment or go to my room if it was nearby. And if that wasn't possible, sometimes, my escape would be as simple as closing my eyes for a minute until I was ready to re-engage again. Other times, I needed much more time, more silence, and more space.

Sometimes my tolerance for being around people lessened. I would either leave or ask them to leave. I would put on a mask and pretend that everything was normal and that I was okay. It was hard to deal with all the emotions swirling inside of me. It had been just over eight months since Ally's passing, and I was back on my roller coaster of emotions. Time was my only gauge to measure how much I had healed. I was always busy, always moving so that I wouldn't have to stand still in time in my grief. Maybe it was because time was taken away from me. My life and future were taken away from me. All because Ally was taken away from me. I really didn't know what to do with my time anymore. Everything I did, I would think Ally would enjoy this or Ally wouldn't like that, and sometimes, I would break down and cry because she wasn't there with me to experience my life, our life together as it once was. My soulmate was now gone.

August 30, 2018 (Ally's Healing Circle)

 Minh Vo
Admin · 30 August 2018 ·

Ally, It has been a year since you had left us. A year since I had last held your hand, kissed your lips, held you in my arms, and told you how much I loved you before I watched you take your very last breath. That was the day my heart broke and shattered into a thousand pieces. And as you laid there still, I remember my last words to you were, "Ally, please wake up, so that we can go home. Please wake up for me, it's time for us to go home now."

Losing you was the most difficult thing that I had ever experienced in my life. Words could not express the pain that I had felt in my heart, the guilt that I carried feeling that I had failed you, and the doubt and anger that it had left deep inside of me. Everyday I would wake up to the what ifs, what could we have done better, what could I have done that would have prevented all of this, so that you would still be here today. And as hard as this year has been without you beside me, each and every day I would be reminded of you by seeing and hearing you in my thoughts, feeling you in my heart, and missing you tremendously. It is through loving you each and every day that I am able to slowly pick up the pieces of my heart. It was you that continued to teach me how to face my greatest pain and suffering, and learn to slowly mend it by simply continuing to love you every single day of my life.

I am so thankful to all of the families, friends, teachers, and healers who helped me get through this extremely difficult year. Thank you all for checking in on me, listening to me, being there for me, and helping me when I needed a hand. Without all of your continued love and support, I would still be imprisoned within the pain and suffering of my own mind. It has allowed me to pickup the tiny pieces of my heart and slowly put them back together again. And although many pieces are still missing, it has allowed me to be here today. And especially because of you Ally, who continues to love me and give me strength to carry on. I will forever carry you in my heart, and love you for all eternity until we meet again.

EPILOGUE

In late October early November, shortly after getting married, Ally began experiencing small bouts of stomach pain. She was still reeling from the nuptials, but knew it was time to detox. Cleanse her body and soul; get her train back on track and finally start using those kettlebells that live underneath the couch. She spent Thanksgiving with her new family AND her newfound pain. She finally got around to seeing the doctor. They sent her for a myriad of labs and x-rays and found nothing, so the discomfort was easily dismissed. In her mind this ruled out what she and Minh had been thinking the past few months: IBS, gluten allergies, celiac disease, diverticulitis, etc.

By late December, the pain had made itself much more present through excruciating abdominal pain, gas, chills, vomiting, and loss of appetite. Ally went to see a second doctor. He touched her stomach and abdomen twice and sent her home with a new prescription, omeprazole or glorified Prilosec... and TUMS.

The new year, 2017, deemed fruitful for Ally and Minh as Ally was gunning at couple of new positions for work and they were both looking forward to a European vacation in the spring. But the pain persisted, so Ally sought care through Minh's doctor. The doctor, a gentle and soft-spoken man, broke sound barriers the day they met. One checkup and a CT scan later; she had cancer.

"I'm afraid to tell you, Ally, that you have cancer... it's large, and rather aggressive. The tumor is located in the mesentery with several lesions trailing behind, so the chance of operability is slim at the moment due to the quantity of the tumors."

I reflected for a minute. It was funny; it was odd. I felt like I was on a crowded train, nobody was paying attention to my cancer or me. My numb feet, my uncertain life expectancy, the loneliness, all coupled with gratitude for being alive, even if it means sharing a world with this beast of a tumor on my cancer train.

The pathologists in Seattle had not seen a cancer like Ally's before, so her slides were sent to a renowned Chief Onco-Pathologist in

Massachusetts. The pathologist determined that the appearance of the cells was undoubtedly peritoneal mesothelioma of the biphasic type. Because Ally's cancer is so rare and Ally is so young, her case was expedited to the tumor board at the Seattle's top cancer center. Currently, Ally is undergoing an insistent treatment of chemotherapy and that may or may not provide positive results.

If the chemotherapy does not prove to be effective, there is a trial in Chicago, in the first phase trial for mesothelioma. In this trial, the immunotherapy drugs have been successfully used to shrink tumors with a sustained and prolonged response. There is no placebo involved, and everybody is getting pembrolizumab. Regardless of treatment, Ally will have excessive medical bills accumulating over time. We are asking family and friends to help us out during this difficult time and give what they can. With help, love and prayers, we feel that she is in God's hands with another new start in life and marriage.

~Ally

As you may have noticed, Ally wrote her one and only entry in the third person. Maybe it was because she was scared to face the fact that she had cancer, and it was her way of detaching herself from the whole experience of it all. The day Ally found out that she had terminal cancer, all her hopes and dreams quickly faded into a living nightmare. The odds of survival were slim, Ally knew she was facing a losing battle, but she still held onto hope. I made her a promise, "We will find a cure, and everything will be OK." I was convinced there was nothing that could stop us from spending the rest of our lives together. We would beat this disease! In Ally's quest for strength and inspiration, she ran across a story about a cancer survivor who blogged about her entire experience. She was inspired to document her own story of survival and triumph in her own battle against cancer. Unfortunately, this was not how the story ended. Immediately after cancer treatment began, Ally was faced with several obstacles, numerous setbacks, and many disappointments that quickly deteriorated her strength, her health and eventually took her life. This excerpt was the only piece that Ally wrote when she began her journey, and she eventually succumbed to cancer.

In this world, we are all connected by a spiritual thread. Some call it God, some call it the Spirit, while others call it by what they are raised to believe. We are born into this world being taken care of by our parents or guardians of our life and eventually learn how to take care of others until it is our time to pass. In my own knowledge and experience with this connection and wanting to be closer to this source, I have relied heavily on meditation to achieve various levels of consciousness. Within these levels of our consciousness, within the spiritual connection that binds us, if we listen close enough, we can hear it speak to us.

Ally's world had been cast into shadows as losing her job enveloped her in a deep and consuming depression. Faced with her despair, I reassured her that everything would be alright. I encouraged her to channel her energy into our wedding planning, embracing this unexpected opportunity for self-reflection and growth. Little did I know that her quest for inner peace would lead us both down a path of shared meditation. In the quiet moments before the dawn, as the world slumbered, we would rise and gather in stillness. Ally, seeking respite from the storm within, expressed a desire to join me in my morning ritual. Eagerly, she sought the sanctuary of meditation, yearning for mental and emotional tranquility amidst the chaos of her inner turmoil.

The August before our wedding Ally was taken off her project and had essentially been laid off. To help deal with the stress of wedding planning and losing her job, Ally asked if she could meditate with me in the morning since I was no longer beside her when she awoke due to my morning meditation ritual. With everything going on, I reconciled my resistance to meditation and anything spiritually related after my failed spiritual career path and restarted my daily morning meditation practice three months prior to the wedding. With Ally joining me, we meditated every morning at around 7 a.m., sitting next to each other on our couch before getting ready for the day. I'd been practicing this for years and had taught my students how to raise their frequency to accelerate into a meditative state faster and for a longer period of time; it was an advantage for anyone to meditate with me. My higher meditative frequency allowed others to access the meditative/psychic state faster and easier. Ally and I started off easy with 20- to 30-minute meditations until Ally was used to waking up every morning to join me. After a few weeks, Ally was up to 30-45 minutes. Sometimes, I'd even have to sit and wait for her to finish.

One morning, I opened my eyes after 40 minutes of meditation and looked over to see Ally sitting quietly, deep in her meditation. Another 20 minutes passed before she took a few deep breaths, grabbed her stomach, and opened her eyes. She looked over at me and said, "That was so intense, Babe."

"You were meditating for a long time. What happened in your meditation that was so intense?" I asked.

"I was holding this big heavy rock in my stomach, and I had to carry it everywhere I went," she told me. "It was as if it was a part of me, a part of my body. It was so intense babe. What do you think it means?"

I reflected back on our one and only energy session I had performed on her back in San Francisco and told her, "Maybe the rock represented all the negative emotional energy and trauma you have been carrying around from your past and is a reminder that of all the things that you still needed to let go of." She began nodding her head. "Don't worry, it's a good thing, the meditation is probably helping you to resolve some of your emotional trauma."

"I'm trying," she said.

"You are doing a great job," I told her. Who would have known that it was actually a premonition of what was in her near future? When Ally was in the last few months of her cancer, she was anorexic, and her stomach protruded greatly as if she was carrying a large rock inside. Who would have known that her meditation would lead to a premonition of what was to come?

In the end, we write books for a reason. We write them so that we can share a story. This is a story of two people, from two different worlds, from opposite ends of the earth, who found each other. Together they found what they had been looking for throughout their lives: unconditional love. When thrown into the fire, I searched far and wide to find something to help prepare myself to be the best caregiver I could be for Ally, my wife, my love, and my life. Unfortunately, there was nothing that could prepare me for what was to come. All we had was our love and the hope that one day we would find a cure and that she would be able to live. But that wasn't the happy ending that was given to us.

With this book, I wish to honor the relentless hard work and dedication of all caregivers. We walk each step of the way with our loved ones to confront cancer, a deadly disease that continues to affect so many lives. Ally's one wish in life was to make a difference in just one other person's life, and she has succeeded by touching many lives with her presence and immeasurable love. Our story serves as a continued effort to help those who have gone through and are still going through the experience of loving and caring for their beloved. Our story shared herein is to let you know that you are not alone. Living through your own battle, you have already shown that you are stronger than you believe by just being present.

The essence and foundation of human nature is love. Without love, we don't have that spiritual connection. Without love, we don't have a union. Without love, we don't have creation. Just like creation, it is the connection of two beings coming together to become one. It is through love that we nurture, evolve, learn, and grow. It is through love that we are drawn to those who we are meant to experience life with, meant to learn from, meant to be with, and meant to grow old with. It is what makes up friendships, relationships, marriages, families, cultures, cities, and countries and connects each and every one of us in this world. The union of everyone here on this planet becomes one. Ally and I found each other at the right place, the right time, and the right moment, and through our love and connection, we helped each other, learned from each other, supported each other, and loved each other until her last breath as in life and as now in death, Ally still teaches me how to not only love myself but also to love others at a deeper level.

If Ally were here today, she would remind us that the way through grief is through self-love. Just like she told me in my vision, "Love yourself as much as I loved you." Only then can you do the work needed to allow grief to be free and leave your body. Transforming it into something greater: Love. It is the reason why it is so important for us to face our fears. Take the first step. Learn to let go of all of the stress, anger, guilt, pain, and suffering that we all experience and hold on to in our daily life. In letting go, we learn to forgive and free ourselves from the mental-emotional burdens that we no longer have to carry. We create more space that helps build us versus keeping us bound within the prison of our minds. We learn to love once again. In doing so, I learned that it was okay not to rush through healing my grief, it was okay to pause sometimes, and it was okay to have those times when I felt blocked, helpless, and alone. It gave me a chance to heal something that I thought I would never be able to. And although I am still far from the finish line, I am still running my race of grief, but now Ally is helping me by running beside me as I ran beside her during her marathon in Greece.

At the same time, I never thought I would meet the blue-eyed girl to whom I would want to give all my love when I was alone in my room at night as a child. Never give up hope. Never give up dreams. Never give up on the ones you love. And never give up, especially on yourself, for there are a lot of people out there who are still fighting for their lives with caregivers and loved ones standing by their side. Know that you are here for a reason, to love and support one another. I hope this story inspires you to continue to hope, to continue to fight, and most of all, to continue to love.

There are moments in life when everything around you just seems to fade away, and nothing else matters. You don't question it. You begin to prepare yourself for the journey ahead. You ready yourself to dig in deep and surrender. You follow with love, faith, and hope with all your heart that everything will be okay. The only thing left to answer is, "Are you willing and able to stay present no matter what?"

THE END

ABOUT THE AUTHOR

Born in Saigon during the Vietnam War, Minh Vo faced his own battle for life. From the moment of birth, he fought severe pneumonia and illness near the point of death until the universe decided to lend a hand and give back the life that was meant to help others.

Immigrating with his family from Vietnam after the war, they found a new home and a new start in the Pacific Northwest of the United States. Minh Vo studied diligently to learn about the different ways of helping people heal, both mentally and physically. In his own journey towards physical, mental, and spiritual advancement, Minh Vo was able to discover truths about healing the body through broadening his personal consciousness.

Today, Dr. Minh Vo uses his knowledge to help many of his patients using chiropractic and energy medicine. Using an alternative integrated approach, Dr. Minh Vo follows the principle that the human body was created to heal itself naturally, that pain and dis-ease are more than clinical definitions, and that they may have a root cause originating from mental states of stress beyond physical explanation.

Exploring this principle, Dr. Minh Vo has shown many of his patients how to let go of their pain and suffering by releasing emotional anchors from their past that hinder a person both physically as well as spiritually. He understands his purpose as sharing this knowledge through his writings and teachings to accelerate humanity's spiritual evolution. Through Dr. Minh Vo's work, knowing and experiencing the greatness of who you really are, becomes achievable within your lifetime.

Minh Vo's latest book is a personal memoir titled *You and Me, No Matter What*. It's a story about two people meeting and falling in love. A modern-day East meets West. A timid Vietnamese immigrant and a fun-loving girl from the south spend their young lives looking and searching for love and eventually finding it and each other in a gay bar in San Francisco.

Three months after their wedding, Ally, his new bride, was diagnosed with terminal cancer, with less than a year to live. *You and Me, No Matter What,* is an unblinking recount of their daily life as a husband and wife, patient and caregiver, battling the intricacies of modern-day cancer treatments, their failures, and eventually how he survived and came back to life after the death of his wife. This memoir is written as a love story and offers hope and solace to those who suffer and grieve from the brutal act of losing a loved one to cancer.

www.ingramcontent.com/pod-product-compliance
Lightning Source LLC
Chambersburg PA
CBHW070504120526
44590CB00013B/748